Office DEPOT®

Taking Care of Business

The First 20 Years

Office DEPOT®

Taking Care of Business

The First 20 Years

Jeffrey L. Rodengen

Edited by Stanimira Stefanova
Design and layout by Sandy Cruz

WRITE STUFF

Write Stuff Enterprises, Inc.
1001 South Andrews Avenue
Fort Lauderdale, FL 33316
1-800-900-Book (1-800-900-2665)
(954) 462-6657
www.writestuffbooks.com

Publisher's Cataloging in Publication
(Prepared by The Donohue Group, Inc.)

Rodengen, Jeffrey L.
    Office Depot : taking care of business : the first 20 years / Jeffrey L. Rodengen ; edited by Stanimira Stefanova ; design and layout by Sandy Cruz.

    p. : ill. ; cm.
Includes bibliographical references and index.
ISBN: 1-932022-21-X

1. Office Depot (Firm)—History. 2. Office equipment and supplies industry—United States—History. I. Stefanova, Stanimira. II. Cruz, Sandy. III. Title.

HD9800.U554 O34 2006
651.2/06   2006903548

Completely produced in the
United States of America
10 9 8 7 6 5 4 3 2 1

Also by Jeffrey L. Rodengen

The Legend of Chris-Craft

*IRON FIST:
The Lives of Carl Kiekhaefer*

*Evinrude-Johnson
and The Legend of OMC*

*Serving the Silent Service:
The Legend of Electric Boat*

The Legend of Dr Pepper/Seven-Up

The Legend of Honeywell

The Legend of Briggs & Stratton

The Legend of Ingersoll-Rand

*The Legend of Stanley:
150 Years of The Stanley Works*

The MicroAge Way

The Legend of Halliburton

The Legend of York International

The Legend of Nucor Corporation

*The Legend of Goodyear:
The First 100 Years*

The Legend of AMP

The Legend of Cessna

The Legend of VF Corporation

The Spirit of AMD

The Legend of Rowan

*New Horizons:
The Story of Ashland Inc.*

The History of American Standard

The Legend of Mercury Marine

The Legend of Federal-Mogul

*Against the Odds:
Inter-Tel—The First 30 Years*

The Legend of Pfizer

*State of the Heart: The Practical Guide
to Your Heart and Heart Surgery*
with Larry W. Stephenson, M.D.

*The Legend of
Worthington Industries*

The Legend of IBP, Inc.

*The Legend of
Trinity Industries, Inc.*

*The Legend of
Cornelius Vanderbilt Whitney*

The Legend of Amdahl

The Legend of Litton Industries

The Legend of Gulfstream

The Legend of Bertram
with David A. Patten

*The Legend of
Ritchie Bros. Auctioneers*

The Legend of ALLTEL
with David A. Patten

*The Yes, you can of
Invacare Corporation*
with Anthony L. Wall

*The Ship in the Balloon:
The Story of Boston Scientific
and the Development of
Less-Invasive Medicine*

The Legend of Day & Zimmermann

The Legend of Noble Drilling

*Fifty Years of Innovation:
Kulicke & Soffa*

*Biomet—From Warsaw
to the World*
with Richard F. Hubbard

NRA: An American Legend

*The Heritage and Values
of RPM, Inc.*

*The Marmon Group:
The First Fifty Years*

The Legend of Grainger

*The Legend of
The Titan Corporation*
with Richard F. Hubbard

The Legend of Discount Tire Co.
with Richard F. Hubbard

The Legend of Polaris
with Richard F. Hubbard

The Legend of La-Z-Boy
with Richard F. Hubbard

The Legend of McCarthy
with Richard F. Hubbard

*InterVoice:
Twenty Years of Innovation*
with Richard F. Hubbard

*Jefferson-Pilot Financial:
A Century of Excellence*
with Richard F. Hubbard

The Legend of HCA
with Richard F. Hubbard

The Legend of Werner Enterprises
with Richard F. Hubbard

The History of J. F. Shea Co.
with Richard F. Hubbard

True to Our Vision
with Richard F. Hubbard

Albert Trostel & Sons
with Richard F. Hubbard

The Legend of Sovereign Bancorp
with Richard F. Hubbard

*Innovation is the Best Medicine: the
extraordinary story of Datascope*
with Richard F. Hubbard

The Legend of Guardian Industries

*The Legend of
Universal Forest Products*

*Polytechnic University:
Changing the World—The First 150 Years*

*In It For The Long Haul:
The Story of CRST*

*Nothing is Impossible: The Legend of
Joe Hardy and 84 Lumber*

The Story of Parsons Corporation

Cerner: From Vision to Value

*New Horizons:
The Story of Federated Investors*

TABLE OF CONTENTS

FOREWORD

by

James L. Heskett

Baker Foundation Professor
Harvard Business School
and
Office Depot Board Member
1996–2006

I JOINED OFFICE DEPOT'S board of directors in 1996—the year the company celebrated its 10th anniversary. Now, one decade later, I have the pleasure of introducing the company's history.

The board recruited me to join an organization that had initiated significant change in the office products industry. The challenge of management and the board was to maintain the company's early momentum that would lead to the spread of its brand globally.

Shortly after joining the board, one of our first major duties involved organizing a combined board of directors that would result from the pending merger of Office Depot and Staples. The Justice Department ultimately challenged the proposed merger, and a federal court upheld its challenge. It was a frustrating period in Office Depot's history, one that had significant repercussions for both companies. It did, however, provide an opportunity to watch the company rise from the setback and evolve into the multichannel, global success that it is today.

From its inception, Office Depot has been characterized by an entrepreneurial spirit that fostered

one of the fastest rates of growth in corporate history. Much of this was achieved through the acquisition of other organizations. In the process of bringing these organizations under one roof, a strong culture evolved—one dedicated to the creation of wealth for investors by meeting the needs of Office Depot's customer base and the realization that neither of these goals could be achieved without addressing the needs of the company's employees and the communities in which they work. These priorities are reflected in leadership's definition of CEO at Office Depot: Customers, Employees, Owners. They continue to key the company's success even as it evolves to meet changing needs today. They are also reflected in the company's vision: *Delivering Winning Solutions That Inspire Worklife*™.

It has been interesting to see how nearly 50,000 associates in the United States and around the world are brought together under one vision and how everyone at Office Depot is comfortable reciting the vision of the company at the beginning of every meeting. While some might regard this as "hokey," they are the same people who probably scoff at those who engage in the Wal-Mart cheer several times a day. It provides a rallying cry around which a large organization can focus its efforts.

Office Depot's management has always focused on the importance of culture, values, and behaviors. But the new initiatives that the company has experienced over the past 18 months have been especially interesting to observe. They both reflect and have been inspired by the company's values: integrity, innovation, inclusion, customer focus, and accountability. Foremost among the initiatives is the concept of shared leadership—the idea behind both the Office Depot Executive Committee and its Global Officer Coalition. The distribution of leadership responsibility is characterized by the goal-oriented accountability of executives and associates at every level throughout the enterprise. Changing goals as a way of meeting them is simply not acceptable. At the same time, the clear message is that one doesn't cut corners or break rules or laws in order to meet goals.

"Inclusion" has characterized the company's policies and practices since its inception. Efforts to increase diversity throughout the ranks of the company's organization are given high priority. The company has always sponsored events of interest to businesswomen, recognizing that they control a large portion of office supply purchases.

Among Office Depot's important no-nonsense initiatives has been the institution of a culture of thrift that has resulted in significant reductions in waste throughout the business. It has been coupled with an even larger effort to marshal information that helps the company build relationships with existing and new customers and find innovative ways to meet diverse, ever-changing needs. Together, these major efforts are designed to fuel the profitable growth of the company.

There are few companies and management teams that have achieved as much as Office Depot in the first 20 years of their existence. Those of us associated with the company have been particularly proud of its strong commitment to employees, customers, communities, and investors. It is this level of commitment that has accounted for Office Depot's success in meeting the promise of its slogan: *Taking Care of Business.*

ACKNOWLEDGEMENTS

MANY PEOPLE ASSISTED IN THE RESEARCH, preparation, and publication of *Office Depot: Taking Care of Business—The First 20 Years.* The development of historical timelines and a large portion of the principal archival research was accomplished by research assistant Melody Maysonet. Her thorough and careful work made it possible to publish a great deal of interesting information on the origins and evolution of this unique company.

The research, however, much less the book itself, would have been impossible without the dedicated assistance of Office Depot executives and associates. Principal among these is Brian Levine, senior director of public relations and internal communications, whose affable guidance made it possible for our research team to locate and identify records and individuals crucial to the Office Depot legacy.

The interest and courtesy of the many interview subjects for the book was most gratifying. All the people interviewed for the book—whether current associates or retirees—were generous with their time and insights. Those who shared their memories and thoughts include Angel Alverde, Lee Ault III, Neil Austrian, George Ballou, Mark Begelman, Brian Benge, Larry Brock, Charlie Brown, George Bryan, Joe Buckley, Cynthia Campbell, Lynn Connelly, John Deaton, David Fannin, Kor de Jonge, Tyler Elm, Kathy Fajardo, Zach Fishbein, Bruce Fong, Annie Frye, David Fuente, Kissell Goldman, Barry Goldstein, Kim Gorman, Myra Hart, Scott Hedrick, James Heskett, George Hill, Mark Holifield, Rolf van Kaldekerken, Jack Kopkin, Gerry Lebel, Paul Larkin, Rick Lepley, Monica Luechtefeld, Patricia McKay, Robert McCormes-Ballou, Mike Myers, Bruce Nelson, Steve Odland, Paula Randolph, Chuck Rubin, Kirby Salgado, Henry Sauls, Dan Schultz, Brett Snyder, Bill Seltzer, Mike Silvers, Tim Toews, Venna Tredway, David Trudnowski, Tony Ueber, Daisy Vanderlinde, and Mary Wong.

Finally, special thanks are extended to the dedicated staff at Write Stuff Enterprises, Inc., who worked on the book. Thanks are due to Stanimira "Sam" Stefanova, executive editor; Ann Gossy, Heather Lewin, and Elizabeth Fernandez, senior editors; Sandy Cruz, vice president/creative director; Rachelle Donley, art director; Elijah Meyer, and Ryan Milewicz, graphic designers; Amy Blakely, Amy Eble, and Martin Schultz, proofreaders; Mary Aaron, transcriptionist; Connie Angelo, indexer; Amy Major, executive assistant to Jeffrey L. Rodengen; Marianne Roberts, executive vice president, publisher, and chief financial officer; Steven Stahl, director of marketing; and Sherry Hasso, bookkeeper.

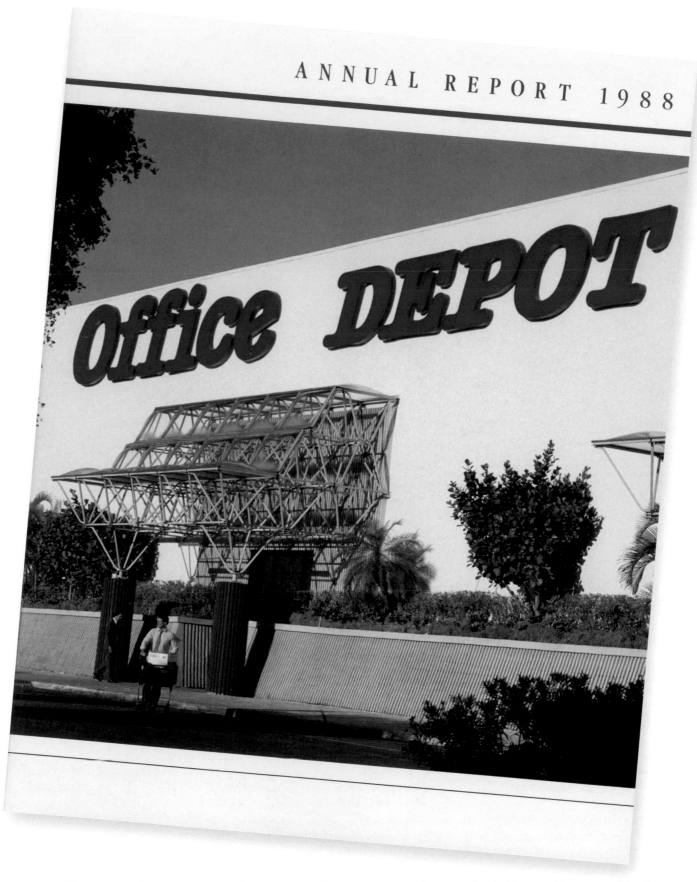

In 1988, Office Depot published its first annual report as a public company. In the letter to shareholders, David Fuente and Stephen Dougherty were understandably proud of the company's progress, reporting a three-fold increase in sales from the previous year.

CHAPTER ONE

BIRTH OF A NOTION

1986 – 1988

Instead of doing $2.5 million out of a [regular-sized] store, you could do five times that volume out of a [warehouse-type] store. This type of approach is a new form of retailing.

—Patrick Sher, cofounder of Office Depot[1]

ONLY ONE YEAR AFTER HE HELPED open the first Office Depot store in 1986, cofounder Patrick Sher was diagnosed with leukemia and learned he had only a 15 percent chance to live. Instead of giving up on his small enterprise, however, Sher forged ahead, even donating his life insurance proceeds to help meet the company's payroll after his death.

Such dedication from him and countless others has certainly borne fruit. Since the company's founding, Office Depot's growth has been extraordinary. In only 20 years, a single office supplies store in Fort Lauderdale, Florida, has grown into a corporate giant, providing more office supplies and services to more customers in more countries than any other company in the world.

As a Fortune 150 company with annual sales of nearly $15 billion and almost 50,000 associates in 23 countries, Office Depot has become an industry leader in every channel, including stores, direct mail, contract delivery, and e-commerce. The company has also been recognized dozens of times for its generous philanthropic and environmental efforts.

Such amazing success, however, did not come without its share of challenges. Office Depot's history is speckled with disappointments and drama—but, without these hardships, the company may not have triumphed to achieve such success.

A Great Idea Made Better

Office Depot is, without a doubt, among the greatest corporations in the world, and its success can be traced back to what seems like a rather simple business concept—warehouse retailing.

When Patrick Sher, Jack Kopkin, and Stephen Dougherty opened the first Office Depot store in October 1986 in Fort Lauderdale, warehouse retailing was not a unique concept. It was, however, an idea in its infancy. When Bernard Marcus and Arthur Blank founded a chain of successful warehouse stores called Home Depot in 1979, it took only a few years for others to notice. Patrick Sher was one of the first such entrepreneurs.

When Sher decided to start his own warehouse retail store in 1981, he was working as president of Lindsley Lumber Company, a chain of stores in Miami. He had witnessed the success of Home Depot and believed he could improve on the concept. "I saw what other people were doing with the warehousing approach to D-I-Y (do-it-yourself)," he said in 1983. "It was a different kind of shopping experience."[2]

Office Depot's first catalogs and print ads featured the "talking" pencil, later dubbed "Stubby," who touted the company's low prices.

In 1982, Sher left his job at Lindsley Lumber and ventured out on his own, eventually bringing fellow Lindsley Lumber executives Stephen Dougherty and Jack Kopkin into the fold. In March 1983, Sher opened the first HomeOwner's Warehouse store (later called Mr. HOW, as in "we'll show you *how* to improve your home") in Coconut Grove, Florida.[3] Mr. HOW was one of Home Depot's first direct competitors.[4]

Sher had originally planned to open four stores but was unable to raise enough capital, so he settled on opening two stores within 60 days of each other. As he noted, "Once the stores get going and making money, it will be a different story. Stores three and four will be no problem."[5]

Sher's Mr. HOW was no mere copycat of other warehouse retailers. As one publication noted, Sher had "done his homework. He was aware that improvements could be made in the warehousing formula. He decided that above all, the new stores would avoid the 'bargain basement' atmosphere that turned certain customers off."[6] According to Paul Bryant, the company's merchandise manager, Mr. HOW's warehouse presentation was more professional compared to other warehouse-style retailers. "Departments and displays ... will be more clearly defined," Bryant said. "There will be broader assortments. Most importantly, the shopping environment will appeal to the female customer as well as to the male."[7]

Above: Cofounder Stephen Dougherty expressed his pride in the company's accomplishments in a 1988 "Happy Holidays" letter to employees. "Office Depot is the leader in its field," he wrote. "It is the leader because we execute our concept better than anyone else ... and because we have by far the best and most dedicated employees in the office supply industry."

Right: Cofounder Jack Kopkin's graduating class at McKenzie College in Chattanooga, Tennessee, voted him most likely to succeed, so it was no wonder he remained confident that Office Depot would prove successful.

The company was a success—perhaps too much so. The same year it was founded, Mr. HOW was purchased by a billion-dollar catalog firm called Service Merchandise Corporation.[8]

"Pat [Sher] called me and asked my advice on whether or not to sell," said Barry Goldstein, who at the time was a partner at Grant Thornton, an accounting firm. "I hated to lose Mr. HOW as a client, but the economy wasn't that great at the time, and with what Service Merchandise was offering, I advised them to sell."[9] Apparently no longer happy in his new role, Sher resigned in 1985 as president of the company he had founded.

Only a year later, Sher, Kopkin, and Dougherty decided to start another warehouse-type store—this time for office products. At first, the three men considered starting a marine supply company, but when they saw the problems and expense in procuring office supplies and furniture for their new enterprise, Jack Kopkin recognized an opportunity. Instead of a marine supply company, the three founders decided to open a warehouse-type store for office products and name their new enterprise Office Depot.[10]

Office Depot is Born

The trio dug into their savings and, along with funding from private investors, managed to raise $2.3 million.[11] Using Mr. HOW as a model, the men set to work, and on October 9, 1986, the first Office Depot store opened its doors in Fort Lauderdale. Sher was CEO of the fledgling enterprise, Dougherty served as president and chief operating officer, and Kopkin was executive vice president and general merchandise manager.

Supply chain training manager Annie Frye, Office Depot's 10th employee, was one of the few current Office Depot employees who worked directly with the three founders in the beginning. In fact, Frye had worked for the founders when they ran Mr. HOW and followed them after they started Office Depot.

"[Pat Sher] was an amazing person," Frye said. "He was very people-oriented. He was very bus-

iness-oriented, too, and dedicated. And he was involved in all the decisions. He was all those things wrapped up in one. I would have followed him anywhere."[12]

"[Kopkin] was the merchandising person," she continued. "He was the one who knew what we needed, how we were going to get it, and who we were going to get it from. He had a great sense of humor, but he was always on top of everything, whether it was finances or strategies or what we needed to bring in. And, like Sher, he was a people person. He always listened."

Frye described Dougherty as "a little bit intimidating. ... He was very tall, somewhere around six feet, six inches, and medium built, and he was serious about everything."[13]

Frye said she revised her opinion of Dougherty after he learned that she intended to accept a different job outside of the company, which offered her travel opportunities. "He came to talk to me," she said. "We talked about everything under the sun except for me leaving. And because I was so young at the time, I thought, 'When is the shoe going to drop?' ... Then we finally talked about Office Depot. He gave me his vision of where he thought the company was going. He told me he'd really like for me to stay and be a part of that. He said he couldn't give me what I was looking for

Above: On October 9, 1986, Office Depot opened its first store in Fort Lauderdale, Florida. Two more stores in South Florida quickly followed.

Below: On the inside of Office Depot's catalogs, Stubby the "talking" pencil explained how company stores could offer such low prices.

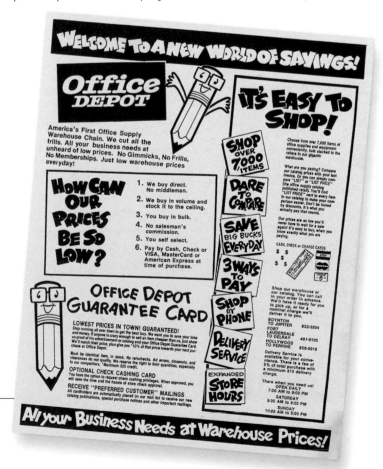

Office Depot offered more than the standard office supply store. Each location featured a wide selection of office furniture designed to fit a variety of décors and budgets.

right now, but in one to two years, I'd have more than I could expect."[14]

Frye ended up staying with Office Depot and never regretted her decision. She was knowledgeable about home improvement supplies from her experience at Mr. HOW, but as part of the crew that helped procure supplies for the first Office Depot store, she wasn't as familiar with office supplies. Frye wasn't alone, however, since most of the crew members who helped open the first store were in similar situations.

"When we received product, we laid it all out on the floor to try to plan how to set it up," she said. "Oftentimes, because we didn't know a lot about office supplies, we just asked ourselves, 'What looks good?' and planned it from there. On the day the store opened, a man asked us for a Montblanc pen, and we looked at each other [inquisitively]."[15]

Despite the learning curve, Office Depot was a hit. It was more than just an office supplies store; it

was an office supplies warehouse store. At that time, most businesses—whether Fortune 500 corporations or small, independent companies—received their office supplies from various mom-and-pop organizations that charged retail prices to buyers who were unable to purchase in mass quantities. Office Depot helped modify that concept.

"We saw that a legal pad was being sold in a local store for a dollar," Kopkin said. "We could sell 12 for four dollars."[16]

By purchasing directly from the manufacturer, the founders were able to cut out the middleman, and because the warehouse store was huge, the company was able to buy supplies in bulk. Consequently, it could afford to offer office supplies—everything from office furniture to pens to typewriters—at discount prices of up to 40 to 60 percent off retail. Although large corporations were often already receiving this type of deal, small- and medium-sized companies were missing out on the savings. Sher, Kopkin, and Dougherty's new warehouse-style stores solved this problem, revolutionizing the way office products were sold.[17] This was also matched by a revolution in office products, especially technology. Personal computers, printers, fax machines, and their supplies were new to businesses. Office Depot gave customers the opportunity to touch and feel the latest innovations in technology.

"I knew the warehouse concept, which was successful in the hardware and building supply industry, could be applied to office products," Kopkin said in early 1988.[18]

"We looked at successful companies, like Wal-Mart, that already have this concept [of purchasing in volume] in place," Dougherty told one reporter. "That's how we wanted to do it—everyday low pricing." Upholding low prices every day rather than hosting intermittent sales, he added, removed some of the confusion and inconvenience involved with sales.[19] Also, Kopkin noted that Office Depot had "created a whole new system of distribution." Even other warehouse-style retailers utilized central distribution centers, but at Office Depot—at least in the company's early days—the store *was* the distribution center.[20]

Above: Each Office Depot store featured a full-service copy and print center for "All Your Printing Needs at Warehouse Prices!"

Left: In the company's early days, its stores were, in fact, warehouses. Product was placed on pallets on the floor, in bins, and stacked floor-to-ceiling on utility shelves.

A Bittersweet Start

Throughout the rest of 1986, the founders concentrated on raising capital, recruiting strong personnel, developing information systems, and selecting inventory and site locations for future stores.[21] By the end of the year, they had opened two more Office Depot stores, and the company's year-end sales had reached $2 million. Clearly, the warehouse style of retailing office products was becoming a success.

In the company's early days, the stores had no frills—product was placed in bins, on wooden pallets on the concrete floor, or stacked floor-to-ceiling on steel utility shelves.[22] Each store measured about 25,000 square feet and carried more than 7,000 different products. Customers could shop by phone or in the store, they could order from the catalog for pickup or delivery, and each store featured a full-service copy and print center.

With three successful stores, Sher, Dougherty, and Kopkin were eager to open more, but they lacked an essential ingredient—funding. So the founders began negotiating with various invest-

Office DEPOT®

IN 1986, PATRICK SHER, STEPHEN DOUGH-erty, and Jack Kopkin had known it was time for a change in the way businesses obtained office products. Taking their cues from consumer warehouse retailing, the three partners had a big idea—to create a one-stop shopping experience that provided all the products companies needed, at the best values. They called the concept "Office Depot."

The trio's first order of business was to establish the Office Depot logo and brand. Since warehouse retailing was in its infancy, the company's brand identity needed to convey value, connote professionalism, and inspire confidence. The team chose a bright shade of red for the company logo in an effort to inject energy into the identity and communicate determination and strength. They also selected a bold and heavy typeface to reinforce the spirit of determination, dependability, and trustworthiness, all while creating a visual impact for consumers.

The three founders also wanted to ensure that the logo communicated the idea of customer focus. To achieve that, the word "Office" appeared more prominently than the word "Depot," emphasizing business customer needs over everything else.

By the time the first Office Depot store opened in Fort Lauderdale in October 1986, the three founders had established a brand identity that clearly communicated their vision. Since then, Office Depot has built significant equity in this identity, and the messages that the logo's design conveys remain relevant to today's customers.

---

ment firms, among them Oak Investment Partners. Unfortunately, one week before they were set to receive the necessary financial backing in June 1987, the unexpected occurred. Doctors diagnosed Pat Sher with leukemia and told him he had only a 15 percent chance to live. When Sher related this news to Gerald Gallagher of Oak Investment Partners, the firm decreased the funding it had planned by 20 percent. This move, of course, made sense from a financial standpoint as Sher was the only founder with financial experience.[23]

According to CFO Barry Goldstein, "We were very, very close to going under because we thought our financing was complete, and we had checks to vendors waiting to go out that now we could not mail."[24]

Even with the cut in financing, Oak Investment Partners, along with several other private investors, purchased $11 million in a private stock placement, providing the young company with its first major funding.[25] Oak Investment, however, requested a major contingency with the deal—they wanted to select Sher's successor, the new CEO of Office Depot.[26]

As one of the company's original venture capitalists, long-time board member Michael Myers remembered negotiating with the other private investors over control of the company. "We negotiated for two or three days," he recalled, "and it was tough, but we [the members of Oak Investment] ultimately agreed that we wanted to have control of [selecting] the next CEO."[27]

Sher died in October 1987, four months after his fatal diagnosis. As a fitting tribute, Sher's life insurance proceeds helped keep the company afloat as it struggled to meet payroll after his death.[28] Perhaps more importantly, Sher's death started a tradition of giving at Office Depot, as contributions toward the treatment and prevention of leukemia were among the first in a long list of philanthropic efforts by the company.

A New Leader

In its quest to find the best candidate to succeed Sher, Oak Investment Partners hired a New York headhunting firm to assist in the selection process. After interviewing 10 candidates,

Gallagher and the other partners at Oak Investment set their sights on David I. Fuente, who at the time was president of Sherwin-Williams' chain of 1,800 paint stores.[29]

"We quickly saw that David [Fuente] was very smart and very quick on the uptake," said Myers. "Also, he was able to immediately see potential of the business model at Office Depot. He had a tremendous retail background."[30]

Fuente did not express much enthusiasm about leaving his position in Cleveland to become CEO of a start-up company. When the executive search firm first contacted him about the position, Fuente was reluctant. He had plans in place to play golf in Fort Meyers, Florida. "I told [the search firm], 'I'm going to play golf. If it rains, I'll drive over to Fort Lauderdale.'"[31]

As fate would have it, Fuente's golf game was rained out, so he went to visit Office Depot. "I saw the first store. It was Sunday afternoon, and it was just as busy as it could be," he said. "I couldn't believe my eyes."[32]

Fuente officially joined Office Depot as the company's CEO in December 1987. By that time, the company had 800 employees and 10 stores in Florida and Georgia, and it had chalked up $34 million in revenue for the year.[33]

"The fact that Office Depot was able to secure a heavyweight executive like Fuente spoke volumes," said longtime employee Brian Benge, director of customer relations, who started out as an assistant manager. Benge remembered the company's first corporate headquarters at Northwest Second Avenue in Boca Raton, Florida, when he interviewed with the company in 1987. "It was in a little strip mall, and it was probably about 2,500 square feet," he said. "There were desks and boxes all up and down the hallways and into these little rooms, and you could barely walk because people were working in hallways … sharing desks."[34]

The Office Depot management team in 1987 (from left): Jack Kopkin, executive vice president and general merchandise manager; Stephen Dougherty, president and chief operating officer; David Fuente, chairman and chief executive officer; and Barry Goldstein, vice president and chief financial officer.

1988 OFFICE DEPOT BOARD OF DIRECTORS

Stephen L. Dougherty
President
Chief Operating Officer
Office Depot, Inc.

David I. Fuente
Chairman
Chief Executive Officer
Office Depot, Inc.

Gerald R. Gallagher
General Partner
Oak Investment Partners, III

David R. Jaffe
General Partner
Chemical Venture Partners

Jack D. Kopkin
Executive Vice President
General Merchandise Manager
Office Depot, Inc.

Michael J. Myers
Senior Vice President and
Managing Director
Barney, Harris, Upham & Co., Inc.
President of First Century Partners, Inc.

Alan L. Wurtzel
Chairman
Circuit City Stores, Inc.

"My kids were out of school by then, and I was ready to do something exciting and new, so I did," Fuente said.[35]

By many accounts, Fuente's respect for people was one of his defining characteristics. "He's very, very people-oriented," said Barry Goldstein, the company's first chief financial officer. "He lets people working for him do their jobs. He's not sitting on your shoulder."[36]

"Dave Fuente is one of my favorite people," said John Deaton, a former vice president who worked under Fuente in the late 1990s. "He is brilliant, and he is knowledgeable about so many different areas of the business. He's fun to work with, and he has such energy, such passion."[37]

Fuente fostered an open atmosphere, and those who worked with him remembered his sense of humor. "He never lost focus in his work [because of his humor]," Deaton said. "It was always direct and pointed."[38]

Case in point was one of Fuente's many witticisms: He once described his own managerial style as "lean and mean, with a little fat around the middle."[39]

Fuente's humor kept him afloat during difficult times. He was no stranger to hardship. In the early 1980s, doctors discovered a cancerous tumor around a bone in his right leg. To save his life, the leg was amputated.[40]

In the beginning, Fuente's goals for the company were simple. For the short term, he wanted to move into Texas.[41] For the longer term, he strove to stay the path and continue "executing the cardinal law of discount retailing: 'pricing, pricing, pricing.'"[42]

Fuente's goal to penetrate the Texas market didn't take long to realize. Store No. 12 opened in Houston in the spring of 1988, and three more stores in the area quickly followed.[43]

Going Public

To continue expanding the business, Fuente, Dougherty, and Goldstein knew that more funding was necessary, but the stock market in late 1987 and early 1988 was considered too weak to achieve a successful public offering. The economy began an incremental upward swing in March 1988, and the company's leaders took a chance on the advice

CFO Barry Goldstein helped take Office Depot public in 1988. Before the initial pubic offering, Goldstein, along with David Fuente and Stephen Dougherty, spent three weeks with the company's investment bankers on a countrywide roadshow to acquire potential investors.

of Office Depot's investment banker, Merrill Lynch.

Goldstein and Fuente embarked on a road show to lure investors, which Goldstein described as "very tough." Rather than using a chartered private jet, the two men traveled commercially, making up to three stops a day for their presentations. "There were a couple of times when we were literally banging on the door of a plane trying to make a connection," Goldstein said.[44]

Despite the challenges of the road show, two months later, on June 1, 1988, Office Depot went public on NASDAQ under the symbol ODEP with a $20 million offering of 2.1 million shares of stock at $10 a share.

Goldstein was understandably proud of the results. "The reception to Office Depot, our business concept, and our results to date were well-received by the institutional investment community and the stock market in general," he told employees upon returning from the road. "We've been told repeatedly that one of the key facts that caused major institutions to invest was the quality and dedication of the people they met in the stores and in our corporate office."[45]

Even so, analysts were skeptical, thinking the fledgling company was moving too quickly. "Our critics argued that we were still too young a company to be going public," said Fuente. "They argued that our management team was perhaps not experienced enough to grow so rapidly. They thought we were trying to grow faster than any sensible company would grow."[46]

Even office supplies manufacturers believed small mom-and-pop distributors had a lock on the industry. "The criticism was based on conventional wisdom," Fuente told *Forbes* magazine. "We were contrarians."[47] As *Forbes* reported:

Fuente based his contrarianism on his understanding that he could afford to grow fast because the warehouse-style, 25,000-square-foot stores had little fashion content; thus, there was little chance they would get stuck with unsaleable merchandise.[48]

The naysayers were proven wrong. Two weeks after the public offering, Office Depot's stock shot up 37.5 percent. "In the same period [after an initial public offering]," the *Wall Street Journal* pointed out, "over-the-counter stocks generally have risen 4 percent."[49]

The influx of cash provided an essential ingredient for the company's expansion. In 1988, Office Depot opened 16 new stores for a total of 26 retail outlets in six states: Florida, Georgia, North Carolina, Texas, Tennessee, and Kentucky. Its 1988 sales reached $132 million, an amazing 292 percent increase from the previous year. That remarkable growth, however, would seem minor compared to what the future would actually bring.

The front cover of this Office Depot 1989 summer/winter catalog celebrates the grand opening of two new company stores in Louisville, Kentucky. For added convenience, the back cover showed the location of each store.

CHAPTER TWO

A NATIONAL PLAYER

1989–1991

We're committed to a strategy of being the dominant supplier of office supplies to small and medium-sized businesses in every market in which we operate.

—Chairman and CEO David Fuente, 1990[1]

THE 1980s INTRODUCED FAR-reaching changes to the United States. Rising interest rates and financial woes, including the Black Monday stock market crash of October 14, 1987, affected millions of Americans.[2]

Despite the economic recession, Office Depot continued to thrive. By 1989, its second year as a public company, Office Depot was the largest and fastest-growing office supply store in the nation, increased competition notwithstanding. Its closest competitor, Staples, owned half as many stores at that time.[3]

Even so, with the industry so highly fragmented, Office Depot's overall market share remained minimal. There was a myriad of other office supply companies, mostly small independents that served local or niche markets. But Office Depot also competed against wholesale clubs, discount stores, mass merchandisers, conventional retail stores, convenience stores, direct-mail companies, grocery stores, drug stores, and catalog companies. Other chain store competitors that dealt exclusively in office supplies were only regional in scope. Although Office Depot's executives continued to focus on saturating the company's existing markets, they had their long-range sights set on becoming a national player.

A New Breed

Office Depot was, as one Florida publication pointed out, a "new breed of superstores."[4] Before Office Depot helped revolutionize the way office supplies were purchased, businesses bought office products mainly from dealers, most of whom owned a few retail stores stocked by a central warehouse.

The dealers bought their inventory from office supply distributors, who, in turn, acquired their merchandise from the manufacturer. Most dealers had salespeople who worked on commission and negotiated with various businesses, offering discounts to those businesses (usually large ones) that purchased in bulk.

Office Depot was one of only a few office products retailers that cut out the middlemen (the dealers and distributors) by purchasing directly from the manufacturer. As a chain of stores, it was also able to purchase in volume, and since its stores served as warehouses, it had no central warehouse to maintain. All of this amounted to significant savings for customers.[5]

"The mom-and-pop suppliers couldn't compete," said Brian Benge, who helped open numerous stores in the company's early days. "Our focus was to keep merchandise in stock and the freight

In 1990, Office Depot began producing recycled paper. This marked the beginning of the company's environmental efforts, which were lauded during the next decade as going above and beyond the norm in terms of corporate stewardship.

flowing because it would fly off the shelves. Some of these small suppliers would charge $60 for a case of paper, and we'd look like heroes coming in at $40 for a case—and we'd blow them away at $25."[6]

"I remember receiving truckloads of merchandise, and we would stack it to the ceiling," said George Ballou, who was hired as a retail sales associate in 1987 and later became a store manager in Fort Lauderdale. "We sold a lot of items in bulk—customers would buy pallets of paper and large boxes of pens, and it was a challenge just to keep the store stocked."[7]

In addition to price discounts, customers enjoyed the one-stop shopping experience and the overall

ease of making purchases at Office Depot. The stores were located in convenient areas with sufficient parking. Items were checked out via swift bar code scanning, which, in the late 1980s, was considered sophisticated technology.

Each store also offered expert customer assistance, with employees attending regular training sessions on customer courtesy, product knowledge, and communications. According to Fuente, stores always had 15 to 20 employees on the floor to help customers.[8] Unlike many office supply stores, Office Depot was open seven days and six evenings a week.

To improve service, the company opened a delivery center in 1990 that consolidated functions for its South Florida stores. As Annie Frye noted, "Our stores became a little hectic trying to be both a warehouse *and* a delivery center, so that's why opening delivery centers was a good idea."[9] That same year,

Office Depot carried top-quality, brand-name products at discounts of up to 75 percent off the list price.

Left: At first, Office Depot offered its "low-price guarantee" exclusively to Office Depot V.I.P. Card holders. The company later offered the guarantee to all of its customers.

Below: In 1989 and 1991, Office Depot fueled its future growth by selling $81.4 million worth of shares to Carrefour, a large and highly esteemed French retailer. CEO David Fuente called Office Depot's involvement with Carrefour one of the most significant events in Office Depot's history.

business customers were able to charge their purchases on an Office Depot private-label credit card.

Furthermore, the company maintained a "no questions asked" return and exchange policy, with an "everyday low-price guarantee." The guarantee meant that if a customer found a product advertised for less, Office Depot would match the lower price and give the customer 50 percent of the difference as credit toward another purchase.

With all of these strategies, the competition was worried, and those who weren't concerned were wearing blinders.[10]

A Picture of Health

Office Depot managed to remain financially healthy. In 1989, the company saw no need to dip into its bank line of credit to continue expanding, as it had sufficient funding from selling shares. In January 1989, a second public stock offering raised $24.1 million, and a few months later, the company raised another $41.4 million by selling 1.8 million shares to a French company called Carrefour, one of the first corporations involved in

warehouse retailing. Office Depot raised another $40 million in 1991 by selling 1.43 million shares to Carrefour, giving the French retailer a 17 percent stake in Office Depot.

Fuente described the Carrefour transaction as one of the most significant events in the early history of Office Depot. "We needed funding for future growth, and Carrefour's $40 million influx saved us from having to do a third round of financing," Fuente explained.[11]

Shareholders remained content, as well. In the spring of 1989, they received a three-for-two stock split in the form of a dividend, as Office Depot's stock value continued to escalate. In December 1991, the company sold 2.3 million shares of its common stock for $42 a share, which was more than four times the stock's value when Office Depot had gone public in 1988.

Smart Merchandising

The secret to Office Depot's rapid, yet well-controlled growth started with smart merchandising, as the company's buyers focused on offering a balanced, in-depth assortment of quality brands. To ensure stores carried items that best met customers' needs, the company's buyers conducted extensive research by testing and evaluating new products to ensure they met Office Depot's high standards. Meanwhile, Office Depot

item by a certain date. That revolutionized the distribution of the office supply industry."[21]

Improved Operations

Since it began operations, Office Depot utilized some of the best information technology available. In 1989, it upgraded to an IBM System AS/400, which was considered state-of-the-art at the time. That year, the company also converted to a shared satellite system for faster and more cost-effective communication between corporate headquarters and stores outside of Florida. The system was also used to conduct "live" meetings across states or broadcast training programs to employees.

In 1990, the company began implementing electronic data interchange (EDI), which allowed Office Depot to order new inventory from suppliers through computer-to-computer transmissions rather than the more cumbersome and expensive exchange via telephone or fax. Office Depot also used advanced inventory control systems to keep track of merchandise and ensure that it was replenished in its stores and delivery centers in a timely and cost-effective manner.

In 1991, the company began working with United Stationers, which provided cross-docking services that helped Office Depot save money in receiving and inventory control. Shipments from 10 vendors were consolidated at United Stationers' distribution center in Norcross, Georgia, before being shipped to Office Depot stores. In later years, Office Depot added more cross docks—which it operated on its own, rather than using a third party—to further reduce costs and simplify purchasing.

"Before we had cross docks, an individual store would sometimes have 15 to 20 trailers outside full of merchandise to stock the shelves," said Kissel Goldman, a district store manager who joined Office Depot in 1987. "The cross docks enabled a system where the stores receive just the right amount of inventory."[22]

Left: After Stephen Dougherty resigned as president in February 1990, Office Depot's top management team consisted of (from left) Jack Kopkin, executive vice president; David Fuente, president, chairman, and CEO; and Barry Goldstein, chief financial officer. Kopkin would retire later that year, and Mark Begelman would join as president and COO the following year.

Below: Office Depot stayed on the cutting edge of new technology to ensure that its information systems ran smoothly. In 1989, the company upgraded to this IBM AS/400 computer system.

Good Relations

Even while the company grew so rapidly, it maintained a fast-paced, entrepreneurial culture that encouraged excellence. In return, Office Depot took great care of its employees. "We try to make it a fun place to work," Fuente said. "As a company, we try to respect our people."[23]

By 1989, Office Depot had already adopted an employee stock purchasing plan. Office Depot executives also wanted employees to help improve the company, encouraging them to provide frequent feedback to their managers. As an example, an employee suggestion program in 1989 paid $1,000 to the first-prize winner for ideas on how Office Depot could remain the leader in office supply warehouses.

An internal newsletter called *Highlighter* celebrated employees' accomplishments, promotions, new store openings, and other company milestones. In addition to reporting significant happenings at corporate headquarters, the newsletter offered employees tips on how to have a successful career and provide better customer service.

Office Depot also began taking steps toward becoming one of the nation's most generous companies in terms of philanthropy. In the spring of 1991, it sponsored the Arthritis Foundation's "All Star Salute to Secretaries" in 36 cities across the United States. The event gave managers the opportunity to honor their secretaries by attending planned events. Overall, Office Depot raised $400,000 for the Arthritis Foundation.[24]

The Founders Move On

A few other noteworthy events occurred in the early part of the decade. In February 1990, cofounder Steve Dougherty abruptly resigned as

Store personnel in Davie, Florida, gather for their November 13, 1989, grand opening. That year, Office Depot opened 41 stores in 29 markets, including 20 new markets.

Office Depot's internal newsletter, *Highlighter*, welcomed Office Club and its associates to the Office Depot family in the summer of 1991.

president, telling the press, "… [It] was just a buildup of things," adding that there were differences between him and Fuente. "I was getting too much aggravation."[25] Fuente, however, had a differing view about his relationship with Dougherty: "He may view it as a falling out," Fuente said, "but I don't."[26]

So in 1990, Fuente accepted the role of president in addition to his duties as chairman and CEO.[27] That same year, Jack Kopkin, cofounder and executive vice president, announced his retirement.[28] Years later, Kopkin said he chose to retire because he was an entrepreneur at heart and

Office Depot—due to its enormous success—had naturally moved away from entrepreneurialism to operate "more like a large corporation."[29]

The First Acquisition

The year 1991 was a successful one for Office Depot. In April, the company acquired Office Club, Inc., an office products retailer, for $137.5 million. The acquisition established Office Depot as "the most dominant and most recognizable office products retailer in the western market," according to the company's annual report.[30] It also transitioned Office Depot from a regional to a national player in the office supply arena. Office Club shareholders received 1.194 shares of Office Depot stock for each common share of Office Club stock they owned.

Office Club operated a chain of 59 warehouse office supply stores in nine western states (37 of them in California). Its customers paid a $10 annual membership fee to receive discounted prices on brand-name office products.

Mark Begelman, who founded Office Club in 1987 in San Francisco, became president and chief operating officer of Office Depot after the acquisition. Years later, he explained why he chose to join Office Depot, despite his own company's success:

The profit margins for all of the office supply superstores were very thin at that time, and to become national in scope, to continue growing, I knew I would have to raise a staggering amount of money. So I decided that if I merged Office Club with another of the big players in the industry, we would have greater access to capital markets. Plus, the combined company would become the dominant office product retailer.[31]

By many accounts, Begelman was smart, entrepreneurial, and different. During the day he was a corporate executive, and at night he played lead guitar in a band called *Eraserhead*.[32]

"There was a culture shift when Mark Begelman came on board," said Benge. "The influx of talent he brought from California was a big change.

Californians seemed to have a different way of doing things with regard to associates and programs. So I actually think he helped a lot in building a more associate-friendly culture."[33]

"It was a bit of an adjustment after Office Depot bought Office Club," said Brett Snyder, who provided audio/video support for most of Office Depot's history. "It was classic East Coast/West Coast lifestyles clashing with each other. The first generation of Office Depot was suit and tie, a very traditional business look, at least at the corporate level. Then you had some of the California management that came to work at headquarters and all of a sudden, you had ideas like casual Friday, and their management style was very different, too."[34]

Begelman also admitted that the cultures of the two companies were decidedly different. "At Office Club, we were a very casual and a very close-knit group, and when the two companies merged, we went through some trials and tribulations of getting Depot people and Club people to stop thinking about two separate companies and start thinking about one company, which was the new Office Depot."[35]

Despite the cultural differences, the synergies were obvious. Besides selling similar product lines, the companies were "very similar in management style and philosophy," Fuente said. "I think it's an excellent mesh."[36]

Scott Hedrick, one of the original investors in Office Club who became an Office Depot board member after the merger, also explained why the two companies melded well. "Office Depot was more retail oriented, while we at Office Club were more business-to-business oriented," he said. "We ended up blending the best aspects of Office Club with the best aspects of Office Depot."[37]

Originally, executives had planned for Office Club to become a wholly owned subsidiary of Office Depot, keeping the Office Club name. But within a year of the acquisition, management decided to convert the Office Club stores to Office Depot ones. "After comparing Office Club's membership format with Office Depot's policy of offering everyone the same low prices every day, we decided that we could best serve our small to midsize business customers by eliminating the annual membership fee," said Begelman. "Once the decision was made to change the membership concept, we felt the 'Club' name might be confusing."[38]

More than 2,000 items were added to the former Office Club stores, so stores company-wide carried the same merchandise assortment. The Office Club stores were also remodeled to accommodate the added inventory and look like traditional Office Depot stores. For a while, the former Office Club stores kept their blue motif (compared to Office Depot's dominating red color), and their Office Depot logo used the same font that Office Club stores had previously used.

Even before Office Depot acquired it, Office Club's marketing strategy was very similar to that of Office Depot, as evidenced by this 1990 catalog supplement advertising "lowest prices guaranteed."

Because Office Club was based in California, Office Depot was able to move into the western third of the United States with already established and profitable stores. One reporter pointed out that the acquisition provided Office Depot with "the upper hand in penetrating the lucrative California office supplies market."[39]

Analysts also approved of the combined companies. "[Office Depot] would become the largest and the most geographically diverse [office supplies] company," said one Dallas-based analyst. "Combining the two forces makes Depot even more competitive."[40] Another analyst in Atlanta said, "This combined Club–Depot entity will have more leverage with their vendors and manufacturers than will Staples."[41]

What Recession?

Though most American companies were mired in the economic recession of the early 1990s, Office Depot continued to thrive. "Someone forgot to tell Office Depot about the recession," wrote one reporter.[42] The *South Florida Business Journal* called Office Depot's stock "enticing," despite the recession. Office Depot "is carving an impressive niche for itself with its no-frills approach," wrote the *Palm Beach Post*.[43] An industry investor pointed out that the recession during which many people were being laid off had resulted in a boom for Office Depot because so many people were starting home businesses.[44]

Office Depot had also continued to grow at a quick pace because the industry was noncyclical, according to company officials.[45] (Noncyclical stocks repeatedly outperform the market when economic growth slows, while cyclical companies are highly correlated to the economy.)

By the end of 1991, Office Depot had 228 stores in 29 states and employed 9,000 people. Sales crossed the $1 billion mark ($1.3 billion) in 1991, an increase of nearly 40 percent over the previous

In 1991, Office Depot moved its headquarters from Boca Raton, Florida, to a nearby campus in Delray Beach, Florida.

year. Even more impressive was the fact that the billion-dollar milestone was achieved in only five years. In December 1991, the company hit the "Big Board" with a listing on the New York Stock Exchange under the ticker symbol ODP. Fuente noted that the listing gave Office Depot better visibility among investors, benefiting both the company and its shareholders.[46]

As evidence of its success, in 1991, Office Depot moved from Boca Raton, Florida, into a new corporate headquarters in Delray Beach, Florida. At first, Office Depot leased the property, but in 1994, after doubling the size of the headquarters and tripling the number of employees, the company purchased the property outright.[47]

With solid financial footing and its first acquisition under its belt, Office Depot was preparing for the future. It continued saturating existing markets to achieve economies of scale, and it continued seeking out new markets. It wouldn't take long for the company to realize its goals, when in just a few months it stepped into the international arena.

Even while the U.S. economy experienced a recession in the early 1990s, Office Depot continued to add big-ticket items such as personal computers to its array of products.

CHAPTER THREE

GLOBAL EXPANSION

1992 – 1995

Office Depot continued to lead the office products industry, remaining first in total sales, first in total number of stores, first in average sales per store, first in average weekly store sales ... and most important to our shareholders, first in net earnings.

—Chairman and CEO David Fuente, 1995[1]

BY ACQUIRING OFFICE CLUB IN 1991, Office Depot set off a flurry of mergers and acquisitions in the office supply industry, as smaller players tried to keep up with the leader in the field. Closest rival Staples moved into Office Depot's backyard when it purchased a chain of 10 WORKplace office superstores in central Florida.[2] And when OfficeMax bought BizMart's 105 stores, it temporarily moved into second place.[3] All over the country, the office supply industry was shaking out. One manager of an independent office supply store estimated that the number of office supply firms had decreased from approximately 14,000 to 8,000 in the past five or six years, with the industry continuing to consolidate.[4] Indeed, by the end of 1993, only Office Depot, Staples, and OfficeMax remained competitive in the "warehouse-style" retail principle.[5]

An International Toe Print

As the early 1990s approached, Office Depot aimed to transform itself into the largest and most successful office supply retailer both in the United States and the rest of the world. As the company explained:

Global expansion makes sense not only because new technologies and improved distribution chan-

nels now make it possible, but because the company's business formula transcends national and cultural boundaries. There is really no difference between a customer in Warsaw and one in Wichita—they both want the best products at the best prices from the best manufacturers.[6]

In February 1992, Office Depot expanded internationally for the first time when it acquired five Great Canadian Office Supplies Warehouse stores and the leases of two other stores, all owned by H.Q. Office International. With all of the stores located in western Canada, the acquisition solidified Office Depot's position as the No. 1 chain of office supply superstores in North America and launched the company's international expansion. The Canadian stores were quickly converted to the Office Depot brand in both appearance and inventory, and by the end of the year, Office Depot owned nine stores in Canada. In subsequent years, Office Depot continued to expand in that country, and by the end of 1995, the company owned 28 Canadian stores: two stores in the province of Saskatchewan, two in Manitoba, seven in Alberta, seven in British

Grand opening celebrations accompany the opening of many new Office Depot stores.

Columbia, and 10 stores in Ontario that operated under the name Office Place.

In 1994, Office Depot's international toe print became a footprint. After the passage of the North American Free Trade Agreement (NAFTA) in January 1994, which encouraged the fair exchange of goods and services among North American countries by lowering trade barriers, Office Depot CEO David Fuente and President and COO Mark Begelman saw opportunities to expand the company's North American operations. To that end, in 1994, Office Depot signed a joint venture agreement with Mexican company Grupo Gigante, which had successfully operated retail stores in Mexico for 33 years.

As Office Depot was preparing to enter Mexico, the Mexican peso became significantly devalued.

As the driving forces behind Office Depot's vision and growth, then-CEO David Fuente (left) and Mark Begelman, then-president and COO, were instrumental in expanding the company, which had already attracted numerous accolades from investors, analysts, and the press. (Photograph is © 1993 Red Morgan with all rights reserved.)

Despite difficult business conditions, the company pressed forward, and the first two stores opened on the same day in Guadalajara, Mexico, in March 1995. Reflecting the economy's poor condition, 7,000 people applied for the 160 positions that were available at the two stores.[7]

Angel Alverde, president of Office Depot–Mexico, was hired in July 1994 as the joint venture's director of marketing, director of merchandising, buyer of furniture, and buyer of copy centers. "We needed to do everything very cheaply," Alverde explained. "The Mexican economy at that time was probably the worst economy of the past 70 years. It was a real disaster, and Office Depot was questioning whether it should move forward with the project. But since Grupo Gigante had been in Mexico for many years and was accustomed to the country's economic ups and downs, Gigante was able to assure Office Depot not to worry."[8]

Office Depot took Grupo Gigante's advice, and Mexico became a strong market for Office Depot. By 2006, Office Depot operated more than 130 stores in five Central American countries: Mexico, Guatemala, Costa Rica, El Salvador, and

Above: When Office Depot ventured into Mexico in 1994 during one of the country's worst economies, Angel Alverde helped the company establish itself as a successful business in the country. Alverde was promoted to president of Office Depot–Mexico in 1996.

Right: Bar code scanning, which was considered sophisticated technology in the early 1990s, helped create quick and easy checkouts for busy shoppers at Office Depot stores.

warehouse in Ashdod and another store in Tel Aviv. According to Fishbein, who became president of Office Depot–Israel, all of Office Depot's stores in Israel proved successful.[11]

Also in 1994, the company entered an international licensing agreement with Centrod Del Futuro in Colombia, opening its first Office Depot store in the city of Bogotá. Three more stores and a delivery warehouse opened in Colombia the following year. A licensing agreement with Retail Investment Concepts (RIC) also allowed Office Depot to build a presence in Poland, with the first Office Depot store opening in Warsaw in 1995.

Aggressive Expansion Continues

Meanwhile, Office Depot continued to expand in the United States, opening numerous stores in its existing marketplaces to enhance industry penetration and spread into new areas of the country. In the spring of 1992, the company came across a unique opportunity for entry into the Washington, D.C. area when six empty stores came up for sale. Office Depot had monitored the highly competitive region for years as office supply retailers vied for a piece of the local market and eventually fell by the

Honduras. The company also planned to open stores in Panama.[9]

Office Depot's leaders also sought out opportunities to move beyond North America's borders. Zach Fishbein, a former pilot in the Israeli air force, who worked as a retail supplier in the United States, had been following Office Depot's progress and believed the company could benefit by opening stores in Israel. So in 1992, he contacted David Fuente via letter and eventually received a call back. The two met in person to discuss the possibility of such an expansion, and at the end of the meeting, Fishbein told Fuente, "I don't take 'no' for an answer." Later, Fuente joked that he had no choice but to expand into Israel because of Fishbein's persistence.[10]

In 1994, Office Depot signed a licensing agreement with several parties in Israel and opened one store each in the cities of Tel Aviv and Haifa. By the end of 1995, Office Depot had opened a delivery

wayside, leaving empty stores behind—ideal locations for Office Depot to fill.[12]

"Part of our expansion plans are a function of the economy," CFO Barry Goldstein said of the company's move into Washington, D.C. "With the number of stores that have closed down, real estate is finally available."[13]

In 1992, Office Depot also entered the important Chicago market with the opening of three stores in metropolitan area retail centers. Three more Chicago stores opened the following year. By 1993, Office Depot had eight stores in the Chicago area and nine stores in and around the nation's capital. By then, to better handle the increase in phone and fax orders, Office Depot had opened two call centers: one in Florida and one in California.

In keeping with its strategy of aggressive expansion, in 1993, Office Depot opened 10 stores in Michigan, including five in the Detroit area. The following year, the company went head-to-head with OfficeMax when it opened four stores in Cincinnati, Ohio; four in Minneapolis, Minnesota; and (in 1995) one store in Cleveland, Ohio.

Also in 1995, Office Depot opened three "megastores" in the New York City metropolitan area. At the time, the New York area was dominated by Staples, which had 70 stores, and OfficeMax, with some 20 stores.[14]

"Because we were going into Staples' territory for the first time, we felt we needed to do something different," said Fuente. "Also, the technology business was exploding, and we thought we could, in essence, combine the idea of an Office Depot and a Comp USA-type store into one monstrous megastore."[15]

Office Depot had already opened one megastore in Las Vegas that year, and the megastore concept seemed a perfect way for Office Depot to debut in the country's largest metropolis. (As it turned out, Office Depot has struggled in New York due mainly to high rental prices, and the company closed three of its four Manhattan stores in 2005.)

Each megastore measured from 45,000 to 50,000 square feet (compared to 25,000 to 30,000 square feet of its traditional "superstores") and carried a wider array of products, including a broader selection of those items that produced higher margins: furniture, computer accessories, and software. The megastores also featured interactive kiosk systems. Through a series of prompts, the kiosk systems helped customers locate the product that best fulfilled their needs by showing pictures and displaying information about each product. Each megastore also contained a larger area for business support than its traditional stores. This included self-service desktop publishing workstations and on-site computer upgrades, repairs, and technical support.

Thinking Outside the Box

Experimenting with different types of stores, Office Depot opened two Images stores in South Florida in 1995, which served as "one-stop resource centers" for copying, graphic design, desktop publishing, and shipping. Customers could rent self-service computer workstations, cell phone services, presentation products, office supplies, and conference rooms. Fuente explained that the

Left: Office Depot copy and print centers offered printing solutions for office documents, including business forms, stationery, and envelopes; specialty items such as labels, plastic cards, tags, and tickets; and promotional printing for direct mail, folders, and binders, among many other services.

Opposite: In-store kiosks in Office Depot's megastores helped customers find the best products to fit their needs.

Images stores were a "research and development" project that was eventually phased out, but not before more Images stores were opened.[16]

Also in 1995, Office Depot opened its first stand-alone furniture store called Furniture At Work, in Austin, Texas. The showroom-style store carried a large selection of premium office furniture, including bookcases, file cabinets, lighting products, artwork, and conference tables. Like Images, Furniture At Work was a research-and-development project. Unfortunately, by 1998, the company realized the stores weren't "performing as satisfactorily as we would like," according to Fuente, so the company pulled the plug.[17]

Taking Care of Business

In 1992, Office Depot launched its most successful marketing slogan—one that the company would revisit several times. The slogan "Taking Care of Business" accompanied a national marketing campaign created by Miami-based Gold Coast

"TAKIN' CARE OF BUSINESS"— THE LEGEND BEHIND THE SONG

IT'S NO SECRET THAT BACHMAN TURNER Overdrive, or BTO, is a legendary rock band. But few people know the legend behind the band's hit song, "Takin' Care of Business." According to George Bryan, vice president of financial services, BTO guitarist Randy Bachman visited Office Depot's campus in Delray Beach from time to time to tell the story behind the song's popularity.

Inspired by the Beatles' "Paperback Writer," "Takin' Care of Business" was originally cast as a ballad but became an upbeat song by accident when it was performed live for the first time, with Bachman singing the lead. Lead singer C. F. Turner had temporarily lost his voice, so Bachman had taken the initiative.

The recorded version has an interesting story, too. Legend has it that on the night the band members recorded the song in their studio, they decided to order a pizza for the group. It so happened that the deliveryman played piano (and he played well), so the band allowed him to contribute to the song. As it turned out, the piano version they created made the final cut.

When the time arrived to compose the song's credits, the band members realized they didn't even know the piano player's name. As Randy Bachman told the story, it took them a long time to find the deliveryman and give him his proper due.[1]

Mark Begelman plays "Takin' Care of Business" with Randy Bachman of Bachman Turner Overdrive on the Office Depot float in the 1994 Miami Orange Bowl Parade.

Actor and comedian Steve Landesberg (above), of sitcom *Barney Miller* fame, served as the first spokesperson for Office Depot's "Taking Care of Business" marketing campaign. Golf legend Arnold Palmer (right) represented the campaign after Landesberg.

my band, Eraserhead, *would play it at every company function.*[20]

In 1994, actor and comedian Steve Landesberg signed on as spokesperson for the "Taking Care of Business" campaign. Office Depot noted that Landesberg's "dry wit and comfortable demeanor" generated a positive response among customers.[21] The following year, golf legend Arnold Palmer served as Office Depot's spokesperson.

Arnold Palmer's involvement with Office Depot came around the same time that the company began its sports marketing campaign. Baseball stadiums, including the Florida Marlins' home stadium, boasted giant Office Depot No. 2 pencils painted on their foul poles. The company sponsored individual golf tournaments, ice-skating events, and tennis matches, and in 1995, it became the official sponsor of the U.S. Volleyball team. In 1994, Office Depot began sponsoring (and participating in) "Corporate Runs" in major cities—a tradition that would continue for many years. Aside from supporting charitable causes such as the Leukemia Society of America, the Corporate Runs promoted

Advertising that combined newspaper, direct mail, national television broadcasts, and local television and radio stations.

As part of the advertising campaign, Office Depot acquired two-year rights to the Bachman Turner Overdrive song, "Takin' Care of Business."[18] The "Taking Care of Business" campaign promised to make 2 billion impressions (reaching 100 million people) and targeted Office Depot's core customers—small and midsize businesses—while building name recognition in an increasingly competitive industry.[19]

Years later, Begelman explained how the idea to use "Taking Care of Business" came about:

In our first managers' meeting after Office Depot and Office Club merged, I chose a theme based around Bachman Turner Overdrive's song, "You Ain't Seen Nothing Yet." The next year, the theme that I picked for the managers' meeting was "Taking Care of Business," another Bachman Turner Overdrive song. Then we decided to adopt that song as our corporate mantra, and

health, fitness, and employee camaraderie. They were open to all employees of any corporation, business, government, or financial institution.[22]

Office Depot also created special marketing promotions. In 1995, for example, it helped launch the much-anticipated Windows '95® from Microsoft and provided customers with the opportunity to preorder the software at Office Depot stores. More than 33,000 customers took advantage of the preorder opportunity. When Office Depot's leaders witnessed the large software demand, they decided to open 185 stores at 12:01 A.M.—literally the minute Windows '95 was officially released.[23]

Office Depot's catalog continued to serve as "the backbone of our marketing efforts," according to the company's 1993 annual report. To reflect its importance, the catalog incorporated a new design in 1993, replacing its black-and-white product drawings with four-color photos. The following year, the catalog reflected an easier-to-follow indexing system. Office Depot also began releasing separate catalogs for back-to-school supplies, furniture, older-model products, recycled paper products, and business machines. In 1993, *Business News*, the

company's "how to" publication for small business owners, changed its name to *BusinessNews* (one word) and transitioned from a newspaper-like format to a glossy, four-color magazine. That year, Office Depot also began publishing a quarterly newsletter called *Home Business Advisor* aimed at people with home offices. *BusinessNews* and *Home Business Advisor* merged into a single publication in 1994.

More Improvements

Office Depot continued to improve its operations across the board. It expanded its lineup of office furniture and business machines, including computers, to better serve the small office/home office customer base. It also opened two centralized production facilities to better handle large-volume printing and copying. Even its stores received a facelift as they transitioned away from the warehouse look with brighter lighting, colorful, easy-to-read signs, and tile floors instead of concrete.

While selling big-ticket technology products, Office Depot also added cell phones and the latest

---

1994
OFFICE DEPOT BOARD OF DIRECTORS

David I. Fuente Chairman Chief Executive Officer Office Depot, Inc.	*W. Scott Hedrick* General Partner InterWest Partners	*Peter J. Solomon* Chairman Chief Executive Officer Peter J. Solomon Company
Mark Begelman President Chief Operating Officer Office Depot, Inc.	*John B. Mumford* President Crosspoint Corporation	*Cynthia R. Cohen* President Marketplace 2000
Denis Defforey Director Carrefour De Noyange, S.A.	*Michael J. Myers* President First Century Partners, Inc. Director Smith Barney Venture Corporation	*Alan L. Wurtzel* Chairman Circuit City Stores, Inc.

computer hardware and software from the four leading computer manufacturers (Apple, Compaq, IBM, and Packard Bell).

"We had a great deal of input into what we wanted to sell," said Mary Wong, a district store manager at the time, who eventually became director of community relations. "We talked frequently among ourselves and to the corporate office as to what was out there—because, at the time, we were heavily into supplies, and we were just emerging into technology."[24]

As computer hardware and software sales increased, the company teamed up with Software Support, Inc., to provide technical support (a department of the Office Depot store called Uptime Services) in such areas as software installation, training, support, and upgrades.[25]

Office Depot improved its customer service as well, educating employees on the "critical importance of customer satisfaction."[26] According to the company's mission statement, "We will achieve success by an uncompromising commitment to Superior Customer Satisfaction—a company-wide attitude that recognizes that customer satisfaction is EVERYTHING."[27]

Fuente told South Florida-based *Sun-Sentinel*, "As we move forward, we're fighting the competition on customer service, not just prices. The fight over prices was a relatively easy one to win."[28]

To help fight the competition on customer service, Mark Begelman spearheaded an initiative in 1992 for "superior customer satisfaction" by assembling a team of 40 employees from headquarters and retail store locations. The team met for problem-solving exercises in an effort to identify, research, and implement solutions that would improve customer satisfaction.[29]

That year, Office Depot also introduced a customer order system that operated more smoothly, while enhancing customer satisfaction. The company also established customer satisfaction teams and focus groups that developed specific ways to improve customer service and relations. Customers mailed in an average of 13,000 sur-

veys each month, which helped Office Depot further refine its business operations. Store managers were given more authority to quickly deal with customer concerns, and a Customer Service Index (CSI) measured service levels in each store to help address concerns at a more targeted level. The CSI compiled several methods, including customer surveys, customer complaints, and mystery shoppers. Also, store personnel were trained to demonstrate and sell the company's more complex items, like furniture and computers. Finally, upgrades in the company's information systems improved response time in addressing customer concerns

Above: Mary Wong joined Office Depot in 1993 and became one of the company's first female district managers. Her involvement with philanthropic causes led to her promotion as director of community relations. *(Photo courtesy of Paul Morris/Morphoto, Inc.)*

Below: Office Depot's employee newsletter featured helpful reminders about the importance of customer service.

and helped every facet of the company's operations run smoothly.

At the same time, Office Depot stepped up its human resources efforts, establishing Office Depot University in 1994 to help recruit, train, and retain top-quality employees. The university offered classes in leadership, business writing, and field management, as well as courses designed to increase personal productivity. "The real emphasis was on getting the company more organized in how it trained managers," said Brian Benge, who facilitated the training and wrote course work for Office Depot University. "Before the university, it was a scattershot approach as to how a new manager was trained for a store. Another gentleman and I wrote training programs on how to train a new manager. The program would take the man-

ager through all the operational training, but it also injected things like performance management and leadership."[30]

The next year, the company established a management training program called Growth and Opportunities Awareness for Leadership Success (GOALS), which identified employees with leadership potential and helped prepare those who wanted to move up the management ladder.[31] Office Depot continued to reward and encourage employees with new programs such as the President's Circle, the Wall of Fame, and other incentives. A courtesy award program rewarded store employees with silver, gold, and diamond pins based on how many compliment letters from customers they acquired. Another program gave "kudos coupons" to those employees who did something "extra special." The coupons were put into a monthly drawing that gave out $50 to the winner.[32]

"We have many advancement opportunities at Office Depot," said Venna Tredway, who joined the company in 1990 as an assistant manager and later became director of human resource operations for North American Retail. "We have training programs to help you advance. We have tuition programs to help you through the education process. If you want a retail career, we're the company to join."[33]

Everyone is Happy

One reporter for the *Sun-Sentinel* credited Fuente with leading Office Depot to "superstore status." If honors and awards were any indication, that reporter was correct. In 1993, Fuente was named Florida Atlantic University's Entrepreneur of the Year, also winning the *Sun-Sentinel* Excalibur Award in Palm Beach County, Florida.[34] "Fuente's ability to stick to the essentials, while at the same time daring to take risks, may help explain his accomplishments," noted the *Sun-Sentinel*.[35]

Office Depot's spring 1993 employee newsletter, *Office Depot Ink*, announced that the *Miami Herald* named Office Depot as Florida's "Company of the Year," recognizing it for its "leadership and achievement."

Office Depot was also honored as a company. In 1992, the *Miami Herald* named it Florida's "Company of the Year" for outstanding leadership and achievement.[36] Office Depot also made the Growth 100 list in *Financial World* magazine in 1995, placing 87th on the list, which was based on a five-year average of earnings-per-share growth and return on equity, plus 1995 earnings-per-share growth.[37]

Office Depot continued to keep shareholders happy with increased profits and conservative financing. The company issued a two-for-one stock split in 1992, a three-for-two split in 1993, and a three-for-two split in 1994. Until December 1992, Office Depot remained mostly debt-free by selling stock to raise money. Then, to spur its aggressive expansion, the company raised $146 million through zero-coupon convertible bonds (called Liquid Yield Option Notes or LYONs™, syndicated by Merrill Lynch) that carried only a 5 percent interest rate.[38] The following year, Office Depot raised another $185 million through an offering of LYONs, this time with only a 4 percent interest rate.

In 1992, the company's earnings increased by an amazing 161 percent to $39.2 million, and the

Meeting its goals, Office Depot operated 504 stores in the United States and Canada by the end of 1995. It continued to enter major new markets and aggressively grow its national delivery network through its Business Services Division.

following year, Office Depot had its "best year ever," according to Fuente, with sales up 49 percent to $2.6 billion.[39] It added 67 new stores, even though it had planned to open only 50 to 60 stores, for a total of 351 stores. The year 1994 topped 1993, with sales increasing 50 percent to $4.3 billion; earnings climbed 48 percent, and the company added 69 new stores.

By the end of 1995, Office Depot had 504 stores; had $5.3 billion in sales; net earnings reached $132.4 million; and stockholders' equity surpassed the $1 billion mark. In an interview, Fuente said the company owed its success to raw aggressiveness and conservative financing.[40] But these qualities could only take the company so far. Office Depot's operations became more complex as it began delving into new areas of business—specifically, the delivery and contract segments of the industry.

Office Depot's next-day delivery guarantee helped increase sales by focusing on even greater customer service. The company's delivery business served companies of all sizes, including Fortune 500 corporations with hundreds of locations around the country.

CHAPTER FOUR

BREAKING NEW GROUND— BUSINESS SERVICES

1992–1995

The company believes that the Business Services Division has the potential to be as big and successful as its retail counterpart.

—Office Depot 1994 annual report[1]

AS THE OFFICE PRODUCTS industry consolidated, the competition became more fierce as the Big Three (Office Depot, Office-Max, and Staples) vied for a bigger piece of the pie. As leader of the pack, Office Depot could not afford to slow the pace. Rather, Office Depot's leaders sought out new areas in which to grow the business. So, while the company expanded outside the U.S. border and opened new stores in the United States, it continued "taking care of business" in other quarters, too. As a result, the new seeds it planted in the early 1990s grew into fresh profit centers.

Soon after Office Depot opened its first store in 1986, customers had started inquiring about delivery options, spurring the company to focus on that segment of its business. According to long-time Office Depot employees, delivery to customers was actually an afterthought. "So, they bought a truck," explained Mark Holifield, former executive vice president of supply chain. "From then on, every store that opened had a truck."[2] Even though Office Depot had always delivered product (it was not a major part of the business), it had charged customers for the service.

During its first few years in business, Office Depot had no need for delivery centers; nearby stores generally delivered catalog and telemarketing orders. With that system becoming less effi-

cient, however, more and more customers ordered office supplies and furniture from the company. In 1990 and 1991, Office Depot tested two delivery centers—one for the company's South Florida stores and one for the San Francisco market (the one it had acquired as a part of Office Club). The test centers confirmed Office Depot's expectations.

While each Office Depot store's inventory met the needs of its local market, the delivery centers allowed the company to offer same-day or next-day delivery for catalog and telemarketing orders without taking away from the stores' inventory. They also helped keep down delivery costs. The success of Office Depot's existing delivery centers prompted the company to open three more centers in 1992—one each for the Atlanta, Baltimore, and Los Angeles areas. The delivery center concept was relatively new and would eventually lead to the development of the Business Services Division (BSD), which was later renamed Business Solution Division.

In 1995, Office Depot continued consolidating within its Business Services Division, creating a cost-effective and customer-focused organization. The division served large, corporate customers.

In 1993, Office Depot acquired several contract stationery companies, including Eastman Office Products, which provided an opportunity for Office Depot to enter a new market.

In 1993, the company began offering guaranteed free delivery on orders over $50, which resulted in a big sales increase in the number of orders and the dollar total of each sale. By then, the scope of Office Depot's delivery network had swept the nation. As nearly 700 Office Depot trucks traveled on the road every business day, each made dozens of deliveries to thousands of customers in total.

A New Area of Business

Enhancing the delivery segment of Office Depot was just the beginning. In May 1993, David Fuente informed shareholders that the company would continue its aggressive expansion, not only by opening new stores but also by capturing business from large companies.[3] Indeed, Office Depot had already started the ball rolling. It entered a whole new area of business when it acquired two contract stationers: Wilson Stationery & Printing Company and Eastman Office Products Corporation, both of which provided Office Depot with a new group of customers—large corporations.

"Dave [Fuente] had the vision to understand the need for and the benefit of a multichannel operation," said Cindy Campbell, executive vice president, Business Solutions Division. "He convinced the board to agree to these contract stationer acquisitions. He understood that customers want to have the ability to shop in a variety of ways."[4]

Monica Luechtefeld, who was an officer at Eastman when Office Depot acquired it and later became Office Depot's executive vice president of information technology, supply chain, and business development, discussed Office Depot's growth plans. "Office Depot made a strategic decision that, at some point, it would need another growth engine in addition to building retail stores," she said. "The company decided that the growth engine would be delivery, not only to small and midsize businesses, but also to larger corporate customers. To enter that business, they decided to make a few strategic acquisitions."[5]

For a discount retailer like Office Depot, the market's contract/delivery segment was a virtual gold mine. As then Office Depot spokesperson Gary Schweikhart said, "Fully one-third of the estimated $100 billion office equipment and sup-

plies sold each year is bought by larger corporate customers. We've been missing that business."[6] Or, as *Office Products Distribution* magazine reported, "Corporate America still consumes the vast majority of office products, and these businesses continue to rely on traditional commercial and contract dealers [contract stationers] as their primary source of supplies. These large commercial and contract dealers move nearly as much product as superstores, warehouse clubs, mail-order houses, and mass merchants combined."[7]

Prior to acquiring the two contract stationers, Office Depot had dealt only with small and medium-sized businesses (those with fewer than 50 employees)—and it didn't fulfill contracts. Smaller businesses generally received discounted office supplies through telemarketing, the Office Depot catalog, or shopping in the company's stores. However, large corporations had little need to purchase from Office Depot, especially because signing on with contract stationers already provided them discounts. They also often required specialized service, and the large volume of their needs did not match Office Depot's existing lines of business.

Office Depot changed that, however, when it purchased the two contract stationers, Wilson and Eastman. Now companies (not always large corporations; oftentimes they were smaller companies that had multiple locations) could meet with an Office Depot account executive and sign a contract to have supplies delivered. Acquiring Wilson and Eastman allowed Office Depot to enter a market it had previously not penetrated, one that had been dominated by independent dealers. At the same time, the contract market fueled Office Depot's ability to continue growing rapidly. Not only did the two acquisitions allow Office Depot to break new ground; they also enhanced the delivery segment of Office Depot's business, adding 10 additional delivery warehouses (six from Eastman and four from Wilson) to its existing five.[8]

Customer orders are automatically transmitted to the nearest delivery warehouse, where workers fill the order. As orders are filled, stock is automatically replenished.

FROM OUT OF THE ASHES: THE OFFICE DEPOT FOUNDATION

WHEN HURRICANE ANDREW RAVAGED parts of Florida and Louisiana in August 1994, many Office Depot employees' lives were devastated. The storm's destruction left many people homeless and struggling for ways to pay for temporary housing until their insurance proceeds helped them pick up the pieces. As entire communities were torn apart, thousands of people were left without food, clean water, or clothing. Many companies also struggled to recover their businesses. Office Depot and its employees wanted to help in any way possible.

"We realized there were no business continuity plans—all those types of things that are in place now," said Mary Wong, director of community relations. "But more importantly, we realized that we needed to do something for our employees."[1]

CEO David Fuente led the company's relief efforts. "We couldn't sit around and wait for FEMA to take care of these people," he said.[2]

After Hurricane Andrew, local stores' shelves were stocked with food, bottled water, baby supplies, batteries, and other necessities. Office Depot and its employees, who lived in all parts of the country, donated these items, which were free not just to Office Depot employees, but to anyone who lived in hurricane-affected areas. The company also provided emergency food, clothing, housing, and transportation to employees in need, and offered grants and short-term, interest-free loans to help them recover. Office Depot also donated emergency supplies, necessary office supplies, and office furnishings to local organizations that helped feed, house, and clothe thousands of people.[3]

Headquartered in southern California, Eastman was the largest contract stationer serving the West Coast, providing office products, including furniture, to thousands of companies. Its annual sales exceeded $300 million.[9]

Texas-based Wilson Business Products contracted with corporations in markets where Office Depot already had a strong presence—namely Houston, Dallas, Austin, San Antonio, and Charlotte, North Carolina.

After the two acquisitions were completed, Schweikhart noted that Office Depot would now be executing approximately $600 million in contract sales.[10] Very serious about entering the contract stationer business, company leaders, and Fuente especially, aimed to create a national network so that a company of any size could select Office Depot for all of its office supply needs. In rapid succession, the company acquired six more contract businesses in 1994:

the L. E. Muran Company; Yorkship Press; Midwest Carbon Company; Silver's; J. A. Kindel; and Allstate Office Products. The six acquisitions added eight more delivery warehouses to Office Depot's network.[11]

Founded in 1867 and based in Boston, L. E. Muran served companies in Massachusetts, Connecticut, Maine, New Hampshire, and Rhode Island.[12] As a well-established company, it served as the market leader for contract stationers in New England.[13]

Yorkship Press was a family-owned business based in Cherry Hill, New Jersey, and filled contracts for companies in Philadelphia, southeastern Pennsylvania, southern New Jersey, and parts of Delaware and Maryland. Its 1993 annual sales reached approximately $30 million.[14]

Midwest Carbon Company, based in Minneapolis, procured office supplies for companies in Minnesota, Illinois, Iowa, Kansas, Michigan,

The South Florida-based *Sun-Sentinel* reported on Office Depot's heroic efforts: "Convoys of Office Depot trucks delivered such huge quantities of supplies to hurricane-ravaged areas that one Miami Office Depot manager took care of an entire block of families left in disarray by the storm."[4]

After the recovery effort, Office Depot decided to establish a more formal program that would help victims and communities. By January 1995, that program had evolved into the Office Depot Foundation, a not-for-profit philanthropic corporation.[5] A cooperative relationship between Office Depot and its employees helped fund the foundation, with employees voluntarily contributing through a weekly payroll deduction and Office Depot matching every cent. "With as little as 25 cents per week, every associate could contribute to the foundation without causing any real hardship in the process," said Andrea Levenson, the foundation's first president.[6]

Today, the foundation continues to grant short-term, interest-free loans to employees who face difficult personal problems, such as an abusive relationship, for example, or a home destroyed by fire. The foundation also offers grants that help defray hotel or transportation costs to those employees who have experienced major financial setbacks due to disasters or personal losses.[7]

"The foundation was established not just for our own associates ... but also for the community at large," Levenson said. "We welcome opportunities to assist in local communities, and we encourage our associates to identify local situations in which the Office Depot Foundation can be of assistance."[8]

Aside from working with community groups, the foundation donates resources and money to national organizations, such as the American Red Cross, the Salvation Army, the U.S. Chamber of Commerce, and Feed the Children. Since its formation, the Office Depot Foundation has supported numerous disaster relief efforts—some quite prominent, like victims of the Oklahoma City bombing; the terrorist attacks of September 11, 2001; the 2004 Indian Ocean tsunami; and Hurricanes Katrina, Rita, and Wilma.

"The people who work here are very giving," said Wong. "It's a huge source of pride for them. You might not always be able to measure it at the register, but you create customer loyalty and employee loyalty by being a good community citizen."[9]

Nebraska, North Dakota, South Dakota, and Wisconsin. It had 1993 sales of $36 million.[15]

Silver's, with 1993 sales of $61 million, was based in Detroit and served companies throughout Michigan. It was one of the largest contract stationers and contract furniture dealers in Michigan.[16]

Cincinnati-based J. A. Kindel, with 300 employees and 1994 sales of $65 million, was the largest privately held office supply company in the United States, serving companies in Ohio, Indiana, Kentucky, Michigan, Pennsylvania, Tennessee, and West Virginia.[17] As Office Depot CFO Barry Goldstein noted, "The Cincinnati deal especially filled in a hole in the Midwest area."[18]

Tampa-based Allstate Office Products, with 1993 sales of $25 million, was a major supplier for north Florida and also served parts of the federal government. "Allstate gives us some access and expertise in government contracting," said Goldstein.[19]

A Consolidating Industry

At that time, the contract stationer industry was still highly fragmented, even though the office supply industry had been consolidating for years. Cindy Campbell remembered one of the reasons she decided to work at Office Depot. "They talked to me about how there were so many participants that the industry was ripe for consolidation," she said. "Office Depot's vision was to serve customers in a way that they had not experienced before, with better cost of product, better process, more streamlined customer service capabilities, better billing and invoicing—all those things that made a compelling business story for businesses out there that were looking for process improvement."[20]

Of course, Office Depot's venture into new territory set off a flurry of acquisitions among the superstores. "Once Office Depot made the deal to acquire Eastman, it triggered a reaction from

Above and inset: By the end of 1995, Office Depot operated 23 delivery centers in the United States, with a fleet of 1,300 delivery trucks that filled orders all across the nation.

Staples and other competitors," said Monica Luechtefeld. "Everyone went on an acquisition binge. Mom-and-pop office suppliers, and then the contract stationers, were rapidly assimilated by the superstores. There were about 16,000 of them that were members of the National Office Products Association (NOPA), and after about two to four years of acquisitions and consolidations, there ended up being about five major players left and probably 4,000 small dealers left. So the industry went through a huge consolidation."[21]

The Business Services Division is Born

With the eight contract stationers under its belt, Office Depot became one of the largest business-to-business office products distributors in the United States. Accordingly, the company formed a Business Services Division (later called the Business Solutions Division) that combined Office Depot's commercial delivery business with the contract stationers. The company hired Judith Rogala, former president of a Michigan hazardous waste treatment company, to head up the division.[22]

Office Depot began integrating the contract stationers into the rest of the company, and slowly, the company started consolidating the contract stationers' administrative, financial, and inventory functions.

In 1995, after opening new delivery warehouses in Chicago and New Orleans, Office Depot consolidated its telemarketing business with its contract stationers to create a national business-to-business network of delivery warehouses (known as Customer Service Centers). While about 6,000 different items were available to in-store shoppers, contract and commercial delivery customers could choose from about 11,000 different items.[23] By then, Office Depot operated 23 delivery warehouses, plus two Telecenters, which received phone and fax orders, and a number of satellite sales offices.[24]

With thousands of customers taking advantage of the far-ranging delivery network, Office Depot's delivery business increased 27 percent in 1995 (to $1.65 billion) and accounted for 31 percent of the company's total sales. By that time, more than 1,300 Office Depot delivery trucks traveled on the road every business day to deliver 45,000 different orders.[25]

The Runaway Train

Despite the creation of the Business Services Division and continued growth in sales and earnings, 1995 was "challenging," according to Fuente, "due to ... additional expenses in our delivery business."[26] Fuente discussed the difficulties associated with integrating the eight contract stationers and the increased competition from retailers like Staples, OfficeMax, and Wal-Mart.

Still, investors and industry analysts saw potential in Office Depot, even as the stock market remained unstable. According to a senior analyst at Merrill Lynch, Office Depot's stock "has been an incredible growth stock. Earnings per share have increased more than 100 percent over the last four years, compounded annually."[27]

Another Wall Street analyst called the company "the runaway train of retail."[28] *Computer Retail Week* reported that Office Depot was "making all the right turns. It is a tremendous success story in retail as well as American business."[29]

In April 1995, during all the high praise and amazing success, Mark Begelman decided to resign as president and chief operating officer, though he remained on the board of directors until 1996. "Although I have no definite plans at this moment," he said, "the excitement of new challenges and a new venture is something I have always relished."[30] Begelman went on to start another company, a chain of music equipment superstores called Mars Music in South Florida.[31]

A Rocky Road Ahead

The company experienced significant problems with starting up the Business Services Division. Rogala announced to BSD employees a plan for 1996 and beyond that would "keep us [as] a world-class organization well into the next century." The goals included "enhancing" overnight delivery; "accepting nothing less" than being the leader in delivery of services; "being the national champion in providing solutions"; and improving communication both within the Business Services Division and between other divisions. To achieve the vision, she wrote, "We all must work together to build the BSD into the most dependable business partner the world has ever seen."[32]

Though those goals would soon be realized, the road would be rocky indeed.

RETAILER
OF THE YEAR AWARD
1996

presented to

DAVID I. FUENTE
CHAIRMAN AND
CHIEF EXECUTIVE OFFICER
OFFICE DEPOT INC

in recognition of his dedicated and outstanding
contribution to American retailing

The Institute of Retail Management
California State University, Los Angeles

David Fuente proudly displays the 1996 Retailer of the Year Award from the Institute of Retail Management at California State University in Los Angeles.

CHAPTER FIVE

GROWING PAINS

1996 – 1997

On a long-term basis, we want to be the premier provider of office products and services to the key and major market segments. We will not be limited to the products and services we currently sell, but we will continue to explore new merchandise and service opportunities that allow us to be a single-source supplier to our customers.

—Dick Bennington,
Business Services Division president, 1998[1]

INSTEAD OF A TIME FOR CELEbration, the 10-year anniversary of Office Depot in 1996 was marked with some of the toughest challenges yet for the fast-growing company. Just as Office Depot had warned analysts to expect flat second-quarter earnings, the company's stock tumbled from a high of $32 in September 1995 to $13 in July 1996.[2] Though sales were up more than 14 percent, earnings were slightly down.[3] To complicate matters, Staples and OfficeMax reported solid earnings, with both chains continuing their aggressive expansion.[4]

The year 1996 began with a major restructuring of senior management at Office Depot. Dick Bennington, vice president of operations and sales in charge of the company's retail division, took over Judith Rogola's position as president of the Business Services Division (BSD). Back in 1986, when the first Office Depot store opened, Bennington served as the store manager, climbing his way up the corporate ladder to accomplish record-setting retail sales growth through diligent execution that included rigorous training requirements. For example, new employees were often tested on their knowledge of product category locations throughout the store. Bennington also enforced strict store standards and remained fervent about customer satisfaction.[5]

"In my 25 years of retail experience, Dick Bennington is the best operator I've ever known,"

said Bill Seltzer, who joined the company in 1991 and retired in 2002 as chief information officer. "The guy is a powerhouse—so full of energy. He is demanding, but also very inspirational."[6]

In addition to the promotions and new hires, other senior management at Office Depot included Harry Brown, executive vice president of merchandising and marketing; Barry Goldstein, executive vice president of finance and CFO; Bill Seltzer, executive vice president of management information systems; and Terry Bean, executive vice president of human resources.[7]

Though Office Depot's stock was flagging, a handful of executives—including David Fuente, chairman and CEO, Bennington, Seltzer, and Goldstein—demonstrated their faith in the company's health by purchasing 123,000 shares. "They went out and purchased [shares]—not only because they felt the stock was grossly undervalued at that point and that we had been slammed by Wall Street more than we should have been—but also to show confidence in the company," said then Office Depot spokesperson Gary Schweikhart.[8] The

---

Office Depot Express was a one-stop center for printing needs, similar in concept to Office Depot's Images stores.

insider buying triggered many analysts to give the company's stock a "buy" rating, which contributed to a ratcheting up of the stock price.[9]

Around the same time, *Fortune* magazine ranked Office Depot as the second most admired company in America in the category of Specialist Retailers. To achieve the ranking, *Fortune* asked executives of various corporations to rate companies in their own industries on such measures as quality of management, financial health, and innovation.[10]

In his 1996 letter to shareholders, Fuente called the year "challenging."[11] In that same letter, Office Depot blamed the slowdown in earnings on an "increasingly sluggish computer hardware market and significant price reductions in paper products."[12] Though other contributing problems existed behind the scenes, these factors had definitely contributed to a slowdown in retail sales and comparable same-store sales (or "comp sales," an important yardstick for appraising retailers' strength).

BSD Challenges

Oddly enough, it was the contract stationer acquisitions—the new vehicle for growth at Office Depot—that had created a temporary hurdle. For starters, the company's plans to integrate the contract stationers into the newly created Business Services Division required more time and funds than executives had anticipated. "We incurred a lot of additional expenses as we integrated the business services side," admitted Barry Goldstein.[13]

"These were old-line companies that had years in the business," said Monica Luechtefeld. "So regionally, we all felt that our product assortment was the perfect assortment for corporate customers, and you really had to take eight entrepreneurial organizations and build them into one cohesive organization, and then you also had to integrate that inside a culture that was a retailing culture at heart."[14]

"The cultures of the contract stationers and Office Depot as a retailer were very different," added Kathy Fajardo, who worked at Wilson before Office Depot acquired it and later became director of supply chain skills and compliance. "The way we dealt with customers on the contract side of the business was different from the way you dealt with

customers on the retail side, so it took some time to adjust on both sides."[15]

Or, as Annie Frye, supply chain training manager, observed, "We were a young company going 90 miles a minute, and we jumped into a business in which we had little experience. We were trying to run these businesses like we do our retail stores, and these customers were very different than our retail customers. It took us a while to realize that."[16]

Cindy Campbell, who was hired in 1995, helped integrate the eight contract stationers through her experience in sales, marketing, and general management. "I ended up at Office Depot in this brand-new environment where they had made eight acquisitions, but they needed to know how to integrate them," she said. "They were very loosely integrated at the time, and there were problems with both the process integration and the cultural integration."[17]

Culturally, Campbell explained, there was a lack of understanding at the store level regarding the vision of BSD at Office Depot:

While senior management clearly understood [Fuente's] vision, I don't think it was well articulated to people in the field. They didn't really understand the benefit to the company in the long term. Office Depot store managers thought you were stealing their customers. I received letters from store managers saying, "I've been doing business with this community college for the last five years, and now you're stealing my customer." Well, the store might have been receiving one-tenth of the business of that junior college. Nine-tenths was going to somebody other than Office Depot. When Office Depot contracted with that junior college, we then became the beneficiary of 100 percent of the revenue stream. The stores suffered the 10 percent loss, but the company gained the other 90 percent.[18]

In addition, the Business Services Division struggled for acceptance in the business community. Campbell continued: "I can recall my sales team sitting outside my office making phone calls to large corporations and, in many cases, they weren't allowed on the bid response list," she said. "That was because they didn't know we had a contract stationer division. We were Office Depot, the retail

After spending 19 years at GTE, Cindy Campbell joined Office Depot in 1995 to help integrate the eight contract stationer acquisitions. Her hard work and business acumen earned her several promotions, and in 2003, she was named executive vice president of the company's Business Services Group (later called the Business Solutions Division). *(Photo courtesy of Paul Morris/Morphoto, Inc.)*

store. They weren't familiar with or didn't have any confidence in our ability as a delivery source of office products to their commercial enterprise."[19]

Other problems arose when the Business Services Division was unable to fill orders completely and on time.[20] As the South Florida-based *Sun-Sentinel* noted, "Delivering office supplies ... was a headache for the company this year."[21]

Trials and tribulations with the computer network at Office Depot had also significantly contributed to the company's delivery challenges. Campbell explained:

Our information systems were up and down. You would come to work in the morning, sign on, and you would crash. You couldn't take customer orders because the systems wouldn't work. You couldn't get the orders to print to the warehouses because the warehouse management system was down, or the tickets wouldn't print because the printers weren't working. I remember one time we tried to save money on labels, and we failed to consider the humidity in some of our warehouses because they're not air-conditioned. The labels would just gum up the printer. They would stick to one another, and it was a mess.[22]

Moreover, Campbell said, the company was unable to narrow down the use of a specific management information system. "We had several different warehouse management systems that we were testing," she said. "In South Florida, we went through three different warehouse management systems in a period of a year and a half. You would barely learn one, and soon you would have to learn the next one. We weren't thinking about the appearance of the invoice or the packing slip. So the customer would see something that looked different, prompting a ton of calls to customer service. This forced our salespeople to serve as customer service people, and it was tough."[23]

Years later, Campbell's memories of those times were marked with wry amusement. "Sometimes I don't know how we made it," she said. "I have a big job today, but back then it was harder. You could work from 7 A.M. to 2 A.M., which I did routinely because we were involved with sales during the day. Then starting at about 9 P.M., you would be in the warehouse working and observing the pick/pack operations. Then you could meet again with the drivers at 6 A.M. before they left to deliver the product to customers. It was exhausting for everyone. My salespeople would sell during the day and literally work the picking line at night. They would place items in their own vehicles to deliver them."[24]

Despite the problems, many analysts believed the Business Services Division reflected true potential. After interviewing several large, corporate Office Depot customers, retail analyst Patrick McCormack of Dean Witter said the company was overcoming many challenges and predicted that the Business Services Division of Office Depot would produce about 30 percent of the company's revenues by 2000.[25]

Continued Expansion

Meanwhile, Office Depot continued to expand in 1996, but at a slower rate. With plans to open 75 to 80 stores, the company opened only 60.[26] Though it improved in-store lighting and signage in more than 60 stores,[27] it pulled away from other remodeling plans once it realized the higher-than-expected cost of integrating the contract stationer acquisitions.[28]

Office Depot also continued its expansion of the Business Services Division. It opened delivery warehouses, or Customer Service Centers, in Chicago and New Orleans, and a third Telecenter in Norcross, Georgia, to keep up with its growing telemarketing operations. The other Office Depot Telecenters were located in Delray Beach, Florida, and Concord, California, both of which were electronically linked via network call routing to improve customer service.[29]

In 1996, the Business Services Division received so many orders that Office Depot opened a third Telecenter in Norcross, Georgia. At the ribbon-cutting ceremony were (from left): Bill Woods, senior manager of the Norcross Telecenter; Cindy Campbell, then-vice president of BSD Zone 2; Marjorie Schwenk, vice president of telemarketing; and Denise Brewer, manager of staff support services.

Office Depot also continued to explore new ways to accelerate growth, such as investing in Furniture At Work, its small chain of stand-alone furniture stores, and Images, its full-service copy and print stores.[30]

A Company in Limbo

One event with a significant impact on the history of Office Depot marked the company's 10-year anniversary when on September 4, 1996, Office Depot announced a merger with one of its chief rivals, Staples, Inc. If the merger was approved, board members agreed that David Fuente would serve as chairman of the new Staples/Office Depot company, while Staples Chief Thomas Stemberg would accept the position of CEO. For six months, associates of both Staples and Office Depot anticipated the merger, but in March 1997, the Federal Trade Commission (FTC) rejected the merger on the basis of antitrust laws, alleging that the new company would harm competition and result in higher consumer prices.[31] According to the FTC, the combined company would have at least twice the overall sales of its closest rival, OfficeMax.[32]

Corporate Growth Weekly pointed out, "The merged company will have 1,100 superstores in 96 percent of the U.S. metropolitan markets, creating a marketing powerhouse."[33] For their part, Office Depot and Staples claimed that savings from the merged companies would result in lower prices for consumers since they would still face competition not only from OfficeMax but from other discount stores like Best Buy and Wal-Mart.

To "remedy any perceived competitive issues," the two companies agreed to sell 63 stores to OfficeMax and contested the FTC's challenge in federal court.[34] Their efforts, however, were unsuccessful. On June 30, three months after the FTC's challenge, the U.S. District Court for the District of Columbia ruled in favor of the FTC. On July 2, Office Depot and Staples announced the merger's cancellation.[35] Fuente described the ordeal as "long and frustrating."[36]

The fallout from the failed merger was extreme, and after the 11-month process, many employees faced an uncertain future. One employee described the mood at headquarters shortly after the merger was announced: "[We were] stunned," she

In the mid- to late-1990s, Office Depot sold a wide range of computer software. Eventually, the company phased out some of the less business-oriented software to better focus on its core group of customers.

said. "Everybody wanted to know what would happen next."[37]

Initially, Office Depot and Staples had planned to combine many of their departments to avoid duplicating efforts, which meant that some employees would lose their jobs. As one newspaper reported a month after the merger was announced, "Because the combined company will be based at the home of Staples ... 1,900 Office Depot workers in Delray Beach have spent the past month wondering whether their jobs will stay put, move, or disappear."[38]

In the months leading up to the federal court's decision to block the merger, Office Depot lost hundreds of associates, many of them mid-level managers.[39] Also, the construction of a three-story, 215,000-square-foot administrative building next to its two existing headquarters buildings was temporarily placed on hold while the company waited to see if its offices would relocate to Framingham, Massachusetts, the headquarters of Staples. In addition, employee morale tanked when

Office Depot lost 500 of the 700 people it had recruited to staff the new building.[40]

"We had always been number one, and all of a sudden, we found out in the matter of a morning that we weren't," explained Henry Sauls, director of merchandising operations. "That took a lot of wind out of our sails. I saw people change during that uncertain time, more than I ever have. When you walked down the hallways, people looked down. They wouldn't greet you. Everyone was wondering if they were going to have a job. We had such pride once, and trying to keep that passion during that time ate me up inside."[41]

As the 12th employee of Office Depot, Paula Randolph also remembered the time of the merger as one of the lowest points in her career. She had

Minute, a weekly internal newsletter that updated employees on the merger's progress and answered all questions that were posted anonymously on the company's "merger hotline." The company also hosted multiple brown-bag lunches, at which high-level executives like CFO Barry Goldstein answered questions.[43] In addition, Office Depot pledged to provide as much advance notice as possible to employees who faced the risk of losing their jobs, even providing severance packages.[44]

Linda Friedman, director of the Center for Career Decisions (an independent outplacement

Left: On September 4, 1996, the leaders of Office Depot and Staples, Inc., surprised company associates, investors, and analysts when they announced plans for a merger. From left: Tom Stemberg, Staples chairman and CEO; David Fuente, Office Depot chairman and CEO; and Marty Hanaka, Staples president and COO.

Below: When Office Depot announced its merger with longtime rival Staples, *The Merger Minute* newsletter kept employees informed on its progress. When federal courts blocked the merger, Office Depot published this last installment of the newsletter.

joined Office Depot in 1986 as a copywriter and retired in 2005 after working in the company's marketing and advertising departments. "It was difficult as a loyal employee to make nice to your fiercest competitor," she said. "I liken that time to somebody striking Office Depot in the knee with a hammer. We were hobbled."[42]

During the due diligence process, officials concluded that Staples owned the stronger real estate department, while Office Depot had the stronger information systems, which meant the layoff or relocation of many Office Depot real estate associates to Framingham. (Information systems employees who worked for Staples faced a similar dilemma.) As a result, Office Depot stopped opening new stores, and many Office Depot employees, especially those in the real estate department, decided to leave the company on their own terms rather than wait for the results of the merger.

While the wait-and-see drama unfolded, Office Depot took a proactive stance to address employees' concerns. A week after the merger was announced, the company published *The Merger*

company) believed Office Depot excelled at handling the distress on employees during the proposed merger. Then-spokesperson Schweikhart also explained, "We wanted to err on the side of openness and disclosure."[45]

After a federal court rejected the merger, most Office Depot employees breathed a deep sigh of relief.

The Untold Story

Unknown to many within Office Depot and Staples, back in 1992, David Fuente had met with Staples CEO Thomas Stemberg shortly after Office Depot acquired Office Club, to discuss the potential acquisition of Staples, whose sales were $883 million in 1992 compared to Office Depot's $1.7 billion that year. "We had reached agreement in price, and we both went to our boards," Fuente said. "But Office Depot hadn't fully absorbed Office Club yet, so it would have been a huge deal to absorb Staples as well. Several people on the Office Depot board were strongly opposed to the deal."[46] Ultimately, the board of Office Depot voted against acquiring Staples.

Then, according to Fuente, in the spring of 1996, "Stemberg and I got cranked up again about marrying the two companies," he explained. "But right in the middle of negotiations, we had a horrible quarter, and Staples had a great quarter. Our stock went down, and their stock went up. We were in the weird position of having this great deal, but it was undoable the way we had originally conceived it because we could no longer afford to buy them. Consolidating the two companies was clearly a good deal for the shareholders, for the customers, and for the companies' futures. So now we had to answer the question: If it was a great deal for Office Depot to acquire Staples, why wouldn't it be a great deal for Staples to acquire Office Depot?"[47]

Thus, the two companies worked out a different arrangement so Staples could potentially acquire Office Depot. The rest, as they say, is history.

Cleaning up After the Fallout

During the merger process, Office Depot's expansion plans came to a near standstill. After the merger was blocked in late June, the company

---

1997 OFFICE DEPOT BOARD OF DIRECTORS

David I. Fuente
Chairman
Chief Executive Officer
Office Depot, Inc.

John C. Macatee
President
Chief Operating Officer
Office Depot, Inc.

Cynthia R. Cohen
President
Marketplace 2000

W. Scott Hedrick
General Partner
InterWest Partners

James L. Heskett
Professor of Business Logistics
UPS Foundation
Harvard Business School

Michael J. Myers
President
First Century Partners

Frank P. Scruggs, Jr.
Shareholder
Greenberg, Traurig, Hoffman,
Lipoff, Rosen & Quental, P.A.

Peter J. Solomon
Chairman
Chief Executive Officer
Peter J. Solomon Company

Above: Office Depot prides itself on its retail stores' friendly and knowledgeable associates.

Below: As president and chief operating officer of Office Depot in the late 1990s, John Macatee oversaw the field operations of the retail stores and the Business Services Division, as well as the merchandising and marketing departments.

opened a flurry of new stores in an attempt to compensate.[48] Since it had lost most of its real estate department during the attempted merger and was eager to catch up and restart the pipeline, Office Depot began opening stores in less than ideal areas. Unfortunately, this rushed process—which usually lasts approximately 36 months from beginning to end—resulted in poor decisions, poor locations, and high prices, and ultimately affected the economics of the company's retail business for the next decade.

The company also scrambled to replace the 200 employees it had lost. As one magazine reported:

Competitors have been thriving for years by getting intimate glimpses into their rivals' inner workings. With some 20 committees looking into how [Office Depot and Staples] could develop efficiencies, it is certain the two will be clubbing each other with details they never should have known. ... For Staples, the blow [of the failed merger] is largely in its pride. ... For Office Depot, jumping back in the race will be more difficult.[49]

In an effort to strengthen its management team after the merger with Staples was scuttled, in August 1997, Office Depot hired John Macatee as the new president and chief operating officer, a position that had not been filled since Mark Begelman resigned in 1995. Interestingly, Macatee had previously served as head of Sherwin-Williams Paint Store

Group, the same position David Fuente held before he joined Office Depot as its CEO. As president and COO, Macatee oversaw the field operations of the retail stores and the Business Services Division, as well as the merchandising and marketing departments.

Throughout his tenure, Macatee placed a strong focus on store operations, furniture sales, and real estate. He wanted to "paint the map red," according to several sources—in other words, open an Office Depot store in every state in the country.[50]

Described as tough and charismatic, Macatee reflected a "big authoritative presence" and a focus on "brute execution," according to several Office Depot executives who knew him.

"The good news was that Macatee was a bulldog kind of guy," Fuente said. "And the bad news was the same. I asked myself, 'what do we need right now?' The answer was: we needed a bulldog."[51]

Also in 1997, Office Depot hired Thomas Kroeger as executive vice president of human resources. The human resources department worked to improve its recruiting, training, development, and evaluation of employees to better reward and retain quality people. The company beefed up other departments, as well. From July to October 1997, Office Depot hired about 200 people, and 100 more positions were left to fill.[52]

There were a few positive aspects to the failed merger with Staples. The companies' integration task forces helped Office Depot learn valuable lessons about its own business. Since the original plan aimed to establish the Office Depot computer information system as the platform for the combined companies, Office Depot significantly strengthened its information technology during the merger process, investing about $25 million to create a highly sophisticated system for both retail and delivery.[53]

Improvements

Throughout 1996 and 1997, Office Depot focused on improving its Business Services Division. As Schweikhart explained, "We have said all along that the contract stationer business has the potential to be equal to our retail division. It's a matter of growing it."[54]

Cindy Campbell, executive vice president of Business Services, was hired in 1995 to integrate two of the eight contract stationer acquisitions—Allstate and Wilson. "They were not integrated when I was hired," she said. "People were still answer-

The Business Services Division vastly improved its warehouse operations in the late 1990s. Here, an Office Depot associate takes completed orders and routes them to the shipping station, where they will be prepared for delivery.

ing the phone, 'Allstate Office Products,' or 'Wilson Stationery & Printing.' "[55]

Eventually, upper management realized that Campbell had implemented a successful process to integrate Allstate and Wilson, rather than rely on guidance from the official integration team of Office Depot. "When you acquire a company, you quickly turn it to the way you prefer it to operate," Campbell said. "I didn't realize that many of the other contract stationers were not fully integrated and wouldn't be for some time."[56]

As Campbell admitted, her approach to integration seemed "self-evident." "There was an integration team, and there were many tasks involved," she said. "I wasn't aware of that. I just did my job, and it worked fine. That was because we had people assigned to the nitty-gritty of the integration."[57]

Clear about her expectations, Campbell measured progress and managed it accordingly. "I expected the phone to be answered 'Office Depot,' she explained. "We paid people on certain bonus plans. We made the compensation plans clear. We priced customers a certain way. All of our correspondence and presentation materials had to say 'Office Depot.' "[58]

Gradually, the company successfully ironed out the wrinkles of the delivery segment. Campbell credited Dick Bennington and Richard Estalella for bringing stability to the warehouses. "Estalella was a great partner," she said. "He was very process-oriented. He took responsibility and accountability for the warehouses, and that is when we started straightening them out."[59]

Switching to a new mainframe computer helped, as well. Since Office Depot had expanded so rapidly, its management information systems were overwrought. As an information technology publication reported:

The company had a plethora of systems supporting various functions. Three systems served individual groups of stores; another supported financial and telemarketing activities; another served human resources, payroll, and word processing; and still another handled software development. And the servers were crashing with alarm-

ing regularity. More often than not, when the servers crashed, databases that were integrated with the operating system became corrupted.[60]

Campbell remembered a time when David Fuente, chairman and CEO, stood up at one Office Depot leadership council meeting and announced he would ensure the company stabilized its computer platforms. His audience, who had worked with unstable systems, cheered him on.[61]

It was up to Bill Seltzer to keep Fuente's promise. "We'd meet every Monday morning at 7 A.M. to discuss every system failure we had in the company," said Seltzer. "We'd seek out the root cause and assign responsibility. It was a relentless pursuit."[62]

As a reward for his diligence, Seltzer received a standing ovation at the next managers' meeting. "I told the other managers that I hoped they had an opportunity to help Dave [Fuente] keep a promise."[63]

Seltzer fixed the company's information systems problems by installing a new mainframe (a large, powerful computer that served multiple connected terminals), and though the decision might have seemed obvious to an outsider, Bill Seltzer explained the dilemma: "It was a serious decision because everyone else in the retail business—everyone else in the world—was, in fact, downsizing," he said.[64]

ComputerWorld magazine called the decision "a risky move" that paid off. "Office Depot willingly forfeited short-term business gains by delaying most of its new application development for 14 months," the magazine reported. "During that time, it stabilized its application portfolio. ... The positive results are showing up on the company's bottom line."[65]

Indeed, the new mainframe architecture was a boon for the company. The system successfully handled over 50 percent more merchandise or-

As the first store manager at Office Depot, Dick Bennington worked his way up to the executive level through hard work, intelligence, and dedication. He was named president of the Business Services Division in 1997.

Bill Seltzer joined Office Depot in 1991 and later became the company's chief information officer. He retired in 2002.

ders, while help-desk calls for service problems dropped 65 percent.[66] *Information Week* magazine agreed. In 1998, Office Depot landed No. 4 on the magazine's list of the 500 most innovative users of information technology in the United States.

By integrating its IBM ES9000 mainframe and IBM System AS/400 computers and investing in customized software, Office Depot was better able to manage stock, order processing, and inventory replenishment. By reducing inventory levels and still maintaining an excellent in-stock position, the company realized less interest expense and an increase in cash.[67]

"Culturally, we thought that technology was the tool to enable business, and it was also the tool that enabled us to work faster and smarter," said Monica Luechtefeld. "Technology was a productivity tool. It was a performance improvement tool. That was just in our DNA."[68]

Luechtefeld credited Seltzer for improving the company's information technology. "He was very good at not only paying attention to the backbone, the infrastructure, system stability, and scalability, but also at articulating the business

value of technology. So we spent a lot of money building infrastructure and architecture."[69]

The Business Services Division also placed a priority on renewing its focus on customer service. In 1996, for example, the year of the Summer Olympics, employees in the Office Depot Telecenters participated in their own "Quality Olympics" to enhance quality and customer service. Through teamwork between supervisors and Telecenter associates, the associates won gold, silver, and bronze medals based on performance. "The goal was to 'catch people doing something right,' and it succeeded," said Denise Brewer, then-manager of staff support services. "It really brought the teams together and opened the lines of communication between associates and supervisors."[70] BSD also implemented a "win back" campaign to win back some of the customers it had lost when it experienced problems.

In September 1997, Dick Bennington was formally appointed president of the Business Services Division. Bennington's previous responsibilities had included both retail and delivery, which had strengthened the delivery segment. Now he aimed to devote himself full time to the Business Services Division.[71]

"On a long-term basis, we want to be the premier provider of office products and services to the key and major market segments," explained Bennington. "We will not be limited to the products and services we currently sell, but we will continue to explore new merchandise and service opportunities that allow us to be a single-source supplier to our customers."[72]

By 1997, the Business Services Division represented 32 percent of the company's sales and was the fastest-growing segment of Office Depot. That year, the division's sales increased 17.5 percent to $2.18 billion. Its ongoing mission was "to become our customers' primary source for business solutions." The division's customers included large corporate customers, government agencies, and medical and educational institutions.

A Pioneer in E-Commerce

While the Business Services Division remedied the issues that had plagued it for the past few years, it also ventured into new ways of conducting business. In late 1995, the company was

selected by the Massachusetts Institute of Technology (MIT) to develop a system through which MIT could order office supplies from Office Depot via MIT's own desktop computers.[73] "We wanted the school community to use the Internet in a way that would eliminate having to make a call, generate a purchase order, and pay an invoice," said Diane Devlin, who was in charge of the MIT team that developed the business-to-business site. "Yet they could still have the item the very next day or sooner."[74]

The technology, which debuted in late 1995, vastly simplified the procurement process of office supplies. "We saw the vision of what the Internet could mean for businesses," said Luechtefeld, who played a significant role in launching e-commerce at Office Depot. "This was very early in the Internet's life cycle. It was just a couple of years after the first browser was created, so there was some doubt as to what the Internet would mean for consumers. But we understood that it was go-

ing to change the way business was conducted between business customers."[75]

Later in 1996, the Business Services Division expanded the business-to-business e-commerce to its other large corporate and government customers, calling it the Office Depot Business Network.[76] (This was a precursor to its public Web site, *www.officedepot.com*, which debuted in January 1998.) Major customers for the Office Depot Business Network included MIT, Boeing, Motorola, GTE, and the U.S. Navy. Employees of these institutions simply used their personal computer to access the Web-based catalogs of Office Depot and placed their orders electronically, much like customers today order from tens of thousands of retail Web sites. The Network even tracked inventory so customers instantly knew if a product was immediately available.

Companies also viewed the site from their own private Office Depot Web page, which displayed negotiated prices rather than regular catalog prices. Though today such procurement methods are commonplace, the Office Depot Business

Above: In 1997, Office Depot finalized its first public, e-commerce Web site—*www.officedepot.com*—designed to benefit the small and home-based business sector, which was the nation's fastest growing business segment at the time.

Right: Monica Luechtefeld laid the groundwork for developing Office Depot's e-commerce capabilities. She started with Eastman in 1993 and later became executive vice president of information technology, supply chain, and business development at Office Depot.

Network was ahead of its time. It functioned more like an intranet, establishing it (at the time) as more secure and private than a public Web site.[77] As the company explained:

> Each link [of the Office Depot Business Network] is individually customized with buying preferences and pricing agreements, plus warehousing and shipping profiles that are unique to each customer's account. Moreover, the Web site is a password-protected place of business for established customers with private access codes for browsing, ordering products, and checking inventory availability.[78]

Indeed, the Internet quickly changed the face of business. "The corporate business customer is really trying to take dollars out of their total purchasing costs," Luechtefeld wrote. "So they are redesigning the way they purchase supplies, to reduce the costs of sourcing items, ordering, tracking, and all the associated expenses."[79]

Discount Store News also explained, "The Internet is an appealing alternative for large business because it costs less, reduces errors, gives them more control over ordering, and eliminates paperwork. The Internet is still an unknown for many retailers, but at Office Depot, it is a channel of distribution that has quickly become an important part of a larger customer service strategy."[80]

New Marketing Campaigns

In an attempt to rejuvenate its marketing, Office Depot switched its television advertising company in the spring of 1996 from Miami-based Gold Coast Advertising, which had handled the Office Depot account for nine years, to J. Walter Thompson in Chicago.[81] A few months later, the company announced its new tagline: "This is where I take care of business" (a spin-off of "Taking Care of Business").[82] New television commercials attempted to broaden the reach of Office Depot "beyond the typical corporate audience," targeting women executives, small business owners, and parents buying back-to-school supplies.[83] One television spot called "Not a hobby" noted, "the real reason why 7.9 million women in this country have opened their own businesses is ... because they can." These women were also the individuals who

An account executive from Office Depot's Business Services Division serves a corporate customer.

made the office's purchasing decisions. Another spot called "On paper" emphasized the importance of paper in business despite the arrival of the digital age, distinguishing Office Depot as an excellent supplier of paper.[84]

The relationship between Office Depot and J. Walter Thompson was short-lived. After the attempted merger with Staples, Office Depot decided to head in a different direction. "Our advertising goal is two-fold," Office Depot announced. "To keep the company 'top of mind' and 'first choice' among current and potential customers; and to continually reinforce our value message of price, selection, service, and convenience."[85]

With those goals in mind, Office Depot signed on with Wyse Advertising based in Cleveland.[86] Then on Thanksgiving Day in 1997, the new Office Depot television ad campaign made its debut with commercials starring the cartoon character Dilbert™.[87] Created by Scott Adams, Dilbert™ was the "cubicle-dwelling comic strip character that fights the idiocies and injustices of upper management and the craziness of the business world." As new advertising spokescharacter of Office Depot, Dilbert™ introduced the company's new tagline: "Business Is Crazy, But Office Depot Makes Sense."[88]

The company continued its multimedia approach of using network and cable television, radio, print advertising, direct mail, and, of course, the Office Depot catalog, which was redesigned in 1997 to make it easier to navigate.[89]

Office Depot also continued its sports and event marketing. The Office Depot name appeared in Madison Square Garden, Los Angeles' Great Western Forum, the MCI Center in Washington, D.C., and in dozens of sports venues, ranging from the NFL to the NHL and Major League Baseball. The company also sponsored several golf events such as the Bay Hill Invitational (hosted by Arnold Palmer), the Office Depot Father/Son Challenge, and an LPGA tournament called The Office Depot.[90] The 1996 Bay Hill Invitational, a televised event, helped raise funds for the Arnold Palmer Hospital for Women & Children.[91]

Around the Globe

By the end of 1997, Office Depot had 45 successful locations outside the United States and Canada. The company recognized the same con-

ditions in the office supply arena in Europe as had existed in the United States a decade earlier. As Office Depot noted, its "global acceptance is attributed to solid, locally based operations that deliver superior service and gain market share by successfully executing a winning retail concept that works in any language."[92]

Office Depot continued its relationship with Carrefour, the France-based retailer, opening two stores in France under a joint venture in 1996, and two more stores plus a delivery center the following year. It continued to expand in Israel, opening four new stores under its license agreement in 1997 for a total of 11. As the company noted, "Office Depot is already the largest supplier of office products in Israel, less than four years after the first store opened."[93]

An electric tram in Warsaw, Poland, traveled through the city, serving as a moving billboard for Office Depot. Poland was the first country to carry Office Depot advertising on electric trams.

An international licensing agreement with Central Department Stores, a large retail corporation in Bangkok, Thailand, allowed Office Depot to open two stores in the country in March 1997.[94] As the company's first undertaking in the Far East, the licensing agreement moved "the giant retailer in Asia ahead of its two major competitors," according to the *Miami Herald*.[95] Office Depot continued expanding its presence in Asia when it established a joint venture with Deo Deo, a large consumer electronics retailer in Japan. In 1997, Office Depot opened one store in Tokyo and a delivery center in Yokohama and had plans to open two stores in Hiroshima in 1998. An Asian newspaper noted that the stores would hold "prices down by selling imported products and buying directly from domestic manufacturers."[96] Also in 1997, Office Depot ventured into Budapest, Hungary, under an international licensing agreement with Retail Investment Concepts (RIC), the same license partner it had in Poland.[97]

In addition, by the end of 1997, Office Depot co-owned 14 stores in Mexico under its joint venture agreement with Gigante. Under license agreements, Office Depot also operated five stores in Colombia and five in Poland.

A Rejuvenated Company

Office Depot made a comeback in 1997 as the world's largest and most profitable office supply business. "The financial condition of the company is the strongest it has ever been," Fuente told shareholders. In October 1997, the company had no short-term debt and more than $50 million in ready cash.[98] For fiscal year 1997, the company's sales reached $6.7 billion, an 11 percent increase—an impressive achievement despite the distractions from the unsuccessful merger with Staples. Its earnings rose to $169.5 million, a 31 percent increase over the previous year.[99]

Office Depot ended 1997 with 602 Office Depot stores (opening 42 that year), five Furniture At Work stores, five Images stores, and one Office Depot Express store. Its national business-to-business delivery network included 70 sales offices throughout the country, 23 delivery warehouses or Customer Service Centers, and three Telecenters.[100]

Office Depot could once again celebrate its good health, but only for a while. Though the company would unleash some major innovations over the next few years, especially in the area of e-commerce, there were more challenges to overcome.

In 1999, Office Depot operated in 17 countries outside of the United States and Canada, including 26 stores in France.

CHAPTER SIX

JOCKEYING FOR POSITION

1998 – 1999

As we enter the new millennium, Office Depot looks forward to a bright and prosperous future. We have a clear strategy for continued growth. Looking ahead, we see great potential to continue to grow our business in every channel worldwide.

—Chairman and CEO David Fuente, 1999[1]

DESPITE THE RECENT AD-vent of office supply superstore chains like Office Depot, the office products industry remained highly fragmented in the last years of the millennium. Office product superstores served only a small fraction of the available market. Retail stores such as Wal-Mart, Target, Best Buy, Kmart, Dell, Kinko's, and other discount retailers also supplied consumers and businesses, as did thousands of contract stationers and mail-order enterprises.

Part of this fragmentation was created to serve the wide range of customers—from individual consumers who needed back-to-school supplies to large corporate customers who needed office products, such as furniture and computers, for thousands of people. There were also multiple categories of products and services to supply, including general office supplies (pens, file folders, paper, etc.); technology products (computers, printers, etc.); communications equipment (telephones, cell phones, fax machines, etc.); and furniture (desks, bookshelves, lamps, etc.). The North American market alone was estimated at more than $200 billion, and 1998 sales for Office Depot were just under $9 billion. So, despite a fragmented industry, ample growth opportunity existed for Office Depot.[2]

The office products industry was expanding, as well. The small office/home office (SOHO) mar-ket remained on the rise, as did white-collar employment. The exponential growth rate of new technologies fueled the industry, as workers sought out the fastest, smallest, smartest, and most powerful tools to take care of business. Along with the office products industry, however, the competition grew as well, so Office Depot—which served customers through stores, catalog, direct mail, contract delivery, and the Internet—relentlessly searched for new techniques that would help it continue on its path of growth.

Viking Office Products

As Office Depot already knew from experience, acquisitions and international expansion had significantly contributed to the financial growth of the company. Office Depot implemented these avenues for growth once again in August 1998, when it purchased Viking Office Products, a highly profitable, well respected mail-order office supply business, for $2.7 billion in a one-for-one stock swap.

The purchase added $1 billion in sales to the Office Depot International Division and positioned

---

As the world's largest seller of office products, Office Depot grew from $2 million in sales to $6.7 billion in just 11 years.

Above: Irwin Helford, former president, CEO, and chairman of Viking Office Products, was named Office Depot's vice chairman when Office Depot purchased Viking Office Products in 1998.

Right: Bruce Nelson served as president of Viking when Office Depot acquired the company. He subsequently became president of Office Depot's International Division, and chairman and CEO of the company.

Office Depot as "the leading provider of office products and services worldwide."[3] Office Depot expected the acquisition to save the combined company tens of millions of dollars a year as it became more efficient in producing catalogs, purchasing, and distribution.[4] The Office Depot International Division immediately began developing a new management information systems platform to consolidate the two companies' order-entry functions, warehouse management, merchandising, and financial reporting.

Founded in 1960, Viking Office Products was purchased in 1988 from its founders by the company's upper management and Dillon Read & Company, a private banking company, in a leveraged buyout. Viking went public on NASDAQ in 1990, and although its home base was in Torrance, California, the company conducted more than two-thirds of its business outside the United States. Throughout its history, the company had successfully charged higher prices than office supply superstores like Office Depot because it offered "fanatical" customer service, as Viking insiders called it.

Lee Ault III, who served on Viking's board since 1992 and joined Office Depot's board after the acquisition, explained the meaning of "fanatical" customer service:

> *Irwin Helford [Viking's chairman and CEO] used to send memos out to employees to the effect that service had slipped to "excellent" and that we couldn't survive in the competitive marketplace unless we truly had fanatical service. When he walked the halls, if he ever heard a phone ring more than a couple of times, it would upset him. After the Los Angeles earthquake in 1994, Irwin sent a letter out to the thousands of customers in California offering regrets and saying that Viking would replace all of their office supplies free of charge, no questions asked.[5]*

Viking's mail-order business model drove its profits. As the *New York Times* reported:

Direct marketers are usually money makers because they have little overhead, and their customers are often less price-sensitive than the smallest companies, which are struggling to survive, and the largest, which have purchasing managers who oversee what the company pays for supplies bought by the truckload.[6]

Once the acquisition was complete, Helford joined Office Depot as vice chairman, while Bruce Nelson, Viking's president, joined the Office Depot board and became president of the International Division. Neil Austrian, a member of Viking's board, also joined Office Depot's board of directors.

Helford, known throughout Viking as a man of honesty and compassion, had a paternalistic influence that would continue long after he retired in 1999. He was reluctant to sell the company he had fostered, but Nelson convinced him that Viking needed to act fast to compete in a changing industry.

"When Irwin [Helford] took over Viking, it was a small, struggling, mail-order company, and he built it into a very significant enterprise," Nelson recalled. "He never wanted to be part of a big company, but in the early part of 1996, I saw a headline in the paper that said Office Depot and Staples were planning to merge. That's when I realized the industry was turning into a world of large-scale players, and we at Viking needed to be larger to compete. We explored some potential acquisitions, but none of them panned out."[7]

So Nelson started searching for companies that could acquire Viking. He recalled how Staples had planned to merge with Viking, but "at the last minute, the Staples board turned down the merger, which led us to a search for a partnership with Office Depot."[8]

Once the two companies started collaborations, the merger process moved quickly. Three months later, the transaction was complete.

David Fuente, Office Depot chairman and CEO, called the Viking purchase "a key step to turning Office Depot from a national company into an international company."[9] Indeed, Viking had direct mail and delivery operations in 11 countries: Australia, Austria, Belgium, France, Germany, Ireland, Italy, Luxembourg, the Netherlands, the United Kingdom, and the United States. With 1997 sales of $1.3 billion, Viking had 26 facilities and more than 2.5 million customers worldwide.[10] *Fortune* magazine

Viking Office Products was well-known in the industry for providing excellent, individualized customer service.

noted that Viking had been "extremely successful in penetrating foreign markets."[11]

"This is a tremendous opportunity for two exciting companies to get together," Fuente said, shortly after the deal was announced. "It creates an opportunity for growth and improvement that neither company could have achieved on its own."[12]

Analysts agreed. "Picking [Viking] up was a real gem for Office Depot," said Aram Rubinson, an analyst with Paine Webber in New York.[13]

"You have two of the market leaders getting together to become a better company," said Peter McMullin of Southeast Research Partners in Boca Raton, Florida.[14]

"It's an extremely positive move," said Amy Ryan, an analyst with Prudential Securities. "It gives Office Depot the platform to expand internationally. It should help to accelerate overall growth."[15]

Under the Office Depot umbrella, Viking operated as a separate subsidiary, maintaining the esteemed Viking brand and its management structure in California. The *Los Angeles Times* reported that both companies planned to keep their "existing product lines and service approach, with Viking offering a higher-end, more service-oriented product, compared with the more price-conscious strategy of Office Depot."[16]

An Influx of Talent

Around the time of the Viking acquisition, Office Depot decided to hire new talent. David Fannin, the company's first general counsel, was recruited in 1998 and built the legal function at Office Depot from the ground up.

"In this post-Staples merger period, the company reached the point where it needed to grow up from having developed as an entrepreneurial-based company," Fannin said. "It had grown very rapidly, but it did not have a lot of the things you would expect to see, like a general counsel, for example. It reached the point where company management and the board concluded they couldn't go further

with the kind of loose structure the company had in the past."[17]

The influx of new talent at Office Depot filled a variety of functions. Shawn McGhee joined the company in 1998 as senior vice president of merchandising and marketing. Charlie Brown, who later became CFO and then president of the International Division, was also hired that year as the company's controller. So was John Deaton, who joined Office Depot as senior manager of supply chain and later became vice president of retail marketing, and then design, print, and ship. Paul Larkin came on board in 1998 as manager of inventory management and went on to become regional vice president of retail sales for Florida.

A Public Web Site

Besides the Viking acquisition, there were other noteworthy events for Office Depot in 1998. The success of the company's business-to-business e-commerce prompted the company to develop a public Web site. "We were doing well online with our corporate customers, and we thought we were ready for something that was more public and more consumer oriented and small-business oriented," said Monica Luechtefeld. "That meant you had to have functionality for offers, and it had to be simpler to use than a corporate Web site."[18]

Office Depot hired a design firm in Silicon Valley to help develop the Web site. "We wanted to be in the hotbed of the Internet to attract Internet-savvy IT people," Luechtefeld explained.[19] Since Office Depot was already familiar with the intricacies of the site and knew how to manage it, the design firm only had to polish the cosmetic pieces.

In January 1998, *www.officedepot.com* made its debut. "We received more than 100 orders on the first day, and that was a soft launch. It was shocking,"

Office Depot's public Web site—*www.officedepot.com*—garnered accolades from technology circles and customers. Even in its debut year of 1998, the site was easy to navigate and saved customers time and money, resulting in increased sales on the site.

This overhead shot of an Office Depot warehouse shows the vastness of the company's operations.

said Tim Toews, who joined the company in 1994 and participated in the development of the corporate e-commerce site. He later became the chief information officer at Office Depot.[20]

It was no surprise that the Web site proved popular. As David Fuente told shareholders, the Internet is "currently the most cost-effective method of servicing our customers 24 hours a day, seven days a week."[21] There was no cost for paper, as with a fax or mail order; there was no cost of human labor, as with a telephone order. Buyers simply logged on to the Web site, searched for items, and placed their order online.

The Web site also helped create brand awareness among consumers and allowed the company to tap new markets. "Our use of the Internet to market our products has allowed us to achieve greater leverage in our merchandising, warehousing, and distribution organizations," Fuente said. After all, Office Depot already had the brick-and-mortar infrastructure, along with the delivery infrastructure, complete with warehouses, delivery trucks, and drivers.

Using the Internet to drive delivery sales was a natural, though not obvious, fit. The public Web site also meant Office Depot could serve every type of customer, large or small, in any way customers preferred to purchase office products. "We had a choice," said Bill Seltzer, then chief information officer at Office Depot. "We could use the Web as another sales channel or as a unifier to lift all channels of our business. We want to be ubiquitous to the customer—to let the customers choose whatever channel they want."[22]

In addition, *www.officedepot.com* "enabled us to build incremental, profitable sales," Fuente explained.[23] The proof was in the pudding. In 1998, sales from the company's combined Web sites reached $66.5 million, but that figure seemed small compared to 1999's sales.[24] That year, the combined Internet site sales increased a whopping 426 percent, to $349.7 million, "well exceeding the goal of $200 million that we set at the beginning of the year," according to Fuente.[25]

Even in its debut year, *www.officedepot.com* was fast and user-friendly, with a flexible search engine and "true-to-life" visuals. It included fea-

Monica Luechtefeld (left), then-vice president of marketing for the contract sales group, discusses the company's Web sites with Elizabeth VanStory, then-vice president of Office Depot Online.

tures that may appear commonplace today but in 1998 were considered advanced, such as customer shopping carts, the ability to create a custom shopping list, real-time access to inventory, flexible delivery and returns, and order tracking. Until Office Depot dropped the Dilbert™ marketing campaign in 1999, the cartoon spokes-character appeared on the Web site to help shoppers locate items and add a touch of humor.

"We've made sure that the site offers the fundamentals," said Elizabeth VanStory, then-vice president of Office Depot Online, "ease of use, clear product presentation, selection and purchase, and readily available help. We asked small and home-based business customers to describe their ideal retail environment, and we built it."[26]

As VanStory implied, *www.officedepot.com* especially benefited the small office/home office (SOHO) market segment, the country's fastest-growing workforce according to the U.S. Small Business Administration,[27] and the source of most of the U.S. economy's new jobs.[28] In addition, the Web site saved time for SOHO buyers. As *Discount Store News* noted,

"Ordering products electronically and having them delivered is a better solution for a time-pressed small business owner than both driving to and shopping at a store."[29] This was a clever "news" approach that not only built goodwill, but pointed customers back to Office Depot to buy the products they would need to accomplish these tasks.

The Web site offered additional assistance to SOHO customers by linking to articles such as "Getting Organized" and "Tax Time." Office Depot published similarly tailored content in its widely distributed *Business News* print magazine.[30]

The year it was introduced, the Web site won several honors from technology circles: the CIO Web Business 50/50 Award, the Retail Network Innovation Award, and Biz Rate Buyers Best Gold Award.[31] As the company noted, "These awards recognize *www.officedepot.com* as a ground-breaking Internet site business model."[32] In September 1998, *BusinessWeek* praised the company's Internet strategy: "As the Internet matures," the magazine reported, "it may be the old brick-and-mortar retailers like Office Depot that have the last laugh. But only if they develop a Web strategy not unlike Office Depot, which is leveraging its strengths in terra firma for success in cyberspace."[33]

Office Depot was undeniably ahead of the game when it came to e-commerce, and those who brought it to reality were understandably proud. "We really took a leadership position when it came to e-commerce," said Luechtefeld. "We spent several years in the leadership position, but then everyone finally decided it was important and threw people and money at it."[34]

Bricks and Mortar: The Stores Division

Throughout 1998, Office Depot worked on rebuilding the real estate staff it had lost after the aborted merger with Staples. It accelerated its new store openings in an attempt to make up for its stagnancy during the 10-month merger period. In their 1998 letter to shareholders, David Fuente and John Macatee shared their goal to increase the company's store count by approximately 15 percent over each of the next five years, essentially doubling the size of the store chain by the end of 2003. "This new store plan includes entry into new markets as well as continued development of existing and under-penetrated markets," they wrote.[35]

In 1998, Office Depot opened 100 stores (57 in December alone) for a total count of 702 in the United States and Canada. It also remodeled about 200 older stores to make them brighter and more customer-friendly.[36] In 1999, the company opened a record 123 stores, for a total of 825 in 46 states, Washington, D.C., and Canada. It also operated 30 customer service centers (delivery warehouses) in North America.

As was its tradition, Office Depot continued to emphasize customer service. The company focused on training employees in communication and sales. Associates received better training in product offerings, especially in terms of technology and furniture, which were the big-ticket items that required the most knowledge to sell.

For 1998, sales in the Stores Division increased 9 percent to $5.1 billion, and store sales increased 15 percent in 1999, reaching $5.8 billion. The division produced the highest average sales per store in

To enhance its customer-friendly reputation, Office Depot periodically remodeled its stores with attractive product displays and easy-to-read signs.

A tech-savvy salesperson helps a customer choose the right computer for his needs. Office Depot took great care in educating its sales floor representatives to ensure they remained knowledgeable about all store products.

the entire industry, and it was the largest contributor of sales to the entire company.[37]

The Business Services Group

The Business Services Group served all of the domestic delivery customers at Office Depot through a contract sales force, a commercial sales force, mail-order operations, domestic call centers, e-commerce Web sites, and warehousing and delivery operations. In 1998 and 1999, the Business Services Group was the second-largest contributor of sales and profit to the company (behind the Stores Division). Sales of the group rose 13 percent in 1998 to $2.7 billion, and sales rose another 9 percent in 1999 to $3.2 billion.[38]

In 1998, the Business Services Group brought Viking's domestic mail-order service, as well as its Internet site, *www.vikingop.com*, into the BSG fold. That same year, BSG expanded its contract sales force to just over 900 account representatives. These salespeople targeted companies that had the

potential to purchase at least $25,000 worth of office products annually, so every account representative theoretically brought in a significant amount of business. To further enhance the contract sales potential, Office Depot combined focused recruiting and improved entry-level training with better territory management.[39] The strength of the sales force was crucial to Office Depot. After all, the salespeople brought in new customers and built a strong relationship with existing customers that would increase sales.

Unlike the contract salespeople, BSG's commercial sales group targeted small businesses (those with up to 25 employees), sending out direct-mail advertising for the Office Depot and Viking brands.

Office Depot quickly realized that Viking maintained an excellent marketing database. Well tuned and analytical, it seemed to understand each and every customer, and Office Depot began using that database as a model for its other marketing databases. "Viking developed the ability to mail to millions, yet speak to one customer at a time with personalized, meaningful offers," said Bruce Nelson, then-president of the International Division and former president of Viking. At the same time, he said, the database "improved catalog response rates and generated the highest net profits, return on assets, and return on investment in the industry."[40] Office

Depot aimed to use the database to "pinpoint the individual needs of our diverse customer base, stimulate greater customer loyalty, and drive incremental sales."[41]

Boosting customer service represented one of BSG's ongoing goals. To that end, in 1998, Monica Luechtefeld headed up a customer service task force that aimed to take better care of customers and standardize customer service, in addition to implementing reporting procedures. Through consistent standards, Office Depot could respond more quickly when customer service issues cropped up.[42]

The Business Services Group maintained an expansive distribution network. In 1999, BSG owned 30 customer service centers (delivery warehouses), 44 satellite centers, and a fleet of more than 2,000 delivery trucks—but the company planned to consolidate and integrate the Viking and Office Depot warehouses, trimming the number from 30 to 21 to lower the cost structure.[43] With the addition of Viking, BSG had eight call centers (formerly

Tim Toews joined Office Depot in 1994 when Office Depot acquired Yorkship. He became chief information officer in 2005.

called Telecenters). Viking's call centers were located in California, Connecticut, Ohio, Texas, and Kansas.

Meanwhile, business from the company's e-commerce Web site grew steadily, but not without overcoming a learning curve, as Luechtefeld explained:

We had to do some evangelizing for the business-to-business site because, in that day, many of our salespeople thought the Internet was going to replace them. Also, the corporations that were our customers weren't sure the Internet would stick around. Many didn't understand it, and if they did, they weren't sure why they needed to pay attention to it. So, the selling cycle to get customers connected was truly Internet 101. We had to educate customers on what it took to be connected, how it could save them time and money, and what it would do to change the way work was done.[44]

In October 1998, Office Depot upgraded its corporate customer business-to-business Web site so it could be accessed through the Internet in addition to private connections. The pages that corporate customers accessed were also modified to meet individual client's needs.[45]

Tim Toews recalled that the upgraded site brought in a significant amount of traffic.[46] Indeed, from 1997 to 1998, the number of contract customers who ordered from Office Depot Internet sites increased from 500 to 11,000.[47] In 1999, the number jumped to 40,000.[48]

Office Depot remained at the forefront of the Internet movement, with its two Internet sites dominating the industry. "We are confident that no other company in our industry offers more ways to conduct electronic commerce than Office Depot, or provides Web sites that surpass our award-winning Internet sites," the company proclaimed.[49]

The International Division

After the Viking acquisition, Office Depot conducted business in 17 countries outside the United States and Canada, either through retail stores, catalog, or Internet sales. The Viking catalog business comprised the bulk of Office Depot's international sales, which were augmented by the launch of *www.viking-direct.co.uk* in the United

SUPPORTING THE NATIONAL PTA

SUPPORTING SCHOOL VALUES

IN 1998, OFFICE DEPOT AND the National Parent Teacher Association (PTA) joined to form a new program called "Supporting School Values" that offered discounts on supplies to teachers and PTA members. The program involved a $250,000 "Back-to-School Sweepstakes" that provided 40 schools a chance to win a $5,000 shopping spree from Office Depot.

To encourage participation in the program, Office Depot gave each state PTA president a computer for his or her office. In addition, the company donated marketing dollars toward raising awareness about the PTA and served as the official source of school supplies for the organization. At the time, the National PTA had 6.5 million members and was the largest volunteer organization for child advocacy.[1]

"For more than 100 years, National PTA has been every parent's best friend, and Office Depot is proud to sponsor them," said then-CEO David Fuente. "As part of our commitment, we want to use our resources to help students, teachers, and families."[2]

Kingdom, where Viking had a particularly strong presence. Debuting in February 1999, the U.K. e-commerce site served as the first international Web site for Office Depot. Modeled after the company's domestic e-commerce sites, the U.K. site reflected many similar features, including real-time inventory tracking.

Throughout 1998 and 1999, the International Division worked at integrating its operations to cut redundant costs. In addition, the division focused on consolidating its purchasing power in the various countries where it operated in an effort to negotiate lower costs from vendors. It lowered catalog merchandising costs and generally reduced operating expenses.[50]

In 1998, the International Division increased its ownership of the two Office Depot stores in Thailand to 80 percent. It purchased the remaining 50 percent ownership of its 26 stores in France and its six stores in Japan. In 1999, the company started Viking mail-order operations in Japan, which, notably, was the second-largest market for office supplies outside of the United States.[51]

In 1999 alone, the International Division added 31 stores, including 11 fully owned stores in France and three in Japan. Office Depot also added one store in Hungary, six in Israel, seven in Mexico, and five in Poland. By the end of 1999, there were 118 Office Depot stores outside the United States and Canada, either fully owned by Office Depot, or operating through joint ventures or licensing agreements.[52]

International sales at Office Depot climbed 26 percent in 1999, to $1.3 billion. The sales growth was largely attributed to a combination of new catalog customers, which grew by 30 percent that year; more catalog orders from existing customers, which grew by 20 percent; and the increased ownership of its operations in France, Japan, and Thailand.[53]

Considering the fragmentation of the international office products industry, experts estimated the market was most likely larger than in North America—that is, it exceeded $200 billion. This created a wide avenue for growth for the International Division. As Bruce Nelson explained, "More than half of the world's demand for office supplies is outside the United States and Canada. ... Some time in the future, we face potential store saturation in North America—but outside North America, there is tremendous potential to grow retail, contract, catalog, and the Internet."[54]

Advertising, Merchandising, and Supply Chain

In December 1998, Office Depot revamped its advertising efforts, ending the Dilbert™ campaign. The company concluded that most customers did not associate Dilbert™ with the purchase of office products. In addition, Dilbert™ seemed to "polarize customers because they tended to either love or hate him," said Deaton. "A lot of people thought that Dilbert™ wasn't representative of their work."[55]

After dropping Dilbert™, Office Depot decided to return to Miami-based Gold Coast Advertising and its highly successful "Taking Care of Business" campaign. "There's no phrase that better describes who we are and what we do," said Gary Schweikhart, Office Depot's spokesperson at the time. "It was the

Right: Office Depot "cranked up the furniture business" by remodeling designated spaces in its stores into "vignette" presentations. The designs included four-way walls, which created an environment that depicted real office areas. This vignette approach to furniture displays served as a turning point for the company and resulted in the rise of furniture sales.

Below: Highly trained Office Depot call center representatives helped ensure that every customer was satisfied with the service they received.

most effective campaign we've ever run and certainly the most memorable."[56]

Unlike the Dilbert™ campaign, "Taking Care of Business" emphasized the expertise in products and services at Office Depot.[57]

On the merchandising front, Office Depot worked on leveraging its purchasing power to negotiate the lowest prices from its vendors. The company offered private-label brands that helped lower costs for customers. In 1998, Office Depot owned three private-label brands (Corner Office, Office Choice, and Office Depot), which it gradually consolidated into a single Office Depot brand. In addition, the company emphasized consultative selling especially for technology items and furniture in order to augment customer service and increase sales.[58]

With 1999 sales of more than $10 billion, Office Depot also "cranked up the furniture business" in the late 1990s, according to Kirby Salgado, divisional merchandising manager for furniture at Office Depot. The company remodeled the space it devoted to furniture throughout the stores into a "vignette" presentation.

"Previously, you walked into the store, and there was just an open floor pad where a section was cordoned off for chairs, the back wall had file cabinets and bookcases, and all the desks were spread out in a big open space. For the vignette presentation, we put up four-way walls and created an environment in each one of those vignettes that showed how the office was displayed with all the pieces together. The furniture business really took off as a result of that move. It was a turning point for us."[59]

By the end of 1999, the Office Depot domestic supply chain consisted of 30 customer service centers (delivery warehouses), which shipped product to customers in the direct and contract channels, while 10 cross docks shipped product from vendors to the stores. As always, the overall goal was to lower shipment and inventory holding costs.

The supply chain continued to improve as a result of the new computer systems at Office Depot. The company's internally developed, customized system distributed and replenished product more efficiently than before. The company also worked with vendors to cut delays within the supply chain and improve order flow and delivery. On any given day, Office Depot could decide what store, customer service center, or cross dock needed restocking, allowing both the company and vendors to cut inventory levels and save money for both parties. In 1998, for example, Office Depot reduced its inventory by $139 million, while adding 100 new stores that year.

Meanwhile, the Stores Division continued to enliven store productivity and streamline the supply chain. John Deaton, who was hired from Ernst & Young consulting in 1998 as senior manager of supply chain, helped vastly improve operations. As always, the company continually reviewed its assortment and evaluated new products to offer customers the finest products and the best values, while also cutting out costs in its own supply chain. Starting in 1998, however, the Stores Division refined its product assortment and improved profit margins by selling more computer supplies and accessories. It also reduced the number of computer brands it carried, thus reducing inventory levels and increasing inventory turns.[60] In 1999, each store had 99 percent of its merchandise in stock at any one point in time, due to a more efficient supply chain.[61]

"Cost was an issue at that time," said Deaton. "We were a fire-ready-aim company. We didn't have a lot of foresight in terms of who we wanted to be or how we wanted to get there, but we were great at going out and executing things and turning on a dime. So my charge was to make sure we were pointing the gun in the right direction—rationalizing our inventory, rationalizing our transportation, rationalizing our distribution centers. We felt we needed to have this enormous amount of safety stock, and eventually we were able to wean ourselves off that lump of inventory. We went through a series of elaborate studies and projects that led us to create the core infrastructure to become one of the premier supply chains in all of retail."[62]

The company's goal for 1999 and beyond aimed to reduce the number of vendors it worked with (nearly 5,000 in 1998) in an effort to lower production costs and simplify replenishment.[63]

The Ups and Downs

In the 1998 Office Depot annual report, Fuente and Macatee announced that the company was "in the best overall financial position in its history," with a debt-to-capital ratio of 18.9 percent and $704.5 million in cash.[64] As Fuente noted, this allowed the company to move fast when acquisitions presented themselves. In 1999, Office Depot sales crossed the $10 billion mark, reaching $10.3 billion, a 14 percent increase over the previous year. Also in 1999, the company issued a three-for-two stock split;[65] Standard & Poor's listed Office Depot on its prestigious S&P 500 list;[66] and the company jumped from No. 239 on the *Fortune* 500 to No. 176.[67]

While Office Depot was in good financial shape under CFO Barry Goldstein and Charlie Brown, its new senior vice president of finance, the sales growth at Office Depot started to slow by mid-1999. In the third quarter of 1999, Office Depot reported a significant loss following the decision to write-off a large number of unproductive assets.

Comparable sales in the stores that remained open for more than a year rose 3 percent in 1998 and 2 percent in 1999, while store-operating

---

Opposite: In 1998, Office Depot acquired the remaining 50 percent ownership of its 26 stores in France. The following year, it added 11 fully owned stores in that country.

David Fuente (left) and John Macatee oversaw some key events at Office Depot in 1998, including the launch of *www.officedepot.com* and the purchase of Viking Office Products.

profit declined in 1999.[68] Office Depot cited "higher occupancy costs in our newer stores, increased advertising spending, and costs to support our sales and re-merchandising initiatives." The company also faced increasingly tough competition from rivals like Wal-Mart and Costco, which honed in on sales of the more profitable items within Office Depot's broad assortment of office products. A sizeable portion of retail sales at Office Depot came from computers and other technology items, which produced low-margin profits thanks to competition from Dell and Gateway (which sold computers directly) and electronics discount stores such as Best Buy and Circuit City.[69]

Office Depot's sluggish performance caused its leaders to re-examine operations in 1999. It was not uncommon for Office Depot to close a few under-performing stores in the United States and Canada, and to exit the pilot operations in Furniture At Work and Images stores. These closures sharpened the focus and strengthened the remaining operations.

When Office Depot reported a loss for the third quarter and said its earnings for the rest of the year would be below analysts' forecasts, the company's stock value plummeted 30 percent in one day. The third-quarter loss of $1.07 million (less than one cent a share) came after the company incurred expenses for closing stores and writing down the value of slow-moving inventory, particularly outdated technology products. It was also feeling the pinch from costs incurred after the Viking acquisition.[70]

As it had in 1996, the company's leaders believed the stock was grossly undervalued, so Office Depot repurchased $500 million worth of its stock in 1999 (and an additional $200 million in 2000).

Just weeks after Office Depot announced its earnings would be below expectations, John Macatee resigned as president and chief operating officer.

Nevertheless, the company tried to inspire confidence among investors. "We have many talented executives in our management structure, who we believe can, and will, provide the strong leadership to pursue our long-term growth objectives," Fuente said.[71]

Office Depot set about reorganizing its upper management and named Shawn McGhee president of North American retail operations. He joined the company in early 1998.

Though investors were concerned about the overall health of Office Depot, the company remained the world leader in all the distribution channels for office products and services. The company also had boasting rights as the largest supplier of office products and services in the world.

Even though it had experienced explosive growth in a short period of time, dramatic changes still lay ahead for the young company. In fact, a significant change occurred in 2000 when David Fuente, the person who had led Office Depot to superstore—and superstar—status, stepped down from his post as the company's CEO.

Looking Forward to the New Millennium

Office DEPOT

As the world's leading seller of office products, Office Depot ensured customers and vendors that its systems would be Y2K compliant. The company released a brochure to assure everyone that business would not be interrupted when the clock struck midnight on December 31, 1999.

CHAPTER SEVEN

THE CHALLENGE

2000–2001

*To return our focus to our core business customers, foster a winning cul-
ture among our employees, and restore credibility with the capital markets, we had to make significant and sometimes difficult decisions. We
see enormous potential for our business to grow and prosper in 2001
and beyond.*

—Chairman and CEO Bruce Nelson, 2001[1]

FOR MANY INDIVIDUALS AND businesses, the new millennium reflected a symbol of hope—a time for new beginnings and great expectations. For Office Depot, however, the year 2000 presented one of the company's most difficult times. While the Office Depot International Division and Business Services Group had fared well, the North American retail stores posted disappointing sales.

In May 2000, the value of Office Depot shares sank 30 percent in one day after the company warned shareholders it wouldn't meet second-quarter earnings expectations. Sluggish technology sales were the main problem, along with slow sales at Office Depot stores that opened between 1996 and 1999—notably the locations that were opened quickly after the aborted merger with Staples.[2] In fact, many of the company's woes traced back to the canceled merger.[3]

An Old Wound

During the 10-month merger process, Office Depot had lost 200 employees in addition to most of its real estate department, nearly freezing expansion in anticipation of transforming into Staples/Office Depot. Many development and internet technology projects had been cancelled, supply-chain expansion had ceased, and new marketing programs were

withdrawn. All of these events had set back Office Depot nearly a decade, forcing the company to open a series of stores in less than ideal locations after the cancelled merger.

"We were racing to catch up," said John Deaton, then-vice president of marketing planning. "We went on a tear of opening stores, but we were building without forethought and strategic intent. We found ourselves in markets where it wasn't cost effective to advertise because you didn't get any efficiencies or economies of scale. We found ourselves in places where we couldn't effectively leverage our existing supply chain."[4]

In its 1999 annual report, Office Depot executives seemed aware of the real estate problem. "Our real estate strategy will stress a more analytical approach," the company reported. "During 1999, we conducted extensive customer and market research that will allow a more precise evaluation of the profit potential and return on investment of each new store opening."[5]

Additionally, the Retail Stores Division was not receiving the necessary guidance. "Retail was our

---

Office Depot associates are well-trained and highly knowledgeable on technology products sold at company stores.

biggest division, yet [we didn't quite focus on managing it]," said Charlie Brown. "It was almost like, 'Well, the retail division is doing okay, so we'll leave it on auto-pilot because we have to get these eight contract stationers integrated.' We put so much focus on those acquisitions that we ignored retail, which then came back to haunt us."[6]

In 2000, the slow and expensive integration of Viking, specifically Viking's warehouse operations, added to the company's lowered earnings. The

integration took longer, in part, because of the cultural differences between Viking and Office Depot. While the two companies had some similarities, they were different enough to cause several problems. David Fannin, executive vice president and general counsel, explained:

We continued operating two different cultures for too long. It was almost like two companies. There was Viking in California, and they operated the Viking way, and there was Office Depot

Office Depot's board of directors in 2000. (Front row, from left): Irwin Helford, vice chairman of Office Depot; Bruce Nelson, CEO of Office Depot; and David Fuente, chairman of Office Depot. (Middle row, from left): Frank Scruggs, Jr., of Greenberg Traurig LLP; Peter Solomon, chairman and CEO of the Peter J. Solomon Company, Ltd.; James Heskett, professor emeritus at Harvard Business School; and Cynthia Cohen, president of Strategic Mindshare. (Back row, from left): Michael Myers, president of First Century Partners; Neil Austrian, president of Dryden & Company; Lee Ault, III, chairman of In-Q-Tel, Inc.; and W. Scott Hedrick, general partner of InterWest Partners.

in Delray Beach. Office Depot culture was more purely entrepreneurial than that of Viking. People just did what needed to be done. It was very instinctive. Viking was almost like an old-fashioned, large family with Irwin Helford and Bruce Nelson as the parents at the head of the dining room table. It was very top-down.

Irwin was very protective of his employees. He really looked out for them and wanted to take care of them. He negotiated an agreement in the merger that essentially said that for the first two years, nothing would change for the Viking employees, including wages and benefit plans. Now I think it helped to get the deal done in some ways, but I think it also led to a prolonged period where those two cultures were almost forced to coexist.[7]

Office Depot stores in Japan are wholly owned and make delivery a huge segment of the company's business in that country. The operations of Viking Office Products and Office Depot, however, are not fully integrated in Japan.

Operating as two separate companies meant Viking and Office Depot were working with parallel structures, so opportunities to realize synergies and consolidate functions were missed.[8] Most of Viking's international operations were faring well, but in countries where Office Depot and Viking both operated, integration issues existed. "Viking and Office Depot were never really fully integrated in Japan," explained Rick Lepley, former executive vice president of North American Retail, who was placed in charge of the Japanese operations in 2001. "So there were two warehouses, two catalogs, two buying groups, and the challenge was to try and put it all together."[9]

Meanwhile, Staples' marketing strategies overshadowed those of Office Depot. Also, instead of opening a flurry of superstores all over the country like Office Depot, Staples had expanded by penetrating areas with clusters of stores that were smaller than its traditional stores. As *BusinessWeek* noted, "Staples is the only office superstore that's increasing its market share—from 34 percent in 1997 to 37 percent in 2000."[10]

The End of an Era

CEO David Fuente had planned to retire once his contract expired in 2001; however, when he announced his intentions to the board of directors in 2000, both he and the board decided to speed up the retirement process and ease the uncertainty that an impending change in leadership could potentially introduce. "I think a board is never happy with someone who knows they are leaving," Fuente said years later. "So they decided that if I was going to leave, they would rather I left when I got it into my mind. So I did."[11]

In July 2000, Fuente retired as CEO of Office Depot after leading the company for 13 years and helping it grow from a local string of stores into the largest office supply chain in the world.

"We have the greatest appreciation and respect for David Fuente's contributions over 13 years of dedicated service, during which he helped build the company into an industry leader," said James Heskett, chairman of the Office Depot governance committee. "However, the company today faces new challenges, and we agreed with David that it was appropriate for him to take a more advisory role."[12]

Bruce Nelson, president of the International Division who had joined Office Depot through the Viking acquisition, was named the new chief executive. Though Fuente remained as a nonexecutive chairman in an advisory role through 2000, Nelson became chairman in 2001. Fuente remained on the board of directors.

2000
OFFICE DEPOT BOARD OF DIRECTORS

Lee A. Ault III
Chairman
In-Q-Tel, Inc.

Neil Austrian
President
Dryden & Company

Cynthia R. Cohen
President
Strategic Mindshare

David I. Fuente
Chairman
Office Depot, Inc.

W. Scott Hedrick
General Partner
InterWest Partners

Irwin Helford
Vice Chairman
Office Depot, Inc.
and
Chairman Emeritus
Viking Office Products

James L. Heskett
Professor Emeritus
Harvard Business School

Michael J. Myers
President
First Century Partners, Inc.

Bruce Nelson
Chief Executive Officer
Office Depot, Inc.

Frank P. Scruggs, Jr.
Shareholder
Greenberg Traurig LLP

Peter J. Solomon
Chairman
Chief Executive Officer
Peter J. Solomon Company

A Tough Road Ahead

As the new chief executive officer of Office Depot, Bruce Nelson had a long and trying task ahead of him, as analyst Mark Mandel, with investment banking firm Robinson-Humphrey, acknowledged. "It's going to be a tough road," he said.[13]

Nelson "inherited some challenging issues," said Daniel Binder, an analyst with Buckingham Research Group, a securities brokerage firm. "He's facing the music and not trying to sugarcoat anything. I think [turning the company around] is something he's up to doing."[14]

Nelson admitted to shareholders how Office Depot had dropped the ball:

Growth in the United States office supply superstore industry was beginning to mature, and we had not responded effectively to the changing competitive environment. We had lost sight of some of our core competencies and competitive advantages, and we had allowed parts of our business to become too complex and inefficient. We had been slow to address issues in underperforming businesses and assets. Worst of all, our company and our management team had lost the loyalty of our shareholders and the confidence of our employees, who viewed our direction as unclear and our future as uncertain.[15]

Just a month before Nelson became CEO, the company's stock had hit an all-time low of $6—down from a high of $25 less than a year before.[16] When Nelson took over the helm in July 2000, the stock stood at $6.63—and that was after the price rose 25 cents upon the company's leadership changing hands.

"We have the building blocks of a good company in place," he said. "I want to build on that foundation and return Office Depot to its position as the premier industry leader. This takes time, but our commitment is to make it happen."[17]

A Compelling Place

In his 2000 letter to shareholders, Nelson reported that upon becoming CEO in July, the company began reviewing all aspects of the business "with an objective to establish Office Depot as a more compelling place to work, shop, and invest."[18]

"Loyal employees create loyal customers," Nelson once explained. "If you are a great place to work, you can become a great place to shop—and if you are a great place to work and shop, you will, by definition, be a great place to invest."[19]

To make Office Depot a more compelling place to work, shop, and invest—and to have it stand out from the competition—the company established new corporate values that stressed fanatical customer service, excellence in execution, and respect for the individual.

Creating a positive work environment at Office Depot meant thinking about the well-being of every employee, whether they worked in the stores, warehouses, customer service centers, corporate offices, or any of the countries where Office Depot conducted business. "We want to provide a rewarding experience that enables them to enjoy a high level of job satisfaction," Nelson said.[20]

Above: In 2000, the board of directors appointed Bruce Nelson, former president of the International Division, as the new chief executive of Office Depot.

Left: With satisfied associates working at its stores, Office Depot hopes its employees will transfer that satisfaction to customers.

Research indicated that employees who were satisfied with their jobs and their management and were rewarded appropriately through fair wages and benefits, preferred to remain in their jobs and even establish stronger customer relationships. "These solid relationships will truly make the difference, driving new revenues and new profitability levels at Office Depot in the future," Nelson said.[21]

Office Depot recognized that customers had a variety of places and conduits through which to shop for office supplies—one reason it was important to distinguish Office Depot from the competition and transform it into a more attractive place to shop. Whether customers shopped in the stores, over the Internet, through catalogs, or through account executives, Office Depot strived to be the company of choice when it came to purchasing office supplies.

"Fanatical customer service"—the deep-rooted mantra from Viking Office Products—served as a key ingredient to turning Office Depot into a more exciting shopping experience. Irwin Helford, who led Viking Office Products for many years, defined "fanatical" service in an Office Depot newsletter. "It's doing more than a customer expected ... and doing it with compassion. It's not found in training manuals, rule books, or posters— it's all in how a customer feels."[22]

Nevertheless, Office Depot leaders realized they had to win back the confidence of shareholders, who saw an uncertain future. They needed to rejuvenate the com-

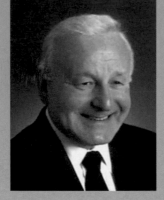

pany and prove that investing in Office Depot was a wise decision.

Strengthening Leadership

Nelson set forth several immediate goals for advancing the company's operations, such as strengthening leadership, assigning managers greater responsibility, and holding them accountable for results. The repositioning of top management involved several promotions, new hires, and retirements.

In 2000, Monica Luechtefeld, who joined Office Depot in 1993 following the Eastman acquisition, was named executive vice president of e-commerce. Steve Embree, who had been with Office Depot since 1987, most recently as senior vice president of technology merchandising, was named executive vice president of merchandising. General Counsel David Fannin, who joined Office Depot in 1998, became an executive vice president in addition to his role as general counsel.

Above: Irwin Helford, retired CEO and chairman of Viking Office Products, defined "fanatical customer service" as accomplishing more than a customer expects.

Below: Office Depot's finely tuned distribution network guarantees next-business-day delivery for in-stock items in most major markets.

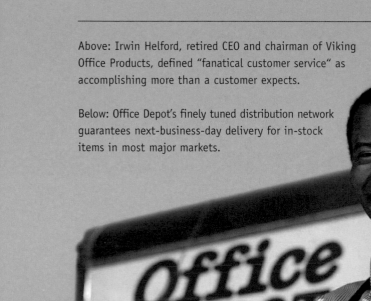

Also in 2000, longtime CFO Barry Goldstein announced his retirement after 14 years with the company. The following year, Charlie Brown, former company controller, became the new chief financial officer after providing interim leadership for over a year.

Shawn McGhee, who was named president of North American operations in early 2000, left the company in August 2000. His role was split into two positions: president of North American retail stores and president of the Business Services Group. Bob Keller, former executive vice president of sales, was promoted to president of BSG in 2000. In February 2001, Jerry Colley was named president of North American retail. Colley was former senior vice president of stores at AutoZone. Also in early 2001, Patricia Morrison was named executive vice president and chief information officer. Previously, Morrison had served as vice president and CIO for The Quaker Oats Company. Rick Lepley was named president of Office Depot–Japan in 2001. He had been an independent licensee with Office Depot since 1993, overseeing Office Depot stores in Eastern Europe.

A Shot of Adrenaline

Disappointing sales in Office Depot North American retail stores was a top concern for Office Depot and its investors. When Office Depot leaders reviewed the company's operations in 2000, they decided "to pursue fewer objectives in a more efficient manner to deliver improved earnings." They also concluded that it was necessary to be "smarter about how to plan and achieve growth."[23]

Analyzing the expense of store locations, including their supply chain, led to Office Depot's withdrawal from five metropolitan markets: Boston, Cleveland, Columbus, Long Island, and Phoenix (where they had established a limited presence), closing a total of 73 underperforming North American stores in 2001.[24] The necessary capital to run those stores was redeployed to more profitable markets. The company also closed six Office Depot Express stores in France.[25] In addition, Office Depot cut the number of stores it had planned to open in 2000 from 125 to

70.[26] In 2001, it opened only 44 new stores, most of them in markets where Office Depot already had a presence so that it could leverage its existing marketing and supply chain synergies.[27]

Closing stores and decelerating the opening of new stores in North America did not mean Office Depot would give up on its retail stores. "It's a necessary step to getting the chain back on the right track," said David Buchsbaum, an analyst with Wachovia Securities. "They're in a very competitive market. Their stores are older and a little bit tired, and they don't sell technology very well out of those stores."[28] As Nelson commented to the press, "We still are a North American leader in retail, and we're not going to give that up."[29]

Office Depot also sought to reduce costs and increase top-line growth.[30] In 2001, Office Depot stopped using its paper-based tracking system for its delivery trucks, instead implementing an automated wireless system. The new system, called Office Depot Signature

Left: Patricia Morrison was named executive vice president and chief information officer in early 2001.

Below left: Bob Keller was promoted to president of the Business Services Group in 2000. He had previously served as executive vice president of sales.

Below right: In 2001, Jerry Colley was named president of Office Depot's North American retail stores.

Tracking and Reporting System (OD STAR), saved Office Depot money and enabled the tracking of packages. Customers were happy because it provided them with real-time information on the delivery of their ordered items. The system served as another example of Office Depot's ability to create and use emerging technologies.[31]

To refocus product inventory on its core business customers, Office Depot planned to reduce or altogether eliminate underperforming inventory, such as DVD players and computer software for children.[32]

All in all, Office Depot cut the number of stock keeping units (SKUs) in its stores by about 20 percent. It also cut the number of SKUs in its

warehouses by about 30 percent.[33] Office Depot also worked on improving the quality and efficiency of its warehouses by continuing to invest in new technologies and consolidating functions to eliminate redundancies. One new technology, a private extranet, allowed suppliers to check inventory in the warehouses and stores within two hours of a sale.[34]

Office Depot also created "Business in a Box" business services, a new area for the company that provided small businesses with bundled business operations services such as payroll, insurance, and 401(k) management. In essence, it helped small businesses manage money and employees. Businesses could sign up for the service via Office Depot's Web site, or at its retail stores.[35]

A Recessionary Economy

Unfortunately, the economy was not cooperating with Office Depot's valiant efforts at rejuvenation. As Neil Cavuto of *Fox News* observed in early 2001, the slowing economy "put a chill" on the number of people who visited Office Depot's stores.[36] Indeed, in the first quarter of 2001, profits fell 42 percent compared to the year before, but analysts were not too concerned. "Most retailers are down today," said analyst Daniel Binder.[37]

Retailers were posting slow sales because of the slow economy. With a weak dollar overseas, overall consumer confidence had dwindled. A report in the *Miami Herald* explained the economy's direct effect on Office Depot:

> *Sales of big-ticket items, particularly computer hardware and software, declined as the chain's small-business customers became increasingly conservative in their spending. While the number of retail transactions increased during the first quarter [of 2001], sales of computer hardware and software fell more than 28 percent. That's a major blow because technology sales represent 25 percent of Office Depot's retail business. Plus, when*

Through good recruiting, training, and incentive programs, Office Depot helps ensure that its store associates are friendly and knowledgeable.

According to many small- and medium-sized businesses, placing orders through the Office Depot catalog is a very convenient method for procuring office supplies.

customers aren't buying computers, it means they aren't buying related products like modems, surge protectors, cables, and ink-jet cartridges.[38]

Unfortunately, events spiraled down even further. On the morning of September 11, 2001, terrorists launched simultaneous attacks on the United States, killing thousands of innocent people in New York, Virginia, and Pennsylvania. When two airplanes crashed into the World Trade Center, Nelson was aboard a plane near Orlando. The pilot landed immediately in compliance with the Federal Aviation Administration's order to ground all civilian aircraft within 15 minutes of the release of the FAA order.

Once Nelson knew that all Office Depot associates were safe, he also realized the long-term economic implications of the attacks. "I don't pretend to be a soothsayer," Nelson told one reporter a few months after September 11. "But deep in my soul, I knew this had to have a huge impact on us and the world."[39]

Indeed, the terrorist attacks had a far-reaching effect on the economy. Companies across the country announced massive layoffs, while businesses and consumers scaled back spending. Retailers all over the country slashed prices in an effort to drive sales.

For its part, Office Depot chose to stay the course. "Nelson and his team made a critical decision," wrote the *Sun-Sentinel.* "The best road out of the danger zone was the one they were already on."[40]

Office Depot recognizes that its most valuable asset is its workforce and that its people make Office Depot a more compelling place to shop each day.

CHAPTER EIGHT

THE BEGINNING OF A JOURNEY

2000–2002

Every journey must have a beginning but never an end.

—Chairman and CEO Bruce Nelson, 2002[1]

THE FIRST YEARS OF THE NEW millennium marked a fresh beginning for Office Depot. While sales still faltered, Office Depot's earnings were on the rise. In 2001, net income rose to $201 million, up from $49.3 million the previous year.[2] Earnings per share climbed 13 percent in 2001, and free cash flow was up to $540 million from $49 million in 2000.[3] Much of this improvement was the result of increased financial discipline and improved processes throughout the company.

A recessionary economy frustrated Office Depot's sales efforts, with total sales declining by 4 percent in 2001.[4] However, in 2002, sales took a modest upturn by reaching $11.4 billion—an incremental rise from its 2001 sales of $11.1 billion.[5] Comparable sales in the company's North American retail stores continued to post negatives throughout every quarter of 2002.

The company's restructuring began to show tangible results by the end of 2001. In an effort to streamline its sales force, Office Depot closed 73 stores in 2001 (announced in 2000) and 13 more in 2002. By sharpening its focus on the customer, reducing costs, and improving operations, Office Depot called itself, "a more compelling place to work, shop, and invest."

Before the tragedies of September 11, 2001, being "the industry's employer of choice" required a concerted effort, as unemployment rates in the United States remained low, and the global economy was healthy. As companies faced stiff competition to attract and retain good employees, Office Depot knew it had to offer more than just competitive wages. It had to provide better-than-average medical, dental, vision, and life insurance plans; an employee stock purchase plan; tuition reimbursement; disability income; employee assistance; and paid sick, personal, and vacation days.

Perhaps more importantly, Office Depot sought to cultivate an environment where employees were treated with dignity and respect by their managers, as well as each other, and where "innovation, communication, and entrepreneurial spirit are recognized, encouraged, and rewarded."[6] To help develop this culture, senior managers communicated with Office Depot associates at all levels of the organization regarding the company's future plans, soliciting the feedback and recommendations necessary to keep those plans on track. Office Depot's leaders also encouraged creativity. For example, Jerry Colley, president of

Office Depot strives to become the most attractive place in the office supply industry to work, shop, and invest. Its exceptionally loyal employees remain dedicated to fulfilling the promise of the Office Depot brand.

"We took great care with regard to audit committee activities," said Jim Heskett, who joined the Office Depot board in 1996. "When Sarbanes-Oxley passed, we were already doing the types of things that many other companies were not doing at the time."[8]

Giving Back

Throughout its history, Office Depot has often given back to the communities where its employees live and work. Its philanthropic efforts started when company founder Pat Sher was diagnosed with leukemia. Whether it was donating to schools, the Leukemia Society of America, the Arthritis Foundation, or any number of other charities, Office Depot was, without a doubt, a champion when it came to corporate philanthropy.

Above left: Despite the challenges faced in the early part of the millennium, Office Depot remains the world's largest supplier of office products and services. Through "fanatical" customer service, Office Depot strives to deliver an unmatched shopping experience through stores, e-commerce sites, catalogs, customer service centers, and sales representatives.

Below: Since much of Office Depot's philanthropy revolves around children, the company instituted a number of back-to-school programs to help children and teachers get the supplies and resources they needed. These programs included the "5% Back-to-Schools" program, the National Backpack Program, and Teacher Appreciation Breakfasts.

North American stores, explained how the innovation of store employees aids in generating revenue. As a store associate, "you can be creative on how you do your floor stacks, end caps, and wings," he stated. "You can appoint a chief revenue officer who is creative and sales-focused to sponsor in-store events to drive business."[7]

Office Depot also afforded associates a wide variety of career paths. It further supported their professional development through training, education, and performance reviews. The company's intranet provided a conduit for employees to learn new skills or brush up on existing ones, and also allowed senior managers to exchange ideas with associates.

Office Depot was a place where hard work and diligence were recognized and rewarded. It was a company where employees could share their opinions and help create solutions. It was also a place that gave back to communities, which was a major source of pride for everyone.

Office Depot employees also appreciated that their employer always acted ethically in all manners of business. Even before the U.S. Congress passed the Sarbanes-Oxley Act in 2002 as a way to prevent corporate and accounting scandals at major U.S. companies, Office Depot had already been compliant with several of the law's edicts.

SPONSORING THE OLYMPICS

Official Sponsor of the 2002 U.S. Olympic Team

36USC220506

IN DECEMBER 2000, OFFICE DEPOT ANnounced its sponsorship of the 2002 and 2004 U.S. Olympic Teams, as well as the 2002 Winter Games in Salt Lake City, Utah.

"The Olympics were a fascinating property," said Lynn Connelly, former director of sponsorships. "At that time, we wanted to find the largest sponsorship that had an emotional connection to people. The goal was to develop some very emotional advertising."[1]

As the official office supply sponsor of the United States Olympic Committee (USOC) and the Salt Lake Organizing Committee (SLOC), Office Depot provided products and services to the organizations and the athletes they supported. Along with the sponsorship, Office Depot developed promotions and special events that revolved around the Olympics. For example, the company began using the familiar USA/5-Ring logo in its promotional campaigns, in the stores, and within *www.officedepot.com.*[2]

Connelly explained the value of the Olympic sponsorship. "It's a great property for global exposure," she said. "It's a good property if you have a message that you're trying to launch or a new product entry because you get a lot of eyeballs in a short period that you can hit with a message."[3]

Or, as Nelson explained, "No other event has the universal appeal of the Olympic Games. It is our goal that Office Depot's sponsorship of the 2002 Olympic Winter Games and the 2004 Olympic Games in Athens empowers us to forge even stronger relationships with our customers, our vendors, and our employees."[4]

Under Chairman and CEO Bruce Nelson, Office Depot's corporate philanthropy took on a new focus—that of helping at-risk and underprivileged children. The company's mission of "Caring and Making a Difference" took on many forms.

Each of Office Depot's retail stores, distribution centers, call centers, and warehouses partnered with a nonprofit organization, often a local one that worked with children. For example, the company supported America's Second Harvest to help feed hungry children and their families. It also donated money to charities such as CHARLEE's Children's Depot, which assisted abused and neglected children. Office Depot and its employees additionally contributed to Toys for Tots, giving toys to needy children during the holidays. It donated or helped raise money for numerous nonprofit organizations that were researching cures for life-threatening illnesses.[9] One such project entailed a corporation-wide fundraising effort for City of Hope, an elite group of cancer centers that has saved thousands of cancer victims' lives, while actively researching new treatments and working towards discovering a cure. Office Depot's efforts, which involved everything from car washes by executive officers to the sale of special "City of Hope" products, raised millions of dollars for the centers.[10]

Office Depot further devoted its focus to supporting education. Through charities such as Gifts in Kind International, it donated essential school supplies. The company also gave both supplies and financial aid to underfunded schools via the Kids in Need Resource Center. Nationwide, Office Depot started a "5% Back-to-Schools" program, giving millions of dollars in store credit to selected schools and donating backpacks loaded with school supplies to children. Office Depot also contributed to Junior Achievement, which educates students about business, economics, and free enterprise.[11]

Office Depot's philanthropic efforts went beyond just helping children. After the tragic events of September 11, 2001, Office Depot became one of the first public companies to donate to relief agencies, which directly supported victims and their families. In total, the company and its employees donated more than $1 million to the United Way, the Red Cross, and the Police, Fireman and Emergency Services Fund. Moreover, Office Depot employees volunteered thousands of hours of their time.[12]

Left: Samuel Mathis Jr. was named Office Depot's vice president of diversity in 2002.

Below: Recognizing the value and importance that diversity plays in the marketplace, Office Depot maintains its commitment to fostering diversity in its management and workforce.

Diversity Programs

To make Office Depot an even more compelling place to work, the company initiated a six-step program in 2001 to improve opportunities for employees and foster diversity in its management and workforce.[13] In essence, the company aimed to transform Office Depot into a workplace "where all employees can feel comfortable, pursue job opportunities, and realize their full potential."[14] The communities where Office Depot's 43,000 employees lived and worked were rich in diversity, just like the company's customers and suppliers. Therefore, it was natural for the company to reflect similar diversity.

Robert McCormes-Ballou, then-director of Office Depot's diversity program, explained why encouraging diversity was important:

Demographic projections indicate an increasingly diverse population; the U.S. Census Bureau estimates that by 2040, ethnic minorities (African Americans, Hispanics, and Asian Americans) will represent more than half of the U.S. population—up from just under 20 percent in 1980. Diversity is not simply "the right thing to do." It is an important aspect of our company culture as well as an essential part of our overall survival and growth.[15]

The first step of the diversity program was to create a new post: vice president of diversity. To that end, the company hired Samuel Mathis Jr. in 2002. Next, the company began a diversity training process and started a career advancement program through mentoring relationships between employees. The company also formed a Diversity Council to promote diversity, not only among employees, but also among

With the knowledge that diversity helps yield corporate excellence, Office Depot established a career advancement program that fosters mentoring relationships between employees and successful Office Depot professionals.

Office Depot's vendors and suppliers. By having a more diverse pool of vendors and suppliers—and by giving all suppliers equal access to purchasing opportunities—Office Depot was able to retain and acquire more contracts. Next, the company began recruiting more minority candidates for internships in management. Finally, Office Depot set out to create a more diverse employee pool by varying its job-posting programs.[16]

In 2000, Office Depot honored women business owners by sponsoring the Working Woman Entrepreneurial Excellence Awards. Organized by *Working Woman* magazine, the program was part of a growing trend to recognize the substantial contributions of professional women.[17] Then in March 2001, Office Depot took a more active step in celebrating the dedication and innovation of female leaders when it created an annual Success Strategies for Businesswomen Conference. The first conference aimed at helping women better run their businesses.[18]

Lynn Connelly, former director of sponsorships, remembered the first women's conference as "a little nerve-wracking" because she did not know if it would prove successful. "We were building this huge event, and it was like creating a party and wondering if anybody was going to show up when you invited them," she said. Fortunately, more than 250 people attended the first conference.[19]

Word of mouth and Office Depot's improved marketing helped the following year's conference sell out with nearly 700 people attending. The three-day event honored six women with Office Depot Visionary Awards and six women with Businesswoman of the Year Awards. A gala dinner was hosted by Robin Roberts, then an ESPN sports commentator and later co-host of ABC's *Good Morning America*. Maya Angelou, author and poet, delivered a closing address and received an Office Depot Visionary Award.[20]

Over the years, the Success Strategies for Businesswomen Conference became increasingly popular and was considered one of the leading women's business conferences in the country. The event attracted a number of noteworthy speakers, including Hillary Clinton, Madeleine Albright, Katie Couric, and Barbara Walters.

In addition to the keynote speakers, Connelly said, "Amazing women, most of whom have started their businesses from nothing, attend this conference. Many of these women share unbelievable,

Above: In 2001, Office Depot initiated an innovative six-step program to improve opportunities for employees and foster diversity, making the company an even more attractive place to work.

Below right: In an effort to provide customers with even more conveniences, Office Depot added UPS shipping centers to all of its stores.

breakthrough stories with the audience, and it's really what, I believe, attracts these attendees. They like to hear the personal side and the journey, and it gives them a role model. It shows them a real person who has done something that they might be dreaming about."[21]

Aside from its contribution to diversity, Office Depot's decision to honor women entrepreneurs made business sense. In 2000, the United States Small Business Administration (SBA) estimated that there were 9 million female-owned businesses in the United States, and those businesses generated some $3.6 trillion in sales.[22] As Monica Luechtefeld, then-executive vice president of e-commerce, explained, "One of the fastest-growing segments of the business community is clearly women-owned businesses. It is important for us to reach out to them."[23]

Office Depot's diversity program attracted quite a bit of positive attention. In 2001, the company won several awards for its innovative programs. Bank of America honored Office Depot with the Supplier Diversity and Development Corporate Advocate of the Year Award. *DiversityBusiness.com*

named Office Depot one of the top 50 U.S. companies dedicated to serving woman-owned and minority-owned businesses for the second consecutive year. In both 2001 and 2002, the company won the Advocate of the Year Award from the Florida Regional Minority Business Council (FRMBC) for its "outstanding" support of the FRMBC.[24] Finally, the Women's Business Enterprise National Council named Office Depot as one of the "Elite Eight" Top Corporations for Women's Business Enterprises.[25]

A More Compelling Place to Shop

By the end of 2001 it was clear that Office Depot had become "a more compelling place to shop," as well. In the stores, customers could choose from a wider array of business supply products, with an emphasis on items they requested most often. An increased number of Office Depot private-label items gave customers access to quality products at a lower cost. Also, the company upgraded most of its U.S. stores by adding UPS shipping centers, which offered a full complement of packaging and shipping supplies, as well as shipping services.

Remodeling all of Office Depot's 800-plus North American stores improved lighting and signage and made the layout more intuitive. As Jerry Colley explained in 2001, "We have reconfigured the store

THE OFFICE DEPOT CENTER

IN SEPTEMBER 2002, OFFICE DEPOT AC-
quired naming rights to the Broward Arena in
Sunrise, Florida, which is located near Office
Depot's Delray Beach headquarters. Formerly
known as the National Car Rental Center and
seating 20,000 people, the arena was home to the
Florida Panthers hockey team and renamed as
the Office Depot Center.[1]

Office Depot believed that associating itself
with the arena provided it with an emotional connection to its home territory and allowed the
company to further extend its brand.[2]

"Jerry Colley felt it was a great opportunity
for us to support the local community and to
enliven our brand here in South Florida," said
Lynn Connelly, former director of sponsorships.[3]

The Florida Panthers approved of the
sponsorship, too. "Office Depot is a great sponsor and a great business, so we're really excited
about having them on board," said Panthers
co-owner Alan Cohen. "I think they basically
did it because of their commitment to the community, and we're just happy to have them as
a partner."[4]

In addition to the marketing opportunities
that the agreement offered, Office Depot successfully turned the sponsorship into a philanthropic opportunity when the Panthers and
Office Depot teamed up to form the Office Depot
Center Foundation, which raised money for
South Florida charities.[5]

so that our busy customers can quickly find what
they need, and we have merchandised our aisles to
reduce shopping time and increase multiple sales."[26]

Before this upgrade, Nelson described the
experience when he and a number of other people from management employed themselves as
"mystery shoppers" at Office Depot stores:

*We were struck by the eight- and nine-foot
shelves. The area was dark, almost like a canyon,
and it wasn't easy to see the product. Also, because
the signs were not always clear, it was difficult to
find our way around the store. It wasn't always
easy to find what we were looking for in those large
aisles, and the large aisles prevented us from easily locating an employee to help.*[27]

In addition to remodeling the stores, Office Depot
took customer service to unparalleled new levels.

Store employees made a point of greeting customers,
and they spent more time providing customer service—whether that meant locating a particular product or identifying the right product to fit customers'
needs. The company also launched a program called
Showtime, in which managers and store employees
put aside other tasks, such as stocking inventory during peak hours, to focus on helping customers.[28]

Once again, Office Depot's efforts bore fruit. The
Customer Service Index (CSI) in its stores increased
15 percent in the fourth quarter of 2000 from the
same period in 1999.[29] The CSI rose a further 21
percent in 2001—an all-time high. At the same time,
the number of complaints fell by more than half.[30]

When analyzing its operations, Office Depot realized that it needed to distinguish itself from the competition. "Right now customers can't tell the difference between Office Depot, OfficeMax, and Staples,"
said Nelson in the spring of 2001. "I want to change

the in-store experience so the customer will remember Office Depot."[31]

In keeping with its entrepreneurial heritage, Office Depot test-marketed a new, smaller store design in 11 locations. Named "Lantana" after the town where the original "test" store was located (Lantana is a coastal community in Palm Beach County, Florida), the store prototype did away with the warehouse look and featured a circular flow, so customers could see the whole store without veering from the main aisle. The new stores featured angled shelves at lower levels so shoppers could better see the merchandise, and many of the racks had built-in lighting to show off selections. The stores featured customer service buttons so shoppers did not have to wander the aisles looking for someone to help them. Products were also grouped together based on customer uses. For example, technology products and their corresponding accessories were contiguously displayed, and lamps were placed near furniture. The stores included an interactive technology center, where customers could check e-mail, test digital cameras, watch videos, and even design virtual office space. Customers could sign up for seminars and classes that educated them about products, such as new software, at a learning center located at the back of store.[32]

Office Depot hoped the new design would distinguish it from the competition, but the prototype stores cost about a third more than Office Depot had originally anticipated. The company and industry analysts were cautiously optimistic.

"I don't want to make any commitments before I know whether [the new store layouts] generate [earnings] results," Nelson told the press. David Buchsbaum, an analyst with Wachovia Securities, said, "There's no question it's a distinct improvement from what they had in the past. Whether that boosts sales depends on the execution of price and customer service."[33]

Beginning in 2002, Office Depot partnered with other retailers to initiate the concept of "a store within a store." The resulting mini-Office Depot stores were located inside larger retail outlets, like supermarkets or military base stores, to serve those with limited time to shop. It intended to be a win-win-win situation. Office Depot leveraged its brand, and customers did not have to visit a separate venue to buy low-cost, high-quality office supplies. The host stores could consolidate multiple vendors for office supplies down to one.

As John Deaton pointed out, "The retailers had much more diversity in their office products offering because we know what items to stock during the different seasons. This is our business, so of course we do it better than they do. There are different strategies for selling certain products at specific times."[34]

On the Internet, *www.officedepot.com* was doing exceptionally well at pleasing large corporate customers. No longer did companies that ordered office supplies via their computers have to deal with the comparatively cumbersome act of connecting from mainframe to mainframe, which electronic data interchange (EDI) involved. Now they could tap into the less expensive and more efficient e-commerce technology presented by Office Depot and fill all of their office supply needs. All corporate customers who signed up on Office Depot's Web site received a customized "virtual store" where they could view the items in stock and place their orders.

The recessionary economy made retail challenging for all product segments, but Office Depot's sales held up in 2002, thanks in part to its renewed commitment to customer service.

By 2001, CEO Bruce Nelson's restructuring efforts had started to show tangible results. Investors were once again excited about Office Depot's stock.

Above: When Office Depot changed its branding campaign, the company produced a special issue of *Ink*, its company newsletter, which encouraged associates to serve as "brand ambassadors ... by embodying the personality and spirit of our brand promise and by communicating it to our customers on a daily basis."

Right: Rolf van Kaldekerken started with Viking in 1994 as country manager for Germany. He joined Office Depot in 1998 and later became president of Office Depot–Europe. He retired in 2005.

A New Strategy

To many customers, Office Depot, Staples, and OfficeMax were indistinguishable. Office Depot wanted to change that perception, and so in 2001, the company abandoned its "Taking Care of Business" marketing theme and sought out a new positioning argument to help differentiate it from its competitors.

Extensive marketing research told Office Depot that many office product consumers did not believe any of the big three office supply superstores met all of their needs. Office Depot hoped its new branding campaign would help consumers and businesses realize that its stores could indeed provide for *all* of their necessities. The new campaign debuted in 2002 with the slogan, "What you need. What you need to know."[35]

As Office Depot explained, the new tagline was "grounded in one of the company's core values, fanatical customer service." The brand let customers know that they could "find not only the office solutions they are looking for, but access to a wide range of product information and guidance necessary to ensure an enjoyable and fulfilling experience."[36]

International Division

During this time, the International Division was faring quite well, despite lower currency values overseas, and Office Depot recognized that there were huge opportunities worldwide to expand the business.

Europe was quickly becoming Office Depot's fastest-growing and highly-profitable market segment. Viking's direct-mail catalog business had operated in the United Kingdom for 10 years, so it made sense when Office Depot launched a Business Services Division in the United Kingdom in 2000.[37]

"Medium- to large-sized business customers have different needs than the small business buyer," explained Rolf van Kaldekerken, then-president of Office Depot–Europe, "and Office Depot will now be able to offer them individual pricing and personalized service through account executives and deliveries to multiple locations through the company's extensive Office Depot and Viking distribution network."[38]

The Viking brand continued to prevail in Europe because of its exceptional database marketing and excellent customer service.[39] "Much of the European market hadn't experienced the quality of service Viking offered," said van Kaldekerken. Also, he said, Viking filled a niche. "Viking's strategy was to serve small- and medium-sized customers. The typical Viking customer was the small company, and few companies in Europe were successful in taking care of that part of the market."[40]

Office Depot's Viking Direct brand plays a key role in the company's international growth strategy. In 2002, new market growth was initiated with the launch of new Viking Office Products Web sites in Ireland, Belgium, Switzerland, and Luxembourg.

In 2001, Office Depot leveraged the Viking brand and Viking's merchandising, warehousing, and distribution systems to launch its Business Services Divisions in Ireland, the Netherlands, and France, each with its own Viking Web site. In total, Office Depot launched nine new international Web sites in eight countries throughout 2000 and 2001:

Germany (*www.viking.de*)
The Netherlands (*www.vikingdirect.nl*)
Italy (*www.vikingop.it*)
Australia (*www.vikingop.com.au*)
Japan (*www.vikingop.co.jp* and
        www.officedepot.co.jp)
France (*www.vikingdirect.fr*)
Austria (*www.vikingdirekt.at*)
United Kingdom (*bsdnet.officedepot.co.uk*)

In 2001, Office Depot entered the Swiss market for the first time, and in 2002, it entered Spain and Portugal. Also in 2002, Office Depot decided that due to its minimal presence in Australia, the company would sell its Australian operations to focus on other long-term growth opportunities.[41]

In 2002, Office Depot formed Business Service Divisions in Italy and Germany, leveraging its strong brand and existing infrastructure to motivate customers.[42] That same year, the company launched Viking e-commerce Web sites in Ireland, Belgium, Switzerland, and Luxembourg.

Office Depot also increased its international retail stores in 2002. Through its licensing agreement with Grupo Gigante, the joint venture opened stores in Guatemala and Costa Rica. It added seven new stores in France, and its operations in Japan improved with the guidance of Rick Lepley, president of Office Depot–Japan.[43]

At the end of 2002, Office Depot had a total of 171 stores outside of North America, compared to 143 stores in 2001. Fifty of these stores were wholly owned by Office Depot, compared to 39 in 2001.[44]

Business Services Group

The North American Business Services Group (BSG) also fared well, as it downsized for the sake of efficiency. The 1,200-member contract sales force was trimmed by 10 percent in 2000 and 2001.[45] BSG consolidated its existing 24 call centers into seven larger, more technologically advanced ones to improve customer service. None of the five Viking call centers were affected.

According to Nelson, customers who called Office Depot before the consolidation were "directed to call centers that may or may not have the capacity or readily available information to handle the call promptly and correctly. This all too often resulted in increased call waiting and call times and reduced customer satisfaction."[46] The new and improved call centers were more like "customer interaction facilities," handling both telephone and e-mail contacts. The telemarketing workstations now allowed service representatives to access the buyers' orders through *www.officedepot.com* and through cash registers at the stores.[47]

Another new technology in the consolidated call centers was an automated speech-recognition customer service system powered by NetByTel in which customers responded to a series of prompts by either speaking their selection or entering it on the keypad of their telephones. Customers could also choose to speak to a live representative. Notably, Office Depot was one of the first direct marketers to use speech-recognition technology. The system saved Office Depot an estimated 87 percent per call.[48]

The Business Services Group also used technology to improve the productivity of its sales force by doing away with paper sales reports. Starting in 2001, salespeople completed their reports on laptops via automated software. Executives and members of the sales force could view the reports online or could have specific reports sent to them via the computer, which saved the company a tremendous amount of money and allowed executives to improve strategic planning.[49]

Beginning in 2000, Office Depot began forming marketing alliances with Internet partners in an effort to reach more customers. Through the partners' Web sites, customers had online access to Office Depot's products. These partners included America Online, Microsoft, Intelisys Electronic Commerce, 2Wire Inc., SupplyWorks, realityBUY, and Epylon.

Office Depot made an important alliance in 2002, when it partnered with *Amazon.com* to have an Office Depot store on the Amazon Web site. Through *Amazon.com*, customers could access more than 50,000 products from Office Depot. This was the largest selection of office products available online.[50]

In the recessionary economy, many Web companies experienced sluggish sales. After the dot-com bubble burst, venture capitalists were no longer throwing money at startup e-commerce companies. At the same time, shares of many public e-commerce companies were sinking. The dot-com revolution had leveled out, presenting a unique opportunity for Office Depot. Without financial help, many Web retailers faced bankruptcy, and Office Depot, which had $134 million in cash at the end of the first quarter of 2001, was in a prime position to bail them out.[51]

The company was selective about the companies it acquired. It only focused on small Web businesses that had "developed a great and loyal customer base," according to Monica Luechtefeld.[52] The small companies had less debt and were easier to negotiate with, and those with loyal customers would now purchase from Office Depot, increasing the company's market share. Moreover, the small dot-coms would easily integrate into Office Depot's existing infrastructure.

Office Depot made its first such acquisition in May 2001, when it purchased *www.officesupplies.com*, a profitable online office supply retailer with 12 employees. A few months later, in July 2001, Office Depot acquired Connecticut-based *4Sure.com*, along with *4Sure.com*'s two Web sites, *www.computers4sure.com*, aimed at home-office customers and individual customers, and *www.solutions4sure.com*, which provided technical support and products for medium-sized businesses.[53]

4Sure.com was an important acquisition for Office Depot primarily because it aimed at business-to-business technology customers. Technology products that were sold in Office Depot's retail stores were more consumer- and small-business oriented. *4Sure.com* sold more sophisticated technology—items that many large corporate customers would need.[54]

Office Depot changed *4Sure.com*'s name to Tech Depot (though it retained the two *4Sure.com* Web sites) and launched a new Web site called *www.techdepot.com*, where customers could purchase everything from computers, memory, servers, and networking technology to cameras, projectors, and scanners. Customers could even build their own

The friendly, knowledgeable, and dedicated staff of the Business Services Group remains committed to Office Depot's core value of Excellence in Execution. Chuck Tharpe, former senior manager of telecommunications, North America, knew that "every team ... is better prepared to face future challenges."

The 2002 Office Depot executive leadership team included (from left): Charlie Brown, executive vice president and CFO; David Fannin, executive vice president, general counsel, and corporate secretary; Monica Luechtefeld, executive vice president of e-commerce; Jerry Colley, president of North America stores; Jay Crosson, executive vice president of human resources; Rolf van Kaldekerken, president of European operations; Bruce Nelson, chairman and CEO; Rick Lepley, president of Office Depot–Japan; Bob Keller, president of BSG; Patricia Morrison, executive vice president and chief information officer; Jocelyn Carter-Miller, executive vice president and chief marketing officer; and David D'Arezzo, executive vice president of merchandising and replenishment.

computers and purchase them through the Web site. Office Depot set up kiosks in more than 800 of its stores that allowed customers to access Tech Depot's 100,000-plus technology products through Office Depot Direct. If customers could not find a particular piece of technology in the store, they could use a store computer to access Office Depot Direct and order items online from a huge selection of products that were in stock and ready to deliver.[55]

Luechtefeld explained one of the challenges of Tech Depot. "Technology products have a very low-profit margin to begin with, so the folks at Tech Depot had to work harder to grow the business dramatically. Also, almost every year after the dot-com bubble burst, you had a reduction in IT spending, and you had the average selling price of tech products go down about 25 percent each year. It got cheaper and cheaper to buy a PC. Since the selling price lowered, you needed substantially more effort to get the same revenue dollars."[56]

Tech Depot dealt with this challenge by ultimately moving away from selling to individual con-

sumers and focusing more on business-to-business needs.

"That became our thrust," Luechtefeld said four years after the acquisition. "Tech Depot has hired great salespeople who do outbound telesales to business customers. Our BSG sales force has partnered with them to introduce them to our corporate clients, and we're beginning to get even more tech sales from our corporate customers." She added that Office Depot worked on leveraging Tech Depot's capabilities and integrating them into Office Depot's system "so we get the benefit of the Tech Depot experience."[57]

BSG redesigned *www.officedepot.com* in 2000 and again in 2002, making it faster and easier to use.[58] The 2002 redesign created a more personalized "mall-style" format that "compartmentalized" Office Depot's products and services, grouping them into logical categories for easy navigation. The newly designed site also included a business resource center that offered links to downloadable business form templates, such as time sheets and balance sheets, and expert advice aimed at small-

and medium-sized businesses. Also, *www.officedepot.com* now featured links to Tech Depot and a new offering, Janitation Depot. As Luechtefeld explained, "We want [customers] to know that we are serious when we say, 'What you need. What you need to know.' We are building out these new virtual "stores" to strengthen our presentation in categories such as technology, break room, and janitation supplies."[59]

Playing a Vital Role

In 2000, *InformationWeek* named Office Depot the top-rated retail company of the most innovative users of information technology in the United States. *Fortune* put Office Depot on its list of 10 "Companies That Do E-commerce Right." That same year, *PC Computing* ranked the company No. 1 in business e-shopping for office supplies, praising *www.officedepot.com* for its shopping convenience and next-day service. Bell Atlantic awarded the company its Supplier Excellence Award for 2000. In 2001, Office Depot won *CIO* magazine's Enterprise Value Award for its technological innovations and strong use of information technology. Also, *Smart Business* magazine named Office Depot one of the top 50 U.S. companies that had successfully used the Internet to drive business.

According to the SBA, two-thirds of newly created jobs in 2002 came from small businesses. Recognizing the importance of small business owners, in 2002, the Business Services Group launched Web Café™, a weekly series of free online seminars led by well-known experts that were geared toward small business owners and entrepreneurs.[60]

Office Depot's worldwide e-commerce sales reached $1.6 billion in 2001 and $2.1 billion in 2002. The company sold more over the Internet than any other company besides *Amazon.com*.

A More Compelling Place to Invest

Thanks to the company's efforts, investors once again showed interest in holding Office Depot stock. In August 2001, billionaire Warren Buffett's holding company, Berkshire Hathaway, acquired $5 million worth of Office Depot shares, signaling that the company was, indeed, "a more compelling place to invest." As a result, Office Depot's shares rose almost 9 percent.[61]

Two months later, in October 2001, Office Depot's shares hit a 52-week high.[62] Earnings per share shot up 48 percent in 2002 over the previous year.[63] Cash flow increased to $540 million in 2001, from $49 million in 2000. In 2002, cash flow swelled to nearly $900 million.[64] The ready cash helped Office Depot repay its short-term debt and provided working capital, as well. These positive indicators helped Office Depot secure a rating in the S&P 500 Index as the second-best-performing stock of 2001.[65]

Despite investor enthusiasm, Office Depot's North American retail stores still required a lot of work. Certainly, the company had taken the first steps toward "fixing" the store divisions, but the road was long. The patience of the investment community would soon, once again, undergo a test.

After the Millennium store design proved too expensive to open and operate, Office Depot designed a new store called Millennium2, or M2. The first M2 store, which opened for business in Venice, Florida, featured a vibrant new color scheme and clear signage.

CHAPTER NINE

FACING CHALLENGING TIMES

2003 – 2004

I remain fully confident in our stated strategies and in our employees as we pursue greater growth and profitability.

—Neil Austrian, interim chairman
and CEO, 2004[1]

THE STRATEGIES THAT OFFICE Depot implemented in the first years of the new millennium had successfully invigorated the company's operations, but unfortunately, 2003 started poorly for Office Depot. Though overall earnings were up in 2002 compared to the year before, comparable store sales (also called same-store sales, or "comp" sales) had been declining quarter after quarter since the first fiscal quarter of 2000.[2] Industry insiders use comparable store sales to measure a retailer's overall health, so the slide in comp sales was understandably troubling for Office Depot and its investors.

The comp sales skid continued in 2003, with first-quarter, same-store sales for North American stores falling 7 percent.[3] Also, 2002 year-end results showed that Staples had overtaken Office Depot as the largest office supply firm in terms of annual sales.[4] Staples had 2002 sales of $11.6 billion, while the sales of Office Depot stood at $11.4 billion—a relatively small difference, but an important one in terms of morale among employees and perception among investors.[5]

A Store of Challenges

Though the company's International Division and Business Services Group (BSG), under the direction of then-president Bob Keller, performed well in

2003, the North American Retail Division continued to drag, despite the company's efforts to battle the waning economy. The company's ongoing struggle with furniture and technology sales remained a component of the problem. In the first quarter of 2003, technology sales were down 20 percent, and furniture sales dropped 5 percent.[6]

An aging portfolio of stores also contributed to the sales slump. According to Nelson, newer stores produced better comp sales than older ones—but despite recent remodeling, many of the company's stores displayed their age.[7] It didn't help that the stores of Staples and OfficeMax were, on average, newer than those of Office Depot.[8]

Moreover, the recently implemented "Lantana" racetrack design for stores did not meet expectations because it was too expensive to build and operate.[9] Adding to the company's woes, a soft real estate market brought on by the weak economy made it difficult for Office Depot to sublet the stores it had closed in 2001 and 2002, which resulted in 2002 fourth-quarter financial results that were lower than expected.[10]

Office Depot's M2 store design featured a series of horseshoe-shaped pods that contained related items. Here, an Office Depot associate at the M2 store in Venice, Florida, helps a customer in the binder pod.

Above: Office Depot pioneered e-commerce in the office supply industry when it introduced *www.officedepot.com* in 1998. Since then, the public Web site has grown more sophisticated with added features and easier navigation.

Right: Chuck Rubin joined Office Depot in 2004 as executive vice president and chief merchandising/marketing officer. In 2006, he was named president of the company's North American Retail Division.

Shifting Responsibilities

In an attempt to rectify some of its problems, Office Depot realigned its top management in the early part of the decade. Mark Holifield, senior vice president of supply chain at the time, was promoted to executive vice president of supply chain in September 2003, and placed in charge of all the company's North American warehousing operations to help improve inventory management and delivery. That same month, Cindy Campbell was promoted to executive vice president of delivery sales, and in her new role, she guided the com-

pany's North American contract, e-commerce, and catalog operations. Office Depot also hired John Lostroscio, who had 20 years of experience in retail at tech-savvy chains such as Gateway, CompUSA, and Sound Advice, as vice president of technology merchandising to help improve the company's sagging technology sales.

Still, industry analysts were concerned over the September 2003 departures of Keller and David D'Arezzo, executive vice president of merchandising. Analysts also worried that Office Depot was still searching for a leader of North American Retail after Jerry Colley's departure.

Office Depot alleviated concerns with a string of hirings and promotions. In March 2004, the company hired Chuck Rubin as executive vice president and chief merchandising and marketing officer. Rubin had previously been a partner with Accenture, a consulting and technology services firm, where he worked with Office Depot on a con-

Office Depot has operated stores in Japan since 1997, when it opened a store in Tokyo and a delivery center in Yokohama. In 2003, the company opened five wholly owned stores in the country. Cliff Shinn (inset), country manager of Japan, oversees all aspects of the company's presence in this area.

tract basis to improve its merchandising. Also in March 2004, Rick Lepley moved from the company's Japanese operations to serve as executive vice president of North American Retail. Frank Scruggs Jr., an employment attorney who had been on the company's board of directors since 1996, joined Office Depot as executive vice president of human resources. (Scruggs relinquished his position on the company's board to join Office Depot full time.) Also in 2004, George Hill, formerly a regional vice president for Home Depot, came aboard as senior vice president of store operations.

The company's board of directors received an influx of talent, too, with four new board members. Myra Hart, one of Staples' founders and a professor of entrepreneurial management at Harvard Business School, joined the board in early 2004. So did Patricia McKay, executive vice president and CFO of Restoration Hardware. David Bernauer, chairman and CEO of Walgreen Company, added his expertise to the board in 2004, as did Abelardo "Al" Bru, retired vice chairman of PepsiCo.

According to Myra Hart, it was no accident that the new board members each possessed strong backgrounds in retail. "I think all of us were brought on board to take a very hard look at how Office Depot was functioning in its retail capacity," she said. "Bringing us on board was the beginning of the company's effort to reposition Office Depot as the No. 1 retailer in the industry."[11]

Also on the board of directors were Neil Austrian, who joined the company's board with the Viking acquisition; Lee Ault, chairman of In-Q-Tel, who also came from Viking; David Fuente, retired chairman and CEO of Office Depot; Brenda Gaines, retired North American president of Diners Club International, a division of Citigroup; W. Scott Hedrick, general partner of InterWest Partners; James Heskett, Baker Foundation professor at Harvard Business School; and Michael Myers, president of First Century Partners.

Guilbert Adds Size in Europe

Office Depot did not allow difficulties in its North American stores to slow it down. Although improving the top line of the company's domestic stores remained a top priority, Office Depot also sought other areas of growth. In his 2003 letter to shareholders, CEO Bruce Nelson wrote that the combined 32 percent growth in the International Division and the Business Services Group "more than offset the $106 million year-on-year decrease in North American Retail segment operating profit."[12] In addition, the 2003 annual report pointed out in bold red lettering that "Office Depot is much more than just a North American retailer. In fact, our North American Retail Division comprises less than half of our overall business."[13]

The International Division received a big boost in June 2003, when Office Depot acquired a major competitor in Europe, Guilbert, S.A. (pronounced "gill-bear"), a well-known and prestigious contract stationer in France that sold office products and services through a direct sales force and e-commerce. Office Depot paid approximately $775 million (after adjustments) for Guilbert and expected the acquisition to bring in $1.5 billion in yearly revenue.[14]

The company's European presence nearly doubled, making Office Depot the leading office supply business in Europe. Aside from adding millions of dollars in annual sales to the company's books, Guilbert's managers, market experience, and pur-

Office Depot has operated in Germany since 1998, when it purchased Viking Office Products. In 2002, it formed a Business Services Division in the country. Pictured here is a distribution center in the city of Lanken.

Above: In 2003, Office Depot acquired Guilbert, S.A., a renowned contract stationer in France. By acquiring Guilbert, Office Depot nearly doubled the size of its European operations.

Below right: David Fannin joined Office Depot in 1998 as senior vice president and general counsel. In 2000, he was promoted to executive vice president.

chasing power "added size, scale, and critical mass to our European business," said Nelson.[15] Guilbert employed 5,700 associates and operated in nine countries: Belgium, France, Germany, Italy, Ireland, the Netherlands, Portugal, Spain, and the United Kingdom.

When Office Depot acquired it, Guilbert operated 18 warehouses and 32 call centers. It owned its own fleet of delivery trucks and retained an excellent delivery network. In fact, Nelson told a South Florida reporter that Guilbert's delivery system "is superior to ours." Moreover, Guilbert had a strong brand presence (under the Guilbert and niceday brands), and it maintained good relations between its sales force and large, corporate customers.[16] Indeed, the acquisition fueled the company's growth in the large, corporate segment, providing Office Depot the capability to serve large companies throughout most of Europe. (Previously, Office Depot had served mainly small- and medium-sized European companies through its Viking brand.) Also, for the first time, Office Depot owned delivery businesses in Belgium, Portugal, and Spain.[17]

The Guilbert acquisition resulted in another advantage, as well. Office Depot temporarily regained the No. 1 sales spot from Staples, though Staples managed to overtake Office Depot later in the year.

Negotiations for the Guilbert acquisition lasted nearly a year, with Charlie Brown, then company CFO, and David Fannin, general counsel, spending much of their time in France at Guilbert's headquarters.[18] "Guilbert itself was a rollup, meaning it had acquired a number of smaller companies

around Europe," explained Fannin. "Since Guilbert hadn't fully integrated its own operations, we had to perform accounting and financial due diligence in each of the nine countries Guilbert served."[19]

After the acquisition was finally complete, Office Depot began integrating Guilbert's systems and processes to conform to its existing ones. However, as Fannin pointed out, the various countries where Guilbert conducted business didn't operate on one global set of systems or processes. Thus, the integration process, by necessity, was gradual.[20] Also, according to Rolf van Kaldekerken, president of Office Depot–Europe, the company's existing Viking operations in Europe had "a very service-oriented culture, but that kind of culture was not as strongly built at Guilbert, and that made the integration of the two companies challenging at times."[21]

Since its European operations had doubled after the Guilbert acquisition, Office Depot needed another leader to help manage the much-larger European segment. To that end, in August 2003,

Office Depot named Rob Vale as senior vice president of European operations. Vale had formerly served as senior vice president of the company's Business Services Division in Europe.

As a side note, Pinault-Printemps-Redoute (PPR), the former owner of Guilbert, had already sold its direct mail-order office supply business to Staples the year before. Bruce Nelson expressed no regrets about the possible missed opportunity that Staples had taken. "We already have a large, profitable, direct mail-order business in nine European countries," he said. "The purchase of mail order would be highly redundant."[22] Additionally, others felt the European commission would potentially block it.

Analysts remained indecisive about the effect of the Guilbert acquisition on the overall operations of Office Depot. "People are still looking for an improvement in North American retail," said Yogeesh Wagle, an analyst with Standard & Poor's. "This acquisition does increase their presence in the big markets of Europe ... but in the short term, it doesn't address the need for change."[23]

In contrast, Douglas Neviera, an industry analyst with Merrill Lynch, had a different take. "Strategically, we are encouraged by Office Depot's decision to acquire Guilbert," he said. "With North American retail facing a challenging economic and competitive environment, international expansion offers a clear second avenue for growth."[24]

The Other Two-Thirds

International expansion did, indeed, offer another growth avenue for Office Depot, just like the Business Services Group's contract delivery business. Unfortunately, in the investment community's eyes, the struggling North American Retail Division eclipsed performance of the International Division and BSG, which were both profitable and growing.

Guilbert's delivery business in Spain gave the International Division a springboard to further expand in that country, and in 2003, Office Depot opened six wholly owned superstores in Madrid. That same year, Office Depot opened five wholly owned stores in Japan and three in France.[25] Adding to its list, Office Depot opened a wholly owned store in Hungary in 2004 and purchased the outstanding interest in the three stores in that country, which had been operating under a license agreement.[26]

By the end of 2004, the International Division had more than 40 public Web sites, 78 wholly owned stores in 14 countries, plus 25 distribution centers and 153 stores under joint ventures or licensing agreements. Although Guilbert was not yet generating the revenue Office Depot expected, the International Division continued to serve as one of the company's most profitable business segments.

The International Division's success could be measured by yet another yardstick, when in 2004, Office Depot was named one of the best workplaces in Europe. The company was ranked No. 1 in Austria, No. 6 in the Netherlands, No. 7 in Belgium, and No. 14 in Germany.[27]

The Business Services Group also expanded. Though Guilbert's operations fell under the International Division's umbrella, Guilbert's large corporate customer base gave the Business Services Group access to a number of large corporate accounts.

BSG further expanded its customer base in 2003 by introducing a Spanish-language Web site

---

Office Depot opened its first store in Hungary in 1997 under an international licensing agreement. By 2006, all of the Office Depot stores in Hungary were wholly owned.

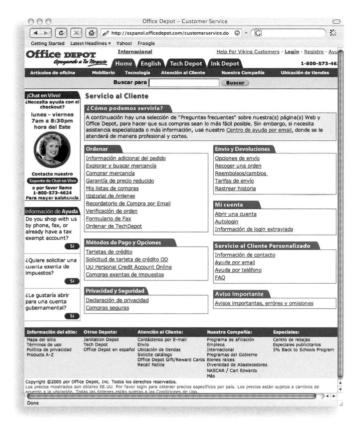

in the United States. At that time, only a few all-Spanish retail Web sites existed, even though 12.5 percent of the U.S. population was Hispanic and about 2 million Hispanics in the United States owned businesses. Even *Amazon.com*, the largest online retailer, did not have an all-Spanish site.[28] Office Depot decided to create the Spanish-language site because market research had revealed that bilingual people preferred reading in their native language about items they could potentially purchase, especially expensive ones.[29]

The Spanish-language site of Office Depot was truly an all-Spanish Web site. "In [other Web sites], a portal will be in Spanish," explained Monica Luechtefeld, then-executive vice president of e-commerce. "But when you click through the site, the start page will be in Spanish and then it becomes the same old [English-language] site."[30]

Since the millennium began, BSG had been adding advanced technologies to facilitate reordering, stocking, the pick-and-pack process, and delivery. The technologies not only streamlined the entire supply chain but significantly lowered its warehouse costs. To further streamline operations, BSG closed two of its Viking Customer Service Centers (delivery warehouses) in 2003 and consolidated their operations into existing Office Depot facilities.[31] From 2000 to 2004, Office Depot had managed to reduce BSG's distribution costs by about $150 million.[32]

While BSG continued to focus on lowering warehouse and delivery expenses, it also strengthened its sales force in 2004, adding more than 100 salespeople.[33] Overall, squeezing out supply chain costs, plus the reinforcement of the sales force, meant that the group was better positioned for future growth. At the end of 2004, BSG operated 22 customer service centers across the United States, including 10 public Web sites.[34]

The Magellan Project

Bruce Nelson recognized that Office Depot's strengths were technical systems (reinforced by e-commerce), but the company needed better organization to succeed and grow. So in 2003, Office Depot rolled out a number of new initiatives designed to further improve the company, including the Magellan Project. Named after Ferdinand Magellan, the first person to circumnavigate the globe, the project represented the same interests that the explorer had pursued nearly 500 years earlier: "the quest for knowledge, a spirit of adventure, and a desire for financial success."[35]

Through the Magellan Project, Office Depot sought to improve its supply chain merchandising systems by implementing a world-class global merchandising system. The new global system would help Office Depot better plan the amount of merchandise it would purchase from suppliers, determine how to price that merchandise, decide how many varieties and brands to carry, and choose where to place the merchandise in stores. These efforts, in turn, would lead to increased sales, healthier margins, and an improved supply chain.[36] Magellan would also help the company divest out-of-date and discontinued items more successfully.[37]

Mark Holifield, who was in charge of the project, called Magellan "the most ambitious systems initiative in Office Depot's history." In essence, Magellan was an enterprise resource planning (ERP) system that would affect the entire organization and provide more accurate, consistent information.[38]

The Magellan Project took root in 2002, when a separate project to improve the company's merchandising revealed the disparate condition of the company's systems, and determined that data was often not easily accessible and was even contradictory. Obviously, good merchandising—the ability to sort product properly and determine pricing, placement, and promotions—needed to be based on accurate information.

"The Magellan Project will ensure that Office Depot can count on a 'single version of the truth' from its business systems and will incorporate the industry's best practices in merchandising," wrote Jay Eisenberg, then-director of merchandising process improvement. "It will enable the company to leverage business data to support merchandising decisions globally."[39]

To implement Magellan, Office Depot worked with several companies. The company's application systems partner, Retek, provided software to build the system. Accenture supplied integration services and helped move Office Depot from its existing systems to the Retek systems. AC Nielsen developed space productivity analysis software that allowed Office Depot to display items in the most productive places in the stores. Or, as Eisenberg explained, the software enabled the company "to put products in the right place in the store, on the right shelf."[40]

Store Revival Strategies

Meanwhile, the North American Retail Division began a slow revival, thanks to new merchandising initiatives. While the division struggled to regain profitability, Office Depot revised its real estate plan to better fit the needs of new and changing markets. The 36 new stores it opened in North America in 2003 averaged only 14,000 square feet in size compared to its older retail stores, which measured 26,000 square feet. The smaller stores, the company reasoned, better matched anticipated demand.[41]

Another initiative began in the spring of 2003, when Office Depot introduced Ink Depot specialty shops in more than 850 stores. Located at the front of the store, Ink Depot was a corralled, 600-square-foot shop dedicated to selling ink, toner, and fax supplies.[42] Notably, ink and toner made up the largest chunk of the company's retail sales, and Ink Depot's assortment of these products was the most extensive in the office products industry.[43] Each Ink Depot corral contained a separate register and its own knowledgeable staff. Ink Depot also contained kiosks where customers could browse through a variety of ink or toner cartridges.[44]

David D'Arezzo, then-executive vice president of merchandising and replenishment, explained how Ink Depot helped separate Office Depot from the competition. "Although many retailers sell ink and toner supplies, no one else has dedicated the space, the staff, and the technology to the extent that we have," he said.[45]

Then in June 2003, Office Depot rolled out an entirely new store prototype—Millennium—in Marietta, Georgia. Designers used computer simulations, focus groups, and surveys to create the prototype, carefully analyzing where best to place merchandise so as to "correspond more closely to the ways customers shop," the company explained. For example, a teacher who was planning an art project could find scissors, glue, construction paper, and other supplies in the same general area. Adding to customer convenience, products were available in multiple locations throughout the store.[46] The stores also featured new signage, much like signs marking grocery store aisles, to help customers find items more quickly.[47]

Though the initial customer feedback on the Millennium stores was positive, ultimately the new format failed to meet the company's expectations, partly because the stores were too costly to open and operate. However, this effort led to the much-improved Millennium2 (M2) design.

The Millennium2 Challenge

Bruce Nelson realized that if Office Depot wanted to truly stand out in an industry ready for change, then the company needed to completely reinvent its retail model. Nelson asked Rick Lepley, then-president of Office Depot–Japan, to com-

CORPORATE GIVING

OFFICE DEPOT HAD LONG BEEN A CHAMpion of corporate giving, with the business community quickly noticing the company's philanthropic efforts.

In December 2003, *BusinessWeek* magazine named Office Depot one of the top corporate philanthropists in the United States, an honor the company earned once again in 2005. In 2004, Office Depot was named to the "Companies That Care" Honor Roll by the Center for Companies That Care, a nonprofit organization that recognizes and encourages companies committed to community service.[1] Also in 2004, Office Depot won the Corporate Stewardship Award for Large Businesses from the U.S. Chamber of Commerce's Center for Corporate Citizenship.[2]

Office Depot continued to serve as a leader in donations for instructional and educational causes. In 2004, the company gave away 250,000 backpacks filled with school supplies to at-risk children through its National Backpack Program. (Office Depot had been running the backpack program since 2000.) For the 2004 backpack giveaway, Office Depot upgraded the backpacks from plain black bags to ones with new color schemes and reflectors. Mary Wong, director of community relations, said giving out the backpacks at the company's retail stores was very emotional. "It's like they received a little Christmas package," she said. "They gave us hugs and were just so thankful."[3]

In addition, Office Depot continued its "5% Back-to-Schools" program, which provided millions of dollars in credit to schools for the purchase of school supplies. With research indicating that teachers in the United States spent about $1 billion of their own money each year for classroom supplies, Office Depot helped alleviate this burden with the Star Teacher program, which gave teachers 5 percent off of school supplies and 15 percent off of copy and print services at Office Depot stores.[4] The company continued hosting Teacher Appreciation Breakfasts, where teachers could enjoy a free breakfast, free school supplies, special discounts on school items, and other prizes.[5]

Office Depot continued its ongoing product donations through a partnership with Gifts in Kind International. Every store grand opening event included donations to local nonprofit organizations. Moreover, Office Depot continued its corporate giving on a grand scale. For example, in 2004, it pledged $1 million to the Scripps Research Institute for research into childhood neurological diseases.[6]

Mary Wong, director of community relations, takes great pride in giving backpacks to underprivileged children via the Office Depot National Backpack Program. Pictured fourth from left, Wong sponsored the backpack program at the grand opening of an Office Depot store in Cherry Hill, New Jersey.

Rick Lepley, who served as executive vice president of North American Retail, retired in May 2006.

plete the task. Lepley had already helped improve the company's stores in Japan, and he had experience with Office Depot stores in Eastern Europe. To keep the project confidential and make certain the approach was fresh, Nelson asked Lepley and his team to develop the new design in secret.[48]

Nelson had already invited Joe Jeffries, who was a rising star in the company's store operations department, to join Lepley's team, along with David Djerf, an analyst in the company's financial department. Lepley then chose the remaining members of the seven-person team: Chad Mikula, director of North American Retail; Jay Eisenberg, then-director of small store formats; Diana Wagner from the company's merchandising department; and Thu Nguyen, also from merchandising.[49]

Nelson set some guiding principles for the new design: The store had to be less expensive to open, operate more efficiently, and provide a comfortable shopping environment. It needed to look, as well as feel, different from the company's existing stores. Nelson said, it had to be "a warmer, more inviting place to shop."[50]

A Covert Operation

Building the M2 prototype was a clandestine operation; only a handful of people among 47,000 Office Depot employees knew about it, as the seven-member team met in a secure, hidden-away room at Office Depot headquarters, where they brainstormed and planned.

Lepley and his team conducted extensive research to identify customers' needs when shopping for office supplies. Part of that research involved visiting competitors' stores such as Wal-Mart, Target, and Costco to observe product displays and packaging. The team members also relied on their own experience with stores in Japan and Europe and with the original Millenni-

um design, as well as with the company's existing vintage stores.

The team's research turned up some simple facts, according to Lepley: "For basic supplies, [customers] want convenience, including help in getting oriented, the ability to find everything on a shopping list, and fast checkout. For technology and furniture, they want information and advice, including assistance and support from knowledgeable staff and the ability to touch and try out various product options."[51]

Realizing that "people are incredibly visual," Lepley decided that building a mockup store would provide a solid venue to test the team's vision. "I tried to explain the vision," Lepley said, "but I wasn't able to accurately describe it. Finally, I just asked to go rent a warehouse and build a store. That way, everybody could experience the store and give input on how to improve it."[52]

Too many people knew about the company's usual test facility, where such an undertaking would normally take place, so Nelson gave the team permission to search elsewhere. The team landed on a vacant Levitz furniture store in Boca Raton, Florida, not far from Office Depot headquarters in Delray Beach, and made a deal with the landlord to lease the space on a temporary basis. Brown paper was placed over the windows of the warehouse to keep the project hidden from the public.[53]

As the mission progressed, Lepley's group introduced a few other key parties who helped bring the vision to life. Some of the company's vendors worked with the team to alter product packaging so the product took less time to stock. A consulting firm helped design the store layout (based on the team's visualization) and created vibrant new signage. Other select experts within Office Depot also helped bring the mockup to life.[54] The entire process of building and stocking the store took only five weeks, according to Lepley, but the team members worked long days and weekends to get the job done.[55]

The M2 Design

Once Nelson and the board of directors saw the M2 mockup, they gave their blessing to open a series of M2 stores. The first M2 store opened on June 30, 2004, in Venice, Florida, and by the end of 2004, the company had opened 101 M2 stores throughout the country.[56]

Just as Nelson had directed, the M2 stores were smaller and cost less to open and operate than both the company's traditional stores and the Millennium design. The M2 cost from $250,000 to $300,000 to open, compared to a $400,000 price tag for the company's other remodels. In addition, M2 reduced information technology (IT) setup costs by 50 to 60 percent and annual IT maintenance by 50 percent.[57]

In addition, the M2 stores took less time to stock, thanks to innovations such as spring-loaded trays that, for example, allowed employees to lay out an entire box of pens rather than feed individual pens onto a hanging peg. Hidden overstock shelves on top of fixtures also reduced labor, and the store's deeper shelves allowed for less-frequent inventory restocking. Items that sold quickly, like paper, were stacked in bulk pallet displays, which reduced labor and reinforced the item's price value. The stores also did not require as many employees (21 compared to the 23 needed at the company's traditional stores). At the same time, the M2 design allowed more people on the sales floor to assist customers.[58]

Customers found their shopping experience in the M2 stores more satisfying because the stores focused on the purchasing decisions people made. Items were grouped in strategically placed, horseshoe-shaped pods, which made navigating the store easier. One pod held binders, for example, and another held pens. The most popular items—such as paper, filing supplies, writing instruments, and ink and toner—were located at the outer perimeter of the store so customers could get in and out of the store quickly if they were buying these basic supplies. For large-ticket items, like furniture and technology, customers wanted to spend more time making their decisions, so those categories were placed in the center of the store where customers could try out various products and receive expert information and advice from salespeople. Moreover, the low steel shelving and open format provided better sight lines, making it easier for store employees to help customers who needed assistance, while also making it easier for customers to find assistance when they needed it.[59]

This inside view of the M2 store shows the clear line of sight available to customers and associates.

The M2 stores also showed off a vibrant new color scheme of cheerful, contemporary colors—bright orange, lime green, aqua, and purple—and featured new signage with photos of products that quickly guided customers.[60] Overall, the store design appealed more to women, who, surveys showed, shopped most often for office supplies. "We found that 60 percent of our customer base is comprised of women," said Lepley. "And half the time they influence the buying decisions of men, who comprise the other 40 percent of our customers."[61]

Nearly three years after the first prototype store was created, M2 was considered a resounding success. According to Henry Sauls, director of merchandising operations, the M2 design kept

evolving: "We not only ask our employees for feedback, but we also bring in a nice cross-section of customer focus groups—some who shop with us, some who don't, some business customers, some individual consumers," he said. "We ask them what they think of the design. We ask what we can do better. We're constantly tweaking the model, and it keeps improving."[62]

The Christopher Lowell Collection

In an effort to boost furniture sales, in the winter of 2003, Office Depot introduced a new line of stylish office furniture called the Christopher Lowell Collection. The ready-to-assemble collection was

Left: By the end of 2004, Office Depot had opened 101 M2 stores throughout the United States.

Below: The open format of Office Depot's M2 stores helps store associates find customers who may need assistance.

available exclusively through Office Depot, and this was the company's first step in moving from private label to private brand. The association between Christopher Lowell and Office Depot was an industry first; never before had such a well-known interior designer teamed up with an office supplier.[63]

In addition to being a nationally known designer, Lowell had an Emmy-winning home-design program, *The Christopher Lowell Show*, which aired every weekday on the Discovery Channel.[64]

The partnership between Office Depot and Lowell helped redefine the way customers shopped for office furniture. For the first time, small businesses and home-office customers had access to high-quality, stylish furniture that was functional as well as affordable. Pieces in the collection were coordinated with each other, so decorating was "foolproof," the company explained. Anybody could "achieve a designer effect at an affordable price."[65]

In 2003, renowned interior designer Christopher Lowell (left) teamed up with Office Depot to present the Christopher Lowell Collection of office furniture and accessories (above). As the author of three books, Lowell also had his own show on the Discovery Channel.

Designed to fit any budget, the collection included everything from desks and chairs to lamps, plants, and clocks. "Many people can't afford fine furniture prices," Lowell said. "We're trying to satisfy that customer."[66]

Lowell also designed the furniture to suit a variety of tastes. The Christopher Lowell Collection featured four different themes: "Town," "Country," "City," and "Shore." The selection evolved, as well. In 2004, Office Depot revamped the City collection and introduced the Spectator Collection, a new line of Christopher Lowell desk accessories that coordinated with all four themes.[67] Also, after

Right: Customers who used Office Depot-brand recycled paper helped conserve 1.3 million fully grown trees a year.

Opposite: Christopher Lowell's Town furniture featured Bordeaux wood and combined simplicity with an upscale look.

listening to customers' feedback, Office Depot introduced a series of multipurpose items, such as armoires that could store audio visual equipment and sofa tables that could also serve as executive desks.[68]

As Office Depot had hoped, the Christopher Lowell Collection was immensely successful. "We launched it in a little more than 200 stores, and from the moment it hit the floor, it really took off," said Kirby Salgado, divisional merchandising manager of furniture. "Then we couldn't roll it out fast enough." Salgado added that Office Depot had "charted new territory with the Christopher Lowell Collection. After we introduced it, several other retailers began offering stylish, ready-to-assemble furniture."[69]

A Private Brand Strategy

With the success of the Christopher Lowell line, Office Depot continued to innovate. Under Chuck Rubin's leadership, the company began focusing more on its private brands, which produced higher profit margins than brand-name merchandise. The quality of its private brands also differentiated Office Depot from the competition.[70]

"[The private brand] is a core building block of our success," Rubin said. "It provides us with an opportunity to present quality, value, and exclusivity in a way that is specific to Office Depot."[71]

As part of the strategy to build up its private brands, the company's merchandising and brand marketing departments redesigned the packaging of Office Depot-brand products to make them appear less "generic," prompting customers to recognize that the company's private-label items were equal in quality to national brands.[72] Under the leadership of Wilson Zhu, vice president of private brand development and global sourcing, Office Depot also began offering private brands for new product groups.

Standing Strong in the Northeast

When Office Depot acquired 124 vacant Kids "R" Us stores in 2004, the company was presented with a unique opportunity. Many of the vacant stores were located in the Northeast, an area where Office Depot lacked a significant presence. The Northeast was Staples' hub, and gaining a foothold in that part of the country had proved challenging for Office Depot.[73] "The Northeast is the country's least-saturated market for office supply superstores," said Rick Lepley.[74] Moreover, the region represented one-third of the nation's gross domestic product, so it embodied an important area of growth for Office Depot.[75]

Thanks in part to the Kids "R" Us stores, Office Depot embarked on a major expansion in the Northeast in 2004. Conveniently, the size of the vacant stores (15,000 to 20,000 square feet) matched the general size of the company's new M2 design, which was smaller than the traditional Office Depot store.[76] Office Depot planned to convert about 80 to 100 of the 124 Kids "R" Us stores to M2 stores, and sell or lease the rest.[77] By the end of

2004, the company's plans were well under way. Office Depot had converted 36 of the former Kids "R" Us stores into M2 stores.[78]

DSN Retailing Today, a trade magazine of the retail industry, reported that Office Depot faced "a difficult challenge" by entering the Northeast, since it would be "competing against a well-established competitor that knows Office Depot is coming." Nelson, too, anticipated a challenge, "but we are ready for the fight," he said. "As we roll out these new stores, customers in the Northeast—for the first time—will have a choice, an alternative to the only place they've been able to purchase office supplies. And what they will find is an Office Depot store that represents a true 'destination experience'—one that is warm, colorful, and exciting, and reflects the latest thinking in everything from

product layout and adjacencies to graphics, replenishment, and service."[79]

Also, according to Nelson, back in 1999 when Office Depot opened stores in the Northeast (and ended up closing most of them because they were underperforming), the company lacked a follow-up plan to add density. "[Through the use of better analytical methods], we know more about density and site selection than we did then," he said. "Today, in markets where we compete with Staples, we do just fine, and our brand awareness is almost as strong in the Northeast as it is anywhere else in the country."[80]

Marketing Initiatives

In 2003 and 2004, Office Depot embarked on a number of marketing initiatives that were designed to increase sales. In the summer of 2003, Office Depot mailed out its newly designed *Big Book* catalog, which featured a number of improvements. Larger-type pricing showed customer savings more clearly. The images were brighter and richer, and new copy better emphasized the various characteristics of the merchandise. Also,

When Office Depot set out to redesign its retail format, the company learned that customers who purchased technology often asked for assistance. As a result, the technology pod of the M2 store was always staffed with a friendly, knowledgeable sales associate.

the catalog was less cluttered than previous editions and had an easier-to-read index and improved shopping tips.[81] The *Big Book* was so well-designed, in fact, that it won *Catalog Age* magazine's 2003 prestigious Gold Award.[82]

In early 2004, Office Depot introduced another marketing strategy designed to boost sales—a customer loyalty program called Office Depot Advantage. Office Depot gave Advantage buyers 10 percent on the value of their purchases if they spent at least $200 in a three-month period. For example, a customer who spent $200 would receive a $20 gift certificate from Office Depot. The maximum store credit a customer could receive in a three-month period was $50.[83]

Office Depot's 2004 back-to-school marketing campaign featured new television and radio ads with the theme, "So Set for School." The ads tied into the company's Olympic sponsorship that encouraged children to achieve academic glory.[84]

Another Office Depot marketing initiative involved one of the most recognized business people in the world, real estate tycoon Donald Trump. In the summer of 2004, Office Depot sponsored Donald

Above: Office Depot's "5% Back-to-Schools" program encouraged customers to shop Office Depot not only for its selection and service, but also for the opportunity to support a school with credits for supplies.

Below: The Office Depot *Big Book* catalog underwent a number of incarnations during the company's history and was redesigned again in 2003. A strong layout, appealing images, and attention-grabbing copy won Office Depot the esteemed Gold Award from *Catalog Age* magazine.

Trump's new radio show, *Trumped!*, which highlighted the entrepreneurial spirit of small business owners. With nearly 300 radio stations broadcasting the show across the country, Trump read Office Depot promotions on the air. In one commercial spot, Trump said of Office Depot, "If you have a small business, these are the guys you want on your side."[85]

In a press release, Trump stated he "couldn't have selected a more appropriate sponsor for *Trumped!* than

For its 18th anniversary in 2004, Office Depot changed the banner of its public Web site to promote the company's special offers.

Office Depot, which shares my passion for providing the tools necessary for people to grow their businesses and be more successful."[86]

Office Depot even centered a marketing campaign around its 18th anniversary in the fall of 2004. Office Depot gave 18 percent discounts on many items and offered other items for a flat $18. The company even gave away $18 bonus gifts with select purchases, and customers who used their Office Depot credit cards were not charged interest for 18 months on purchases of $499 or more. Office Depot extensively promoted the special savings through newspaper inserts, direct mail, signs in the stores, its Web site, flyers, e-mail, and on Trump's radio show. The tagline for the promotion was "It's our 18th anniversary, and we're celebrating *you*!"[87]

An Environmental Policy with Tangible Benefits

Even the company's environmental policies helped increase sales. Office Depot had long been an industry leader with regards to environmental stewardship, but in 2003, Office Depot stepped up its commitment to the environment, hiring environmental specialist Tyler Elm as director of environmental affairs.[88] Elm had worked as an environmental consultant for Office Depot for nine months before he joined the company. He explained how the company's green strategy improved the environment, boosted sales, and helped Office Depot customers report solid environmental performance:

> We started to differentiate Office Depot-branded paper products by their environmental performance, and we started making that an attribute that could be easily quantified. By buying Office Depot's brand of environmental paper [EnviroCopy], the business customer could declare that their company was environmentally conscious. They could tout that the paper they purchased required 35 fewer trees to produce than most other paper, that it resulted in 15 percent fewer greenhouse gas emissions. They could say the paper they bought produced 30 percent fewer hazardous air pollutants, that it generated 17 percent less solid waste. So, by having those figures, the business could say it was an environmentally conscious company and have these tangible numbers to back it up."[89]

Elm helped Office Depot develop an environmental policy that went beyond offering recycled paper products. The company's environmental initiatives centered on three principles: reducing pollution through recycling and other means, managing sustainable forests, and developing environmentally preferable products while creating awareness and demand for those products.[90]

As part of the Earth Day celebration in March 2003, Office Depot introduced a new Environmental Paper Procurement Policy that helped conserve natural resources and protect the environment. The policy involved Office Depot working with its suppliers to sell recycled paper made of "postconsumer" recycled material—that is, paper collected from office and community recycling programs. The company ultimately aimed to use a percentage of postconsumer recycled material in all the paper products it sold. As another part of the Environmental Paper Procurement Policy, Office Depot made a point of selling paper products made without chlorine bleach. Chlorine bleach made paper brighter, but it formed dioxins that remained in the environment for years. Office Depot also sold paper products from forests that had been certified as sustainable by independent organizations. The company made it a policy not to sell paper that came from endangered forest ecosystems or forests that had been planted with genetically modified trees.[91]

In addition, Office Depot sought to increase demand for sustainable paper products. The company educated store employees on how its environmentally friendly products helped preserve the environment so they could then pass that knowledge on to customers. Also, the company's copy centers used EnviroCopy recycled paper as the default. (EnviroCopy was Office Depot's private brand of recycled paper that contained 5 percent more recycled fiber than federal guidelines required.) Moreover, Office Depot hired a consulting firm called GreenOrder to encourage Office Depot's large corporate customers to switch to environmentally sustainable products.[92]

Office Depot even offered incentives to convince people to recycle their used ink and toner cartridges. For every cartridge brought to an Office Depot store for recycling, the customer was rewarded with either a free ream of EnviroCopy paper or a discount off their next purchase of a remanufactured cartridge. (Remanufactured cartridges are created by replacing the ink and worn parts of used cartridges before being resold.)

"That incentive produced business benefits as well as environmental benefits," Elm explained. "First, it kept those cartridges out of the landfill. Also, it drove traffic to the stores, and it helped Office Depot accumulate a supply of cartridges for recycling, which could then turn into a remanufactured product for resale." Moreover, Elm said, giving away recycled paper or offering a discount on a remanufactured ink or toner cartridge enabled customers to try the environmental products at little or no risk.

"Many people formed their opinions about recycled products a couple of decades ago, and the technology to produce recycled products has changed tremendously," Elm said. "With this in-

centive, customers learn that the environmental products are just as good as others. That then helps switch customer demand over to recycled paper and recycled cartridges."[93]

Office Depot knew that recycling cartridges was extremely important to preserving the environment. Worldwide, more than 300 million cartridges are thrown away every year, only to end up in landfills. In the United States alone, an estimated eight cartridges are discarded every second. The remanufacturing of a single cartridge conserves the equivalent of half a gallon of oil.[94]

In another environmental initiative, Office Depot teamed up with Hewlett-Packard in 2004 to form the nation's first free electronic products recycling program. People could bring to an Office Depot store any unwanted electronic products—from cell phones and scanners to computers and televisions (anything smaller than a 27-inch TV). Office Depot then turned the items over to Hewlett-Packard, an expert in recycling electronics.[95]

Also in 2004, Office Depot introduced its *Green Book* catalog, which con-

Left: After working with Office Depot as a consultant for nine months, Tyler Elm was named Office Depot's director of environmental affairs.

Below: Office Depot's EnviroCopy paper contained 5 percent more recycled fiber than state and federal laws required of recycled paper.

tained only environmentally preferable products. The catalog itself was also printed on chlorine-free recycled paper.[96] That same year, Office Depot published an *Environmental Stewardship Report* for its own company. This was the office supply industry's only independently audited environmental report, and it detailed not only the company's environmental performance but also that of its customers. As an environmental trade magazine noted, "The report holds Office Depot to a higher environmental standard while making its environmental performance more transparent."[97]

The Office Depot *Green Book* catalog contained a wide range of environmentally preferable, high-quality products that could offer substitutes for traditional office supplies.

Stormy Times

The various strategies that Office Depot had undertaken to revive its North American stores were clearly working. In the first quarter of 2004, comparable store sales rose 3 percent, and comp sales rose another 3 percent in the second quarter. The gain reversed the company's 15-quarter streak of declining comps.

"That was a huge morale booster," said Rubin. "We needed to show people that we could break through this glass ceiling and reverse the declines."[98]

Also, sales of two troubled product categories for Office Depot were on the rise. Technology sales in the second quarter were up 18 percent, and furniture sales were up 4 percent.[99]

Unfortunately, the company's fortunes changed once again, when a series of hurricanes and tropical storms swept over Florida in the fall of 2004. Tropical Storm Bonnie and Hurricanes Charley, Ivan, Frances, and Jeanne (four hurricanes in just six weeks) damaged many Office Depot stores, causing some to shut down for several days. "A significant portion of the company's North American revenue base comes from the areas impacted by the recent storms," Bruce Nelson told the press. After Hurricane Frances, the company's headquarters lost power and closed for four business days.[100]

Office Depot lost sales, not just because it was forced to temporarily close stores, but also because many other area businesses experienced the same problems. Companies that were out of commission were not buying supplies from Office Depot.

A weak back-to-school season combined with the disruptive impact of the hurricanes contributed to flat comp sales for the third quarter of 2004. Adding to the overall bleak picture, the Business Services Group produced lower-than-expected sales growth. In the International Division, catalog sales were below expectations for the month of August. Also, operations from the Guilbert acquisition had yet to show a profit; Guilbert's sales actually fell after Office Depot acquired it.

"The integration of Guilbert did not fully appreciate the cultural differences," explained Charlie Brown, who was CFO when Office Depot acquired Guilbert and later became president of the International Division. "We had some contract

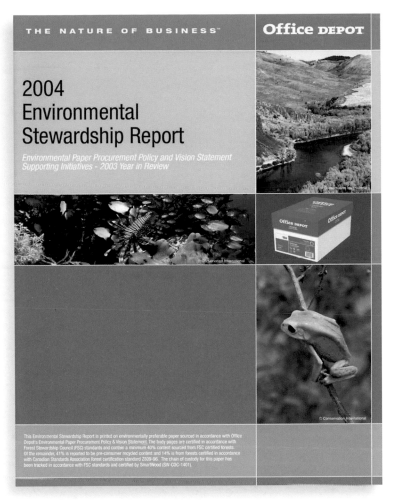

THE NATURE OF BUSINESS™   Office DEPOT

2004
Environmental
Stewardship Report

*Environmental Paper Procurement Policy and Vision Statement
Supporting Initiatives - 2003 Year in Review*

This Environmental Stewardship Report is printed on environmentally preferable paper sourced in accordance with Office Depot's Environmental Paper Procurement Policy & Vision Statement. The body pages are certified in accordance with Forest Stewardship Council (FSC) standards and contain a minimum 40% content sourced from FSC certified forests. Of the remainder, 41% is reported to be pre-consumer recycled content and 14% is from forests certified in accordance with Canadian Standards Association forest certification standard Z809-96. The chain of custody for this paper has been tracked in accordance with FSC standards and certified by SmartWood (SW-COC-1401).

The Office Depot *Environmental Stewardship Report* provided the company's suppliers, employees, customers, and shareholders with an overview of Office Depot's environmental policies and its progress on integrating those policies. The report also presented measurable outcomes that had resulted from the company's environmental initiatives.

business in Europe, but most of our business in Europe was mail order, and all of the people who ran that business were of a mail-order culture. They didn't necessarily understand how to run a contract business."[101]

Kor de Jonge, vice president of international human resources, agreed. "Though Guilbert doubled our organization, it also complicated it significantly because, up until that time, our European operations were basically mail order, with some retail activities, and Guilbert's contract business added a whole new level of complexity."[102]

Brown added, "We had a different culture in our European operations. So, for example, our financial discipline was much weaker in Europe." Moreover, Nelson had not yet replaced himself as president of the International Division. "Bruce and I split oversight of the international operations," Brown said. "So in terms of growing our business in other parts of the world, essentially it was part-time effort for both of us. CEOs and CFOs typically don't have a lot of spare time, which meant we weren't aggressive enough as new opportunities opened up."[103]

Some industry pundits were sympathetic to the plight of Office Depot. As *Office Products International*, a trade publication, reported:

> *In the face of such a stuttering [2004 third] quarter, the last thing the company needed were forces out of its control to compound matters. However, the slings and arrows of outrageous fortune came in the shape of tropical storms that tore into the Florida Panhandle. There is obviously never a good time for this kind of natural disaster to happen, but if there was a quarter when Depot could have most done without it, this was probably the one.[104]*

A Change at the Top

Damage from the storms, combined with unexpectedly weak sales in all three of the company's operating units, caused Office Depot to cut its profit estimates for the third quarter of 2004.[105] The company's shares fell 7 percent as a result, but the weak third quarter had greater repercussions.

The board of directors decided it was time for new leadership at the top. By mutual agreement with the board, Nelson, whose employment agreement expired at the end of December 2004, resigned from his post as chairman and CEO in early October 2004.

The board asked Neil Austrian to serve as interim chairman and CEO until a permanent replacement was assigned. As a director of the company, Austrian said he felt "a personal responsibility" to accept the role.[106] Austrian had been on the board since Office Depot acquired Viking Office Products in 1998 and was head of the board's finance committee. From 1991 through 1999, he was president and chief operating officer of the National Football League, and from 1987 through 1991, he served as managing director of Dillon, Read & Company.

WEATHERING THE STORMS

This fallen tree, caused by Hurricane Frances, is a simple but powerful illustration of the destruction Florida residents suffered during an entire season of vicious storms. *(Photo courtesy of Melody Maysonet.)*

THE 2004 HURRICANE SEASON PRO-duced a series of devastating storms that wreaked havoc on the southeastern United States. Alex, Bonnie, Charley, Frances, and Ivan knocked out power lines, uprooted trees, tore off roofs, and caused extensive flooding. Residents from New Orleans to the Florida Panhandle, and all along Florida's east coast, including many Office Depot employees, suffered from the series of tropical events. The emotional stress of waiting and wondering where and when the storms would hit took a toll on many. When the storms made landfall near a community, people were often left without electricity, phone service, clean water, and other basic necessities.

As a testament to the company's values-based culture, Office Depot associates all over the country rallied to help the victims of the hurricanes and tropical storms. Even those who were victims themselves came together to offer help, making donations and volunteering their time to ease the suffering of others.

For its part, Office Depot made in-kind donations valued at about $300,000 to help in the recovery process. The Office Depot Disaster Relief Foundation also donated $500,000 to the American Red Cross' Disaster Relief Fund and $100,000 to America's Second Harvest, which helped provide much-needed food to the worst-hit communities. Also, for many of its employees who were affected by the storms, Office Depot provided financial assistance in the form of grants and low-interest loans.[1]

Office Depot offered a number of free services through its retail stores to help residents and business owners contact friends, family, and associates. In areas hit by the storms, Office Depot set up workstations in many stores and provided free Internet, fax, and copy services. Some of the Office Depot stores also held in-store food drives to assist local food banks.[2]

There was a feeling that Office Depot had too many initiatives and too many disparate strategies, and lacked a focus. Austrian simplified the gameplan with three strategies to which people could relate.

"The major issue up to now has been execution and accountability," Austrian said in a conference call to investors and analysts shortly after he assumed his new post. "We don't feel we need new plans, just better and more rapid execution of the plans we already have in place."[107]

Or as one analyst said, Office Depot "needs someone who has three skills: execution, execution, execution."[108]

Also during the conference call, Austrian said the company's first objective was to improve profits of its North American Retail operations. The second priority was to apply a new approach to the Business Services Group, which had been losing market share. Third, he aimed to wring out the performance and synergies that were expected from the Guilbert acquisition.[109]

Immediately after Nelson's departure, Office Depot began a widespread initiative to cut costs. The company had purchased land in nearby Boca Raton, Florida, in March 2004 for a new headquarters but now decided to put the move on hold. The company also cut 97 jobs at its corporate offices and about 800 others in retail stores, call centers, and in Europe.[110]

While Office Depot suffered through this painful transition, it began searching for a new CEO, someone "with the energy and drive to jump-start the business," according to Austrian. "We want someone who holds people accountable." The new CEO, Austrian added, would have to hold true to the values of the company and put forth respect for the individual, fanatical customer service, and excellence in execution.[111]

The Millennium2 (M2) store design helped customers distinguish Office Depot from the competition.

CHAPTER TEN

A NEW ERA

2005 AND BEYOND

We believe progress has been made in reshaping our company, but we believe that much work lies ahead of us.

—Chairman and CEO Steve Odland, 2006[1]

WHILE THE OFFICE DEPOT board of directors proceeded with an extensive search for a new leader, the company's interim chairman and CEO, Neil Austrian, began preparing Office Depot for a transition into a new era. Or perhaps more precisely, his efforts guided Office Depot back to its roots.

In 1986, when Office Depot was founded, it primarily served the business customer—and as a result, the company was exceedingly successful. Under Austrian's leadership, Office Depot renewed its dedication to serving the business customer segment, which comprised approximately 80 percent of the company's sales.[2]

As part of its commitment to the business customer, in January 2005, Office Depot resurrected its popular "Taking Care of Business" tagline, set to the tune of Bachman Turner Overdrive's hit song from the 1970s.

"The 'Taking Care of Business' tagline has served as a rallying point for the entire company, both externally and internally," said Brian Levine, who joined Office Depot in 2003 to spearhead the company's communications efforts. "Externally, it reinforces that our business customers are the lifeblood of Office Depot and that all of the things we do are based around meeting the needs of business customers. Internally, 'Taking Care of Business' highlights the fact that it is essential for us to take care of

our own business as an operation so we can drive profitable growth and be successful in the future."[3]

Extensive research told Office Depot that its most recent tagline, "What you need. What you need to know," did not resonate with many business owners. Also, according to Tony Ueber, who joined Office Depot in 2003 as vice president of marketing strategy, "We felt that we, along with our competitors, were relying too much on humor that poked fun at the customer as opposed to demonstrating to our customers what we could actually deliver and portraying that in an inspirational manner."[4]

Office Depot evaluated a number of brand alternatives, one of which was to revisit the "Taking Care of Business" theme. Studies had concluded that this classic tagline—a slogan Office Depot had employed twice before in its history—"was the clear winner," according to Ueber.[5] Not only did the saying renew customer awareness of Office Depot's product offerings, but it also resonated more strongly than either of the taglines for other retailers.[6]

In January 2005, Office Depot became the official office products partner of NASCAR and the primary sponsor of Roush Racing driver Carl Edwards.

For those who argued that "Taking Care of Business" was losing its appeal, Ueber pointed out that several other well-known corporations had moved away from successful taglines only to return to them later. In addition, some distinguished brands, such as Campbell's soup and Maxwell House coffee, had kept the same tagline for decades. "We realized that if you have something that's really good, don't move away from it because a good tagline can stand the test of time," Ueber said. "And we learned that if you do move away from a successful tagline, you shouldn't be afraid to come back to it."[7]

Once executives decided to revive "Taking Care of Business," Office Depot launched a major marketing campaign that involved radio and television spots created by New York-based broadcast advertising agency BBDO. To ensure customers knew Office Depot was a "one-stop business supplier," Office Depot stores increased their inventory of business-related supplies (including a large assortment of Office Depot brand products) and bulk items, such as paper.[8]

"Going back to 'Taking Care of Business' rallied the field," said Austrian. "The people in the field have to be excited about what they're saying about the company, and the 'Taking Care of Business' slogan really got them re-enervated."[9]

Steve Odland Recruited

Meanwhile, Office Depot demonstrated that it was taking care of its own business, when in March 2005, the board of directors recruited Steve Odland as the company's new chairman and CEO.

Odland had served as chairman, president, and CEO of AutoZone from 2001 to 2005, where, under his leadership, the company's stock had quadrupled. Prior to overseeing AutoZone, Odland was an executive with Ahold USA and president of the Foodservice Division of Sara Lee Bakery. In his early career, he

had served in various executive positions at The Quaker Oats Company.

In an Office Depot newsletter, Neil Austrian outlined Odland's credentials and commended his past performance:

Steve's track record in delivering strong operating performance and excellent financial results in challenging business environments makes him the ideal person to lead our company to the next level. With his background in marketing and merchandising, his demonstrated focus on building loyalty through customer service and satisfaction, and an unparalleled record in the creation of shareholder value, we could not have found a better fit for our company. We are delighted that Steve has agreed to join us.[10]

Austrian performed a critical role during his interim term. He began a cost-reduction process and introduced much-needed energy and optimism into the company.

The board of directors' response to Austrian's performance was overwhelmingly positive. "Neil was the right choice for our interim chairman and CEO," said Michael Myers, who was among the company's first venture capitalists and had served on the board since Office Depot went public in 1989. "He did an excellent job of not just holding the bag, but actually making some important operating decisions in the company. He got management to start working together, and in a sense, he started the turnaround even before Steve got there. We're all in Neil's debt for doing a good job."[11]

Steve Odland joined Office Depot in March 2005 as the new chairman and CEO. Previously, he had served as chairman, president, and CEO of AutoZone. Odland was known in business circles as a leader who excelled in improving financial results, building shareholder value, and improving customer service and satisfaction. *(Photo courtesy of Paul Morris/Morphoto, Inc.)*

2006
OFFICE DEPOT BOARD OF DIRECTORS

LEE A. AULT III
Chairman of the Board,
In-Q-Tel, Inc.

NEIL R. AUSTRIAN
President and CEO
(retired),
National Football League

DAVID W. BERNAUER
Chairman and CEO,
Walgreen Company

ABELARDO (AL) E. BRU
Vice Chairman
(retired),
PepsiCo, Inc.

DAVID I. FUENTE
Managing Partner,
Dash Ventures

BRENDA J. GAINES
North American
President (retired),
Diners Club International
Division of Citigroup

MYRA M. HART
Entrepreneurial
Management Professor,
Harvard Business School

W. SCOTT HEDRICK
General Partner,
InterWest Partners

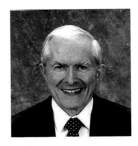

JAMES L. HESKETT
Baker Foundation
Professor (retired),
Harvard Business School

MICHAEL J. MYERS
President,
First Century Partners

STEVE ODLAND
CEO and Chairman,
Office Depot

PAUL MORRIS/MORPHOTO, INC.

After Odland was hired, Austrian resumed his place on the board of directors as head of the finance committee. At that time, the board was comprised of nine members besides Odland and Austrian: Lee Ault III, David Bernauer, Abelardo (Al) Bru, David Fuente, Brenda Gaines, Myra Hart, W. Scott Hedrick, James Heskett, and Michael Myers. In May 2006, Heskett retired from the board after 10 years of service.

All the Right Moves

Wall Street rallied behind the board's decision to bring in Odland as chairman and CEO. Office Depot's shares rose 12 percent after it made the announcement, and analysts relayed many positive statements about Odland's past performance.[12]

"It's a good hire and a win for Office Depot," said Joseph Feldman, a retail analyst with SG Cowen & Company. "He's a smart man, and he has done a terrific job everywhere he has been. I don't see why he won't be able to do that here."[13]

"Odland is a highly analytical executive, disciplined about spending and focused on returns," wrote Matthew Fassler, an analyst with Goldman, Sachs & Company.[14]

One of Odland's many strong points was his consistent focus on ethics. While at AutoZone, his corporate governance guidelines were more rigorous than those established by Sarbanes-Oxley's corporate reform legislation.[15] Odland had also chaired the Business Roundtable's Corporate Governance Task Force since 2004.[16] (The Business Roundtable is an association of chief executives committed to fostering U.S. and global economies. They address specific issues that direct research, recommend policy, and lobby Congress on select issues. The Roundtable seeks to identify issues early and tries to understand the problems faced by government and business.)

As expected, Odland applied his high ethical standards to Office Depot. "My mantra is always, 'We have to do the right thing and have the highest level of ethics every single day,'" he told a throng of gathered employees on his first day of work. "We have to do the right thing for our customers, for all our employees, and, of course, for our shareholders."[17] Indeed, Office Depot required that associates receive ethics training, and the company hired an independent contractor to run an ethics hotline that associates could call if they ever had questions or concerns about ethical behavior inside the company.[18]

Even on his first day at work, Odland's enthusiasm and optimism permeated through the company. Office Depot associates cheered when, during his inaugural speech, he announced his commitment to transforming Office Depot into "the

On his first day at work in March 2005, Steve Odland spoke to a crowd of headquarters associates and emphasized his commitment to the company's three constituencies represented by the letters in his title of "CEO," which stood for Customers, Employees, and Owners. *(Photo courtesy of Paul Morris/Morphoto, Inc.)*

president of North American Retail since 2004, retired in May 2006.

Office Depot experienced other changes in its top management. In 2005, Tim Toews, who had joined Office Depot in 1994, was promoted to senior vice president and chief information officer, and Patricia McKay came on board as the new CFO. McKay was former CFO of Restoration Hardware, a home furnishings retailer, and had served on the Office Depot board of directors since 2004. Also in 2005, Daisy Vanderlinde was hired as executive vice president of human resources. Prior

Left: In 2005, Charlie Brown was promoted to president of the Office Depot International Division. In his newly expanded role, Brown was responsible for all operations outside of North America.

Below: Patricia McKay came to Office Depot in 2005 as executive vice president and chief financial officer. Previously, McKay served as executive vice president and CFO of Restoration Hardware. She was also on the Office Depot board of directors in 2004. *(Photos courtesy of Paul Morris/Morphoto, Inc.)*

clear No. 1 office products supplier in the world."[19] Office Depot's recent slide to the No. 2 spot behind Staples had been a significant morale buster, and employees were ready for change, which Odland promised to deliver.

Corporate Leadership Evolves

Shortly after Odland came on board, Office Depot announced changes in senior leadership that would allow it to better concentrate on its three growth priorities: North American Retail, North American Business Solutions (formerly the Business Services Group), and International.

In April 2005, CFO Charlie Brown was promoted to president of the International Division. Also that month, Monica Luechtefeld, who had led the company's online initiatives since 1994, was promoted to executive vice president of information technology, supply chain, and business development. The North American Retail president position remained vacant until January 2006, when Chuck Rubin, former executive vice president and chief merchandising/marketing officer, assumed the post. Rick Lepley, who had served as executive vice

Above: Daisy Vanderlinde joined Office Depot in 2005 as executive vice president of human resources. She previously served as senior vice president of human resources and loss prevention at AutoZone. *(Photo courtesy of Paul Morris/Morphoto, Inc.)*

Right: In 2006, Dirk Collin came on board as executive vice president and managing director of Office Depot–Europe. He succeeded Rolf van Kaldekerken, who retired in September 2005.

managing director of the division. Previously, Collin had been with Xerox for 25 years and had also worked for StorageTek Corporation as general manager of northern Europe and vice president of sales operations for Europe, Asia, and the Middle East.[20]

One Vision, One Culture

One of Odland's first tasks as the company's new chief executive was to unite the company's departments and direct them toward the common good of Office Depot. His overarching goal was to create a culture of shared leadership through a single management team that worked cross-functionally. To that end, Odland formed an Executive Committee (EC) comprised of himself, the company's presidents and executive vice presidents, and a Global Officer Coalition (OC), which included the EC and roughly 80 top officers of Office Depot. In addition, Odland instituted monthly Open Forum

to joining Office Depot, Vanderlinde had served as senior vice president of human resources and loss prevention at AutoZone.

The press lauded the company's diverse pool of leadership and made note of the fact that Patricia McKay was the company's first female CFO. Indeed, in a corporate world dominated by men, half of the people who reported directly to Odland were women.

Also, in September 2005, Rolf van Kaldekerken retired from his post as president of Office Depot–Europe, and in early 2006, Office Depot hired Dirk Collin as executive vice president and

meetings in which officers from around the globe updated each other and their own departments on all corporate activities.

"Steve wants us to be able to complete one another's sentences," said Cindy Campbell, executive vice president of North American Business Solutions. "He wants to create an environment where we are encouraged to share our concerns without fear of retribution. Then he wants us to translate that philosophy to the entire employee population."[21]

According to Brian Levine, "Steve has always said that one person cannot make all decisions for the company, so he created a process of shared leadership. The company is driven by the Executive Committee, which meets extensively every Monday, and the Officer Coalition, which meets monthly, and these two bodies really make the decisions and drive the business of the company."[22]

"Office Depot has a very open, candid culture," said Lee Ault III, who served on the Office Depot board since the company acquired Viking in 1998. "Steve has all of his senior people involved in the overall business. They're sort of quasi-CEOs on their own because they have a voice in everything."[23]

Odland also established a new cooperative problem-solving tradition at Office Depot. When managers thought there was a problem or that a process was "broken," they would declare a "breakdown," and then Office Depot associates would collaborate to solve the problem.[24]

Perhaps Odland's most far-reaching cultural initiative was his focus on "Breakthrough Performance," the idea that Office Depot should do more than merely *meet* performance expectations; it should break through hidden barriers to *exceed* expectations. To achieve Breakthrough Performance, however, Office Depot first needed to develop a shared vision and shared values—and then it needed to develop the social fabric of the company to execute that vision and those values.

In an internal company video, Office Depot explained why it needed Breakthrough Performance:

For years, Office Depot struggled with the same problem. It was siloed [sic]—with departments reaching individual goals, but not working together as a team. Breakthrough Performance changes that—it clears the air between departments—and helps Office Depot become one, singular force.

At meetings in both the United States and Europe, members of the Officer Coalition were

Left: Brian Levine, senior director of public relations and internal communications, joined Office Depot in 2003. *(Photo courtesy of Paul Morris/Morphoto, Inc.)*

Below: By the end of 2005, Office Depot had 42 stores in France, all wholly owned by the company. Office Depot has operated in France since 1996, when it opened two stores there under a joint venture with Carrefour.

asked to write down their honest opinion about every division in the company. The opinions were then posted around the room for the other officers to view. Some of the perceptions, in the words of one Office Depot officer, "were not pretty," but the group pushed through the sometimes uncomfortable discussions.

"We decided that what we put on the wall was really yesterday's news, but it wasn't going to write the future," said Luechtefeld. "To write that future script, we had to put the past away and celebrate the things we shared in common."[25]

With the air cleared, the officers began to form a shared vision statement, "something that inspires us but that also gives us something to aspire to," said Vanderlinde.[26]

Office Depot sales associates receive specialized training in both customer service and product knowledge to ensure customer satisfaction.

Chuck Rubin described the importance of a company's vision statement:

A vision statement unifies the company. It's something that is never quite fully achieved, but it's always motivating. When you look at a company like Office Depot, with people in so many countries and so many different locations, all trying to achieve the same objective, everybody had to be clear on what we're working for, and that's really the purpose of the vision statement.[27]

Working together from around the world, members of the Officer Coalition spent weeks exchanging and debating ideas until at last they settled on the exact words to describe their shared vision: *Delivering Winning Solutions That Inspire Worklife*™.

The deliberate words of the new vision reflected nearly as many connotations as there were people involved in crafting the phrase. Among its many implications, "Delivering" meant meeting and exceeding expectations, not just for customers but for associates and shareholders, as well. It meant providing customers with the highest quality at the lowest price. "Delivering" suggested execution and implied that actions speak louder than words.

"Winning" connoted positive energy, achieving goals, and landing the No. 1 spot in the office supplies industry. It meant striving for the best with respect to associates, customers, vendors, suppliers, and shareholders.

Providing "Solutions" was an opportunity to help customers resolve problems. "Solutions" meant providing *all* of the tools customers required for their businesses. It meant following through after a sale was completed.

The word "Inspire" stirred passion, creativity, and energy. It meant enabling customers to become motivated, innovative, and enthusiastic so they could better achieve their goals.

Though "Worklife," the last word in the vision statement, was not found in the dictionary, it was a term the officers created to better characterize working in the modern world. The officers who fashioned the term spoke 15 different languages, yet all of the nationalities, except the British, assumed that "worklife" was a real word because it perfectly described the convergence of work and life. "Work" was no longer a separate place that people visited

Regional and assistant managers for Office Depot District No. 33 in South Florida gather for a group photo. Front row, from left: Robin Cohen, Marlynn Martin, Yuri Salas, Manny Perez, and Louise Murdoch. Middle row, from left: Chris Marco, Cesar Orejarena, Rob Cousins, Melvin Robinson, Julius Tieszler, Stephen Garraway, Nick Konoulas, Charles Campenni, Lazaro Hernandez, and Julio Quintana. Back row, from left: Keith Ferguson, Casey Cohen, Mike Brown, Brad Mellette, Mike Silvers, Robert Morony, Paul Koterba, Javier Manso, and Michael Corey.

to bring home a paycheck. Instead, people's work had become integrated with their personal lives, so *Delivering Winning Solutions That Inspire Worklife* meant providing solutions that addressed how people worked *and* lived. It was a seemingly simple statement, but it held complex undertones. In essence, the vision embodied everything for which Office Depot stood.

Odland was understandably proud of the company's vision. "It wasn't something that a consultant created and handed to the company, and that is inspirational unto itself," he said. "The officers understand the meaning behind the words because they were the ones who debated and came up with them. The vision isn't meant to be a slogan that you hang up on the wall, or a poster that everybody walks by. It's meant to be a reservoir that people can go to when they're stuck, a compass that guides them."[28]

Once the company's vision had been put into words, the Officer Coalition needed a set of shared values to reflect that vision. Odland explained the importance of establishing such values:

How do we make sure that our 47,000 associates are doing the right thing every single day? There's the Sarbanes-Oxley Act that we're required by law to follow. But a rules-based approach will only take you so far, and there cannot possibly be enough rules to govern everything that goes on in a company, especially when you have 47,000 employees making millions of customer interactions every day. That means you have to take a values-based approach. You have to articulate what you stand for and what is important for your company. If you have a values-based approach, you are empow-

ered to operate consistently with that set of values. The values-based approach means we're not going to tell you exactly how to behave with every customer interaction. We're not going to write a rule for everything, but we're going to tell you to do the right thing consistent with our values.[29]

The Officer Coalition created values that centered around five ideals: Integrity, Innovation, Inclusion, Customer Focus, and Accountability. Office Depot described its values as follows:

*   **Integrity***: We earn the trust and confidence of associates, customers, suppliers, and shareholders by being open, honest, and truthful in all that we do.*
    Innovation*: With a culture of creativity and a thirst for intelligent risk-taking, we aspire to do what has never been done.*

This page: On St. Patrick's Day in 2005, Office Depot associates in Delray Beach "got green" when they participated in a local St. Patrick's Day parade to build awareness of environmental issues, encourage recycling, and exhibit the wide variety of office products that contain recycled material.

*   **Inclusion***: We approach all opportunities and challenges by respecting the diverse thoughts, beliefs, backgrounds, cultures, and energies of all associates, customers, and suppliers.*
    Customer Focus*: We fuel our customers' dreams by anticipating and listening to their needs and passionately delivering on our promises. Failure is not an option, as we promise to "wow" on recovery.*
    Accountability*: We are responsible for achieving and sustaining unprecedented results that create extraordinary value to our shareholders and stakeholders through personal commitment, sensible thrift, collaboration, and shared leadership.*

After spending weeks creating the statements that reflected Office Depot's vision and values, company officers were ready to live by them. As Odland remarked, "We are embarking on the development of a global Office Depot. Not a North American Office Depot and a European Office Depot. Not Office Depot and Viking. We are creating a global business that we can carry around the world with one vision and one culture."

In its internal video about Breakthrough Performance, Office Depot summed up the achievements of the Officer Coalition: "Breakthrough Performance has developed a team, a new vision and values, and a foundation to build a trusting environment, where open communication will continue after the meetings end."

After nearly a year at the company's helm, Odland concluded that Office Depot associates were responding well to the new, trusting environment. "Even tough news and tough messages of change are easier to accept because we're being open and honest about them," he said. "Gossip around the company has been reduced to a minimum because there's no need to float ideas to see if they're right. People know that if they have a question about something, they can come ask, and we'll tell them."[30]

Celebrating Diversity

While Office Depot concentrated on Breakthrough Performance, the company continued to make great strides in promoting diversity. "Our unwavering commitment to diversity enables us to be an employer of choice," the company told its shareholders. This quality enabled Office Depot to "serve the needs of our customers and stand as a valued corporate citizen in the communities in which we do business."[31]

Office Depot celebrated diversity, as well. In 2005, Office Depot held its fifth annual Success Strategies for Businesswomen Conference, in which poet Maya Angelou and supermodel Kathy Ireland participated. The conference was a sold-out event, with more than 1,000 attendees. A

Barbara Walters received a standing ovation at the 2005 Success Strategies for Businesswomen Conference. Supermodel Kathy Ireland (inset right) was one of the keynote speakers.

Women's Business Enterprise National Council

Creating Opportunities…Recognizing Excellence

In 2006, Women's Business Enterprise National Council (WBENC) named Office Depot as one of 18 "America's Top Corporations for Women's Business Enterprises." Office Depot was honored because of its supplier diversity programs and dedication to offering equal access to women-owned supplier companies. Additionally, Office Depot has been the only retailer named to this prestigious list the past five years in a row. Since 1997, WBENC has dedicated itself to fostering diversity in commerce for women's business enterprises.

South Florida newspaper described the conference as "one of the nation's preeminent confabs for female small business owners."[32] At the opening session, Office Depot honored nine women with its prestigious 2005 "Businesswomen of the Year" award.[33] At the closing luncheon, Office Depot and Xerox presented a $25,000 grant to the National Ovarian Cancer Coalition.[34]

The 2006 Businesswomen Conference was equally successful. Actress and comedienne Lily Tomlin, former New Jersey Governor Christine Todd Whitman, and former U.S. Secretary of Labor Alexis Herman were among the keynote speakers.

Office Depot also continued its vendor and supplier diversity programs to ensure that it gave historically underutilized businesses (HUBs) equal opportunities. Robert McCormes-Ballou, director of vendor development and diversity, explained that a historically underutilized business included not just minority-owned or women-owned businesses but also businesses owned by service-disabled veterans, and, perhaps surprisingly, any small business, no matter what the gender or ethnicity of the owner. In fact, he said, "Small businesses are the heartbeat of our retail business. By buying from small businesses and creating opportunities for them to grow, Office Depot benefits, because our revenue is tied

directly to how much they buy from us. Taking care of diversity is taking care of business."[35]

McCormes-Ballou also explained how Office Depot's diversity program augmented the drive for its transformation into a truly global company. "If you want to be a global company, you can't be mono-ethnic and mono-cultural," he said. "If a company has a hard time being diversity-sensitive in the United States, it's going to have an even harder time when it crosses the border."[36]

In 2005, *DiversityBusiness.com*, a multicultural company that linked large buyers with multicultural business owners, included Office Depot for the fourth consecutive year on its Top 50 Corporations for Multicultural Business Opportunities list.[37] In 2006, Women's Business Enterprise National Council (WBENC), which certified women-owned businesses, named Office Depot one of 18 of "America's Top Corporations for Women's Business Enterprises." Office Depot was honored because it provided "equal access for women-owned suppliers" and had an excellent supplier diversity program.[38]

Commitment to the Environment

Office Depot took its environmental stewardship to new levels in 2005. The company's *Green Book* catalog included 84 percent more environmentally preferable products than the previous year's catalog. Delivered to nearly 40,000 companies, the *Green Book* provided detailed information about the environmental benefits of its 2,500 products and offered tips to companies that attempted to take a more environmentally friendly business approach. As Tyler Elm, then-director of the company's environmental affairs, said, Office Depot acted as a business partner to its customers. "As their partner, we help them achieve their business goals, including those related to the environment."[39]

Elm was awarded the 2004 Forest Leadership Communication Award for his commitment to sustaining forests around the world.[40] Unfortunately for Office Depot, another large corporation recruited him in 2005 to help straighten its own environmental affairs.

Office Depot's commitment to improving the environment did not slow down with Elm's departure. In 2005, the company joined a group of businesses called the Environmental Paper Assessment

Tool (EPAT) Early Adopter Circle that wanted to help develop a universal tool that evaluated environmentally preferable paper in purchasing decisions. Office Depot became the first office products company that was listed in the U.S. and global indexes of FTSE4Good, an independent company that creates and manages indexes and associated data services on an international scale. Office Depot had met the criteria of environmental sustainability, positive stakeholder relationships, and universal human rights support.[41]

In April 2006, Yalmaz Siddiqui replaced Tyler Elm to head up Office Depot's environmental strategy. Previously, Siddiqui had served as a senior consultant in customer relationship management at IBM Business Consulting in Toronto and also authored the first global study on the environmental purchasing of wood and paper products.[42]

"Yalmaz's role at Office Depot reinforces our commitment to superior environmental performance," Odland announced. "He comes to us with a very market-oriented view of environmental issues and will help us deliver the most comprehensive and customer-focused environmental program in the office products industry."[43]

In addition to furthering the company's environmental goals, Siddiqui oversees its five-year Forest & Biodiversity Conservation Alliance, which develops standards and tools for forest and biodiversity conservation around the world. As part of the alliance, Office Depot partnered with three highly respected conservation organizations: NatureServe, Conservation International, and The Nature Conservancy.

As in past years, the company's environmental stewardship continued to earn awards. In April 2005, Office Depot received the Outstanding Retailer Award from the International Council of Shopping Centers and the Environmental Protection Agency for its "outstanding efforts" at helping to conserve the environment.[44]

Project Streamline

One of Odland's initiatives, "Project Streamline," aimed at "implementing a culture of thrift." Odland believed that Office Depot needed more discipline with the ways it spent money, so he encouraged the Executive Committee and the Officer Coalition to begin a corporate-wide review of the company's operations to search for inefficiencies and ways to lower costs.[45] Mark Holifield served as the executive sponsor of Project Streamline, though all company officers were in charge of analyzing their own areas for ways to improve the bottom line through better cost discipline.

"Sometimes when people hear the term 'cost reduction,' they automatically think of layoffs and massive job losses," said Joe Buckley, vice president of procurement, who joined Office Depot in 2002. "Project Streamline isn't about that. It's about taking a look at everything around us and asking

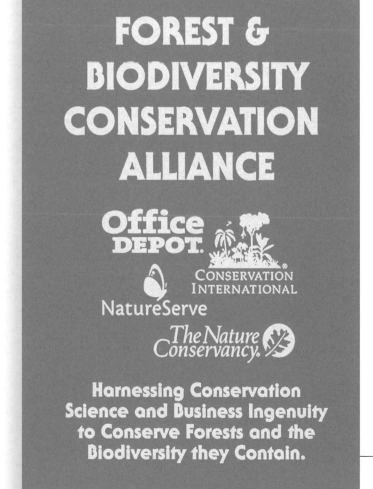

As another example of Office Depot's leadership in addressing conservation issues within the supply chain, the company collaborated on a $2.2 million agreement with NatureServe, Conservation International, and The Nature Conservancy to form the Forest & Biodiversity Conservation Alliance.

NASCAR SPONSORSHIP

FOR YEARS, MUCH OF OFFICE DEPOT'S marketing was focused on brand awareness. Besides the Olympics, Office Depot sponsored 26 different sports teams around the world, and its name was featured on the Office Depot Center arena in Sunrise, Florida.

"We had a very good plan for brand awareness, but as the company started to shift, and metrics started to become more important, we realized we wanted to focus our sponsorship dollars so as to better track our return on investment," said Tony Ueber, senior vice president of marketing strategy. "We wanted a program that was more national in scope so that we could execute one program coast to coast."[1]

To that end, Office Depot relinquished its naming rights to the arena in South Florida and discontinued its sponsorship of the Olympics.

Instead, in January 2005, Office Depot became the first "official office products partner" of NASCAR.[2]

When Office Depot sponsored the Olympics, it received marketing exposure for only a few months every two years. NASCAR, however, provided Office Depot with a much broader marketing platform since the stock car season lasted for 10 months of the year. Moreover, NASCAR had grown in popularity, especially among women (who made most of the buying decisions for office supplies) and small business owners, two of the company's target constituencies. Office Depot conducted a survey of NASCAR fans and concluded that if it sponsored NASCAR, more than 44 percent of people shopping at competitors' stores would switch to Office Depot as their office supply store of choice.[3]

This page and opposite: In 2005, Office Depot became the primary sponsor for Roush Racing driver Carl Edwards. Driving the Office Depot No. 99 Ford Taurus, Edwards placed third in the Nextel Cup. For the 2006 racing season, Edwards drove the Office Depot No. 99 Ford Fusion (below). *(Photo left: Image by Action Sports Photography Inc./ Matthew T. Thacker.)*

"NASCAR has a 75 million fan base that actively supports the sponsors of the sport," said Ueber. "It's really hard to argue with the numbers."[4]

Chuck Rubin, then-executive vice president and chief merchandising/marketing officer, said the company had conducted a thorough analysis of sponsorship opportunities before settling on NASCAR. "NASCAR's increasing popularity and passionate, loyal following give us an opportunity to target not only the small business community that makes up much of the fan base but also NASCAR's powerful team of marketing sponsors."[5]

In addition to the multiyear agreement with NASCAR, Office Depot became the primary sponsor for Roush Racing driver Carl Edwards, who drove the Office Depot No. 99 Ford Taurus in the 2005 racing season. (For 2006, Edwards drove the Office Depot No. 99 Ford Fusion.) Though Edwards was a rookie, his name carried a lot of weight in racing circles. Personable as well as talented, he was fast becoming a favorite among NASCAR fans. Moreover, *People* magazine named him one of its "50 Hottest Bachelors,"[6] and the National PTA named him an Ambassador for Youth for his dedication to promoting family nutrition and wellness and encouraging children to excel in school.[7]

"Carl embodies the kind of work ethic and attitude and team spirit that everybody within Office Depot exhibits as well," said Rubin.[8]

In addition, the NASCAR sponsorship allowed Office Depot to feature NASCAR in its advertising and promotions. One very popular promotion offered small businesses a chance to become the "Official Small Business of NASCAR." The partnership also meant Office Depot could advertise with signs on the racetrack and reserve commercial spots during NASCAR race telecasts.[9]

Office Depot celebrated the partnership by holding a private tailgate party at its headquarters, where more than 2,000 associates were invited to meet Edwards.[10]

With his modest demeanor and celebratory signature back flip from his car's window frame, Edwards made Office Depot proud. For the 2005 racing season, he finished third in the Nextel Cup. He was also named the Busch Series Rookie of the Year.[11]

Office Depot made NASCAR proud, as well. The company was awarded NASCAR's Marketing Excellence Award for 2005. According to Brian Levine, senior director of public relations and internal communications, Office Depot's sweepstakes aimed at small businesses, and its joint promotions with other NASCAR sponsors did an excellent job of boosting brand awareness and increasing NASCAR sales.[12]

Mark Holifield joined Office Depot in 1994 as director of transportation and was promoted to senior vice president of supply chain in 1997. He was later named executive vice president of supply chain with responsibility for all distribution, transportation, inventory management, and supply chain development activities in North America. He left Office Depot in June 2006. *(Photo courtesy of Paul Morris/Morphoto, Inc.)*

ourselves, 'Do we need it to run the business?' And if we need it, can we buy it better, or can we utilize it in a different way?"[46]

Buckley recalled how Project Streamline helped Office Depot reduce its annual cellular phone bill by $600,000. The company had distributed about 1,600 cell phones among delivery drivers and people who worked in the warehouses. But "when we looked at who those cell phones were assigned to, we discovered that we were paying for 300 rate plans for people who were no longer with the company," he said. "Then we dove into the spending aspect and realized we had 85 different programs with 25 different accounts. We pooled all of the bills into two rate plans and managed the pooled minutes, and all of a sudden, something that was costing us $1.4 million a year now costs us $800,000."[47]

Reducing the cell phone bill was just one example of how Project Streamline saved Office Depot millions of dollars a year. Throughout the corporation, Office Depot associates, inspired by the new shared leadership approach, searched for ways to cut costs or perform tasks more efficiently. The company even installed more energy-efficient light fixtures in the stores and upgraded its energy-monitoring systems so it could adjust store electricity usage in real time. It worked out more favorable lease agreements for the stores' cash registers and copy center equipment, and it ended multiyear contracts, which invariably cost the company more than if contracts were re-bid every year. The company also switched the store's broadband communications from frame relay to DSL, which was less expensive.[48]

One of Office Depot's seemingly negligible ideas for cutting costs quickly became legendary for its simplicity and ingenuity. It involved the register receipts in the stores. Odland explained:

When I went into the stores, I bought a couple of pens, and I got a receipt that was a foot long. I asked why we needed to use so much paper for a register receipt, and I was told we needed the return policy on the receipt. I said to post the return policy somewhere else. I wanted every receipt in the store to be six inches long. And you know what? By shortening the receipts and using a lighter-weight paper, we're saving a million dollars a year in register tape.[49]

Buckley explained that Project Streamline was a mindset. "We have to educate our associates about this culture of thrift so that when it comes time to take a business trip, they're asking themselves, 'Can I do this by conference call instead?' Or when a customer goes through the checkout line, the clerk doesn't automatically grab the large bag if it's a box of pens the customer bought. They grab the small bag that costs a half-cent less."[50]

In just a few months, Project Streamline successfully cut millions from the company's expenditures. "The savings from any individual program isn't a home run," Odland explained. "They represent the singles and the doubles that will add up to substantial cost savings over time."[51]

Or as Neil Austrian noted, "These substantial cost savings are a result of hundreds of initiatives that have somebody's name next to them. Even if the initiative only takes out $200,000, somebody's name is attached to it, and there is accountability."[52]

North American Retail

With newly formed vision and values statements under shared leadership, Office Depot was ready to take care of business. In May 2005, at the company's first shareholders' meeting with Odland at the helm, it was reiterated that the North American Retail Division was the company's first priority. "We hope to improve store productivity while continuing our store build-out program," Odland said.[53]

Though skeptics wondered if any market share remained for more office supply superstores in the United States, Odland pointed out that office supply superstores had less than a 10 percent share of the $311 billion U.S. market for office supplies and services. Odland aimed to open 100 stores a year, but—unlike the period after the scuttled merger with Staples—the company would take meticulous care in finding the best locations for those 100 stores.[54]

In 2005, Office Depot did, indeed, open 100 new stores, all of which were M2 designs. For 2006, with a new real estate and construction team led by Senior Vice President Rob Koch, the company planned to open an additional 100 M2 stores and continue its conversion of existing stores to the M2 design.[55] By then, the original M2 design, after continual fine-tuning, had evolved into the M2 Maximized store—"the best of all the M2 teachings"—according to George Hill, senior vice president of operations.[56]

The M2 Maximized store had evolved largely through the leadership and expertise of Chuck Rubin. Customers in M2 Maximized stores could walk freely through the center of the stores without the hassle of shelving in their path. Technology products were placed on lower shelves for added visibility, and the technology area itself

Above: George Hill joined Office Depot in 2004 as a regional vice president for North American Retail. He was later promoted to senior vice president. *(Photo courtesy of Paul Morris/Morphoto, Inc.)*

Below: Sales of ink and toner supplies are robust at Office Depot, thanks in part to the company's knowledgeable and friendly salespeople.

The technology areas of Office Depot's M2 stores are staffed with knowledgeable sales associates who specialize in helping customers find the specific products that fit their needs and budget.

was no longer cordoned off, providing better access. In addition, the M2 Maximized stores featured a "strike zone" near the center, where popular items were located.

Part of the M2's fine-tuning involved a more varied product assortment that better met customers' needs and budgets, which meant offering more Office Depot private-brand merchandise. Private-brand products gave customers high-quality merchandise while also producing higher profit margins for Office Depot because they cut out the middle man. In addition, private brands required little or no advertising expense. Under Rubin's leadership, the company's private-brand sector reached 15 percent of North American sales in 2004, up 2 percent from the year before.[57] Odland desired to see that figure grow to 20 percent by the end of 2005.[58]

In addition, performance at the company's retail stores benefited from the corporate-wide belt-tightening, which included not only the trimming of register receipts and the use of more energy-efficient light fixtures. It also forced Office Depot to close 16 stores in North America in 2005.[59]

1,000 Stores

Even as it shut down several underperforming stores, Office Depot continued to celebrate the opening of new ones. No celebration was as large or as impressive as the grand opening of its 1,000th North American store in Countryside, Illinois, a suburb of Chicago. The June 2005 celebration included many special events and relayed the message that Office Depot was healthy and growing.[60]

As usual when Office Depot opened a new store, local charities benefited. For its 1,000th store grand opening, Office Depot donated $125,000 to Feed the Children and gave in-kind donations of $1,000 each to the Helping Hand Rehabilitation Center, America's Second Harvest/Chicago Food Depository, Chicago Youth Programs, and the

National Arbor Day Foundation. Moreover, Office Depot planted numerous trees and seedlings in the Chicago area, which the National Arbor Day Foundation had donated. The company also gave out 1,000 backpacks filled with school supplies to two local children's nonprofit organizations, hosted a food drive at its 40-plus Chicago-area stores, and helped serve hot lunches to children at Beatrice Caffrey Youth Services in Hyde Park.[61]

"Office Depot's charitable mission is to enhance the quality of life in the communities in which we live and work," said John Mullen, regional vice president, who oversaw the company's festivities in Countryside. "Therefore, it gives us a great sense of pride to be able to leverage our 1,000th store as another opportunity to support organizations that make such a meaningful difference in the lives of children.[62]

The 1,000th store was certainly a milestone, but Office Depot didn't stop there. By April 2006, the North American Retail Division boasted 1,049 stores, with plans to continue expanding both in the United States and Canada. Also, Office Depot had racked up nine straight quarters of positive retail comp sales after 16 consecutive quarters of negative comps. Clearly, the company's efforts to cut costs, improve merchandising, and enliven marketing were on the right track.

Business Solutions

The North American Business Solutions Division (BSD) continued to improve operating efficiencies, which resulted in significant cost savings. During 2005, the company closed two of its warehouses in the United States and consolidated some of its call centers. Also, instead of offering two separate catalogs in the United States—one for Viking and one for Office Depot—the company consolidated them under the Office Depot brand.[63]

As it had since the 1990s, Office Depot continued to lead the office products industry in e-commerce. In 2005, Office Depot chalked up $3.8 billion in online sales, about 25 percent of the company's

In June 2005, Office Depot celebrated the grand opening of its 1,000th store in Countryside, Illinois.

HELPING HURRICANE VICTIMS

THE 2005 HURRICANE SEASON MADE history as one of the most active and destructive seasons of all time due to the devastation wreaked by Hurricanes Katrina, Rita, Wilma, and a record number of other tropical events.

Based in the heart of hurricane territory, Office Depot anxiously monitored the path of each storm. Even though Hurricane Katrina was only a Category 1 storm when it approached the company's headquarters, Office Depot followed through with a proactive response. After driving cautiously through the storm on his way home from the airport, CEO Steve Odland watched from his television as the hurricane ambled toward the Gulf Coast.

"I remember thinking, 'This is going to be enormously disastrous,'" he said. " 'Somebody needs to do something here.'"[1]

So Odland acted upon his intuition. Even before Hurricane Katrina reached New Orleans and the Mississippi Valley, Office Depot pledged $1 million to the Red Cross to aid in relief efforts and issued a challenge to the other CEOs of the Business Roundtable to match that pledge.[2]

To help victims of Hurricane Katrina, Office Depot donated more than $18 million in cash and in-kind donations to the American Red Cross and other organizations.

revenue. According to *Internet Retailer*, Office Depot was the second-largest e-tailer behind Amazon based on 2005 sales.[64]

Even though Office Depot was a leader in providing business-to-business solutions, Monica Luechtefeld warned that Office Depot would have to continually raise the bar. "What was breakthrough and leading-edge eight months ago is old news now," she said. "It's been replicated, and now it's expected by the customers."[65]

Looking to the future, the Business Solutions Division sought new ways to grow its market share. "We need to penetrate new business and retain those new customers," said David Trudnowski, senior vice president of BSD sales. "We continue to look at different product categories to complement our basic office supply offerings. We might, for example, introduce promotional product opportunities or print and

copy opportunities. We're also expanding our furniture services—everything from designing services to complex furniture installations. And we continue to grow the large private and public sector portion of our business such as serving school districts, higher education, and state, federal, and local governments."[66]

BSD also planned to further refine its direct marketing capabilities. "We lost track of the fact that we need to continue investing in our sales force," said Cindy Campbell, executive vice president of Business Solutions. We reduced our sales force at a time when the industry was growing. Meanwhile, our competition continued to invest in their sales force, so we found ourselves behind."[67]

Even so, BSD showed robust growth, fiscal quarter after fiscal quarter. For the fourth quarter of

"We have many associates and facilities in harm's way tonight, and thousands of our customers will suffer greatly as a result of this storm," Odland said on the night he issued the challenge. "We want to make a substantial pledge of assistance in advance of the devastation that we recognize is coming. And we want to encourage other companies that have significant business assets in this area—as well as those who do not—to join us in a massive relief effort for our fellow citizens who will be suffering in the days and weeks ahead."[3]

Odland's challenge resulted in 100 corporations donating more than $300 million in cash and in-kind donations.[4]

Four of the company's 10 stores in the New Orleans area successfully dodged the worst of the storm's effects. Though the stores lost power, Office Depot brought in generators and used the stores as staging areas where Office Depot employees and other local residents could pick up care packages and receive aid. Office Depot worked with FEMA and local agencies to help local businesses restore operations and provide aid to affected residents of the Gulf Coast region. Moreover, Office Depot donated the contents of its five hardest-hit stores to the city of New Orleans.[5]

Office Depot also donated water, batteries, and office and school supplies through its partnership with Feed the Children, and gave 1,000 backpacks filled with school supplies to local children. In addition, the Office Depot Disaster Relief Foundation matched employees' contributions. The company's total cash and in-kind donations for relief after Hurricane Katrina exceeded $18 million.[6]

When Hurricane Wilma struck South Florida shortly thereafter, it was the most intense storm ever recorded in the Atlantic basin. It passed directly over the company's home turf, affecting not only operations at Office Depot headquarters but also at about 50 of the company's Florida stores. For weeks, much of the area remained without power. Office Depot brought generators to stores that suffered the least amount of damage, and those stores accomplished everything possible to help local residents, inviting people to charge their cell phone or laptop batteries. Mike Silvers, a store manager in North Miami Beach, enabled Wi-Fi capability in his store so people could connect to the Internet. When Office Depot headquarters heard about Silvers' inventiveness, the company set up network wireless technology at 40 other stores in areas affected by the hurricane.[7]

2005, the division's sales rose 11 percent,[68] and sales increased 8 percent in the first quarter of 2006 compared to the same period in 2005, the first increase in at least two years.[69]

Overall, Campbell was optimistic about the division's capabilities. "Looking at the future is really exciting," she said. "We have the cash generation in place, and we're fleet of foot because we don't need a lot of infrastructure. There are so many opportunities for us to grow and invest."[70]

The International Division

Even though the International Division had carried Office Depot for many years, it was not faring as well as North American Retail or BSD. For the third and fourth quarters of 2005, sales in the International Division actually declined. More strin-

gent competition, less favorable exchange rates, and a depressed economy contributed to the drop, but the International Division experienced other challenges that required attention.[71]

"It may take us some time to stabilize the situation [in International]," Odland told the press. "We need to reignite profitable growth in Europe and over time increase our geographical reach."[72]

Reigniting profitable growth meant closing underperforming stores. The company's retail stores in Spain had posted losses since they opened in 2003, so Office Depot made the tough decision to exit the retail business in Spain, closing its six stores in that country. Office Depot retained its mail-order and contract businesses in Spain through the Viking and Guilbert subsidiaries.[73]

Above: The Office Depot–International headquarters is located in the city of Venlo in the Limburg province of the Netherlands.

Right: Jim Walker, senior vice president, Finance International, played an integral role in the establishment of the International Division. A seven-year veteran of the company, Walker passed away unexpectedly in July 2006 after being involved in a motorcycle accident.

Below: Office Depot stores in France are fully owned by the company. Some, like this one in Paris, are located in the heart of the city.

Charlie Brown, president of Office Depot–International, explained why the stores in Spain had not performed well. "Our people there were from Viking, whose expertise was in mail-order, so they had very little expertise in retail," he said. "We knew our quickest path to profitability was to focus on our core businesses, which were contract and mail-order."[74]

Office Depot also closed a handful of under-performing stores in France and had plans to close six call centers in that country. To further cut costs, the company intended to outsource its call center in Japan.[75]

Brown also worked on improving the business from the Guilbert acquisition, which had thus far produced disappointing results.[76] The company's leaders pulled together to streamline processes and identify a number of areas where efficiency required improvement.[77] Also, Office Depot decided to phase out the Guilbert brand in Europe, just as it had phased out the Viking brand in the United States.

Office Depot, however, took the offensive in its

international operations. In 2006, the company acquired a majority interest in South Korea's Best Office Company, a leading office supply provider. With annual revenues of more than $44 million, Best Office had a delivery sales network and more than 70 retail stores.[78]

"Acquiring a majority ownership of Best Office will strengthen Office Depot's global presence in a rapidly growing area of the world and extend our ability to service our global customers," Odland told a group of analysts and investors.[79]

Office Depot also increased its ownership in Office Depot–Israel, from 22 percent to 51 percent, giving Office Depot a controlling interest. Office Depot–Israel operated 33 stores in Israel and had annual income of more than $100 million.[80]

After buying into Best Office in South Korea, Office Depot–International had delivery and catalog operations in 21 countries outside of the United States and Canada. It owned a total of 70 Office Depot stores in France, Japan, and Hungary and operated more than 200 other international stores under joint venture or licensing agreements. It also maintained 30-plus public Web sites outside of the United States.

Above: In 2006, Office Depot had 24 wholly owned stores in Japan. Due to the country's dense population, most of the stores do not have their own parking lots, so shoppers tend to buy only what they can carry—one reason delivery service is so important in Japan.

Below: In the spring of 2006, Office Depot gained majority ownership of its 22 stores in Israel.

In May 2006, Office Depot–Mexico opened its 100th store in Mexico City. By June 2006, Office Depot operated 102 stores in Mexico under a joint venture agreement with Grupo Gigante.

By the first quarter of 2006, the company's efforts to strengthen the International Division had shown promising results. First-quarter sales were up 2 percent in local currencies compared to the same period in 2005. Also, comparable store sales in Europe grew by 4 percent, and the division's direct and contract sales showed increases as well.[81]

Office Depot's future plans included expanding its international footprint, and it is considering expansion in South America and Asia in an effort to transform into a truly global company.

Magellan and Project Simplify

Magellan, the long-term project that aimed at improving the company's supply chain systems, continued moving forward and received high praise throughout the company. Since Office Depot began implementing it in 2003, the Magellan Project had improved the accuracy of inventory forecasts, financial planning, and pricing data.[82] Moreover, in the spring of 2006, Office Depot reported 20 consecutive quarters (more than five years) of improved cost performance in its supply chain. "That performance came on top of higher fuel prices, higher transportation costs, and higher benefits costs," said Mark Holifield, former executive vice president of supply chain. "We're proud of that."[83]

Though the Magellan Project was a resounding success, Odland recognized that Office Depot needed more than a world-class merchandising and supply chain system; it needed a single global platform that integrated all of the company's systems. The information technology (IT) program that Office Depot had built in the 1990s had worked well, but as Office Depot expanded into new areas of business, the amount of computer programming and resources required to maintain the system grew increasingly cumbersome. The complexity of the system was, in fact, slowing the company down.[84]

Thus, Office Depot began a new initiative dubbed "Project Simplify."

"Project Simplify was more than an IT project," said Tim Toews, senior vice president and chief information officer. "It was designed to simplify, globalize, consolidate, and standardize business processes and practices, and support them with common applications and platforms. It was based on a global Oracle ERP system that replaced the many separate platforms Office Depot utilized to run the entire corporation. Aiming to narrow the company's 19 different warehouse management systems to one, the project also involved using software packages "out of the box" rather than altering them to meet the company's specific business needs. As Gerry Lebel, manager of international IT system development who joined Office Depot in 1986, described it, Project Simplify is "one global solution that we can maneuver quickly to fit either a new acquisition or to make it more global."[85]

Project Simplify promised to reduce system administration costs and enable easier integration of future acquisitions. In the past, each time Office Depot acquired a company, it brought in that com-pany's IT processes. Once Project Simplify was complete, the IT systems of future acquisitions would transmit to the single global application system.

Office Depot aimed to complete Project Simplify by the end of 2007. Bruce Fong, a system administrator who had been with Office Depot since 1986 and was heavily involved in the technicalities of the project, likened the transition to "changing a tire on a moving car," but said the process, thus far, was running smoothly.[86]

Corporate Giving

Odland remained equally as dedicated to corporate philanthropy as the company's past CEOs. In March 2005, Office Depot hosted a two-day conference called "Best Practices in Employee Giving," which was created by Charities @ Work as an opportunity for businesses to share ideas about

Office Depot–Europe has a number of distribution and call centers, such as this combined facility in Puurs, Belgium.

corporate giving and learn new ways to give back to communities.[87]

Office Depot also contributed to higher education, donating $4.5 million to three South Florida universities and two nonprofit organizations that promoted opportunities for minority students. Collectively, the donations represented the largest corporate gift in the company's history.

"Office Depot has an unwavering commitment to education and the community," Odland announced. "We clearly understand the critical role that education plays in our society and our lives. Universities, in particular, are engines of economic development and entrepreneurship in their communities, our nation, and the world.

They are instrumental in developing the business leaders of the future and provide unmistakable value to our customers, as well as to our current and future associates."[88]

Also, Office Depot continued to help students and teachers during the back-to-school shopping season with its signature National Backpack Program, "5% Back-to-Schools" program, Star Teacher program, and teacher appreciation breakfasts.

The accolades for outstanding corporate philanthropy continued to roll in, too. In 2005, *Business Ethics* magazine named Office Depot one of the best corporate citizens in the United States, and in 2006—for the third consecutive year—the Center for Companies That Care named Office Depot to its "Companies That Care" Honor Roll.

Breakthrough Results

By the end of the second quarter of 2005, Office Depot's fortunes had clearly turned around, thanks to the united efforts of Odland, the Executive

Supporting children's education, Office Depot provides backpacks filled with school supplies to at-risk children all around the world. It also provides millions of dollars in credit to schools for the purchase of school supplies.

Office Depot has long supported children's education by hosting teacher appreciation breakfasts and offering teachers discounts on school supplies.

Committee, the Officer Coalition, and the tens of thousands of Office Depot associates around the globe. Just four months after Odland took over the top spot at Office Depot, the company produced higher-than-expected earnings. Total sales were up 6 percent, and North American comp sales increased 3 percent. In fact, all three of the company's divisions performed well that quarter, contributing to a 26 percent rise in earnings.[89]

For the fourth quarter of 2005, earnings at Office Depot actually doubled, thanks to higher revenue and lower costs. Comparable store sales for the North American Retail Division were up 5 percent, due in part to robust technology sales during the holiday season.[90] Year-end results for 2005 showed a 3 percent gain in North American comp store sales, with total earnings for the year reaching $14.3 billion, a 5 percent increase over 2004.[91]

The value of Office Depot shares had also risen 80 percent over the previous year, prompting

CNNMoney.com to name Office Depot among its hottest stocks of 2005. "After meeting or only slightly beating earnings estimates in 2004, the company trounced them in the first and third quarters of 2005," the online publication noted.[92]

Investors were clearly pleased with the company's performance. Throughout the early weeks of 2006, the company's share price rose steadily. In February 2006, Office Depot shares closed at a 52-week high of $34.84, a significant jump compared to their $18.58 value in April 2005.[93] By late March,

Above: The North American Business Solutions Division delivers office products and services to more than two million customers a year. Customers can place orders through the Office Depot catalog, through Office Depot salespeople or account executives, or on one of the company's Web sites.

Right: Office Depot store managers are arguably the most important element of the company's North American Retail Division. The store manager influences positive interaction among associates and customers. District and regional managers are chosen from among a pool of experienced store managers.

the stock closed at $37.91.[94] After the company reported first-quarter results for 2006, the value of Office Depot shares topped $40.[95]

Perhaps more importantly than Wall Street's approval, Office Depot associates had regained the sense of pride they previously felt about working for one of the great companies of the world. Office Depot was no longer racing to catch up with its competitors; instead, it plowed ahead at a steady, healthy pace. The board of directors, the Executive Committee, the

Officer Coalition, and associates at all levels of the company celebrated the rejuvenation.

"This organization feels they can win, and I'm very confident that they *are* going to win," said Scott Hedrick, who has served on Office Depot's board of directors since the company acquired Office Club in 1991.[96]

According to George Hill, senior vice president of operations, "We now have every business unit on the same page, and that was a huge transformation. Now we are able to make smart, quick decisions based on what is good for the entire company."[97]

Henry Sauls, director of merchandising operations, agreed. "We brought back a lot of our hope. We were like a train trying to get over the hill. We would get the momentum, and all of a sudden we would lose focus and roll backwards. We now believe we have the sustained momentum, and we're doing it through the people."[98]

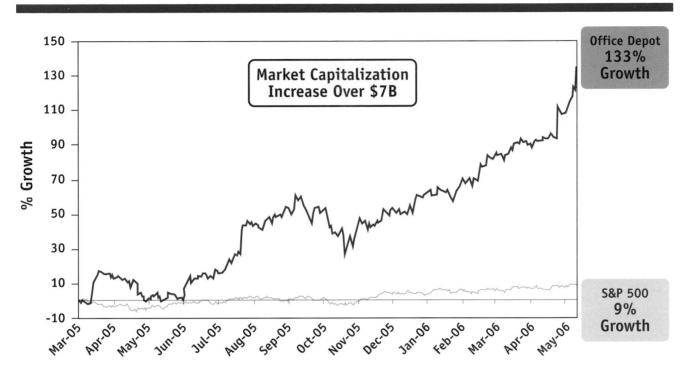

Office Depot Share Price Growth vs. S&P 500

Market Capitalization Increase Over $7B

Office Depot **133% Growth**

S&P 500 **9% Growth**

Office Depot displayed this chart at a shareholder's meeting in the spring of 2006, showing how the company's share price has vastly outperformed the S&P 500.

Since Office Depot was, once again, on a healthy track, company officials also decided it was time to move from the crowded Delray Beach location to a new headquarters in nearby Boca Raton, Florida.[99]

"Our company is clearly headed in the right strategic direction," Odland told a group of shareholders and analysts in the spring of 2006.

"We are pleased with the results that we have achieved in 2005, but we are mindful of the significant work that still must be accomplished to drive continuous improvement in those operating results."[100]

Office Depot had proven that the company can drive that continuous improvement and move to the next level. "We have three constituencies in our company," said Odland. "I remember them by my title: C-E-O—Customers, Employees, and Owners. That's who we're trying to take care of; that's who we're trying to perform for; that's the group for whom we're trying to provide solutions."[101]

NOTES TO SOURCES

Chapter One: Birth of a Notion

1. "Home Centers in the Making; Home Owner's Warehouse," *Chilton's Hardware Age*, February 1983, 49.
2. Ibid.
3. James M. Cory, "Warehouse Retailing: Tough Competition; Part I," *Chilton's Hardware Age*, February 1984, 71.
4. Annie Frye, interview by Jeffrey L. Rodengen, audio recording, 12 January 2006, Write Stuff Enterprises.
5. "Home Centers in the Making; Home Owner's Warehouse."
6. Ibid.
7. Ibid.
8. "Warehouse Retailing: Tough Competition; Part I."
9. Barry Goldstein, interview by Jeffrey L. Rodengen, audio recording, 23 March 2006, Write Stuff Enterprises.
10. David Fuente, interview by Jeffrey L. Rodengen, audio recording, 9 March 2006, Write Stuff Enterprises.
11. Robert Douglas, "Office Depot's Roots Remain Here," *Palm Beach Post*, 13 September 1996, 1D.
12. Annie Frye, interview.
13. Ibid.
14. Ibid.
15. Ibid.
16. Zina Moukheiber, "A Lousy Day for Golf," *Forbes*, 9 May 1994, 60.
17. Denise Deveau, "Office Depot Excels in Warehouse Retailing," *Computer Dealer News*, 18 October 1993, 18.
18. Unnamed Office Depot newsletter, 18 March 1988, 3.
19. Steve Frandzel, "A Bullet-Proof Balance Sheet," *Business Atlanta*, December 1989, 30.
20. Jack Kopkin, interview by Jeffrey L. Rodengen, audio recording, 17 April 2006, Write Stuff Enterprises.
21. Office Depot 1988 annual report, 11.
22. David Sedore, "Office Depot Going Public," *South Florida Business Journal*, 2 May 1988, 1.
23. "A Lousy Day for Golf."
24. Barry Goldstein, interview.
25. Elaine Walker, "New Era at Office Depot," *Miami Herald*, 19 July 2000, 1C.
26. Michael Selz, "Tough Day at the Office," *Florida Trend*, November 1990, 28.
27. Michael Myers, interview by Jeffrey L. Rodengen, audio recording, 6 March 2006, Write Stuff Enterprises.
28. Charlie Brown, interview by Jeffrey L. Rodengen, audio recording, 30 November 2005, Write Stuff Enterprises.
29. "Tough Day at the Office."
30. Michael Myers, interview.
31. "A Lousy Day for Golf."
32. Ibid.
33. Robert McCabe, "Giving At the Office: Office Depot Penciled in David Fuente as CEO, and He's Led It to Superstore Status," *Sun-Sentinel*, 30 January 1994, 1D.
34. Brian Benge, interview by Jeffrey L. Rodengen, audio recording, 11 January 2006, Write Stuff Enterprises.
35. David Fuente, interview.
36. "Giving At the Office ... ."
37. John Deaton, interview by Jeffrey L. Rodengen, audio recording, 30 November 2005, Write Stuff Enterprises.
38. Ibid.
39. "Introducing the New Management Team," *Office Depot Ink*, Winter 1996, 6.
40. "A Lousy Day for Golf."
41. "Office Depot Going Public."
42. James A. McConville, "Solid Growth Keeps Office Depot Firm on Track," *HFD—The Weekly Home Furnishings Newspaper*, 12 November 1990, 120.
43. Unnamed Office Depot newsletter, March 1988, 1.
44. Barry Goldstein, interview.
45. Ibid.
46. David Fuente, interview.
47. "A Lousy Day for Golf."
48. Ibid.
49. Udayan Gupta, *Wall Street Journal*, 13 June 1988, section 1, column 1, 35.

Chapter Two: A National Player

1. James A. McConville, "Solid Growth Keeps Office Depot Firm on Track," *HFD–The Home Furnishings Newspaper*, 12 November 1990, 120.
2. John Taylor, *Circus of Ambition: The Culture of Wealth and Power in the Eighties* (Warner Books, 1989); Vincent Virga, *The Eighties: Images of America* (HarperCollins, 1992).
3. Mark Albright, "Pencil Pushers: Workplace, Office Depot Battle for Tampa Bay's Office Supplies Business," *St. Petersburg Times*, 24 September 1989, 1I.
4. Ibid.
5. Office Depot 1990 annual report, Form 10-K, 1-2.
6. Brian Benge, interview by Jeffrey L. Rodengen, audio recording, 11 January 2006, Write Stuff Enterprises.
7. George Ballou, interview by Jeffrey L. Rodengen, audio recording, 16 March 2006, Write Stuff Enterprises.
8. Jan Luken, "Office Depot Looking to Open Another Store," *The Business Journal–Jacksonville*, 18 December 1989, 19.
9. Annie Frye, interview by Jeffrey L. Rodengen, audio recording, 12 January 2006, Write Stuff Enterprises.
10. Stacey Butler, "Office Depot, Staples to Take on Area Office Suppliers," *Baltimore Business Journal*, 27 November 1989, 3.
11. David Fuente, interview by Jeffrey L. Rodengen, audio recording, 9 March 2006, Write Stuff Enterprises.
12. Paula Randolph, interview by Jeffrey L. Rodengen, audio recording, 17 March 2006, Write Stuff Enterprises.
13. Office Depot 1989 annual report, 3.
14. "Office Depot, Staples to Take on Area Office Suppliers."
15. "Office Depot Looking to Open Another Store."

16. Chip Ricketts, "Office Depot Says Three's No Crowd," *Dallas Business Journal*, 16 October 1989, 1A.
17. Ibid.
18. "Office Depot, Staples to Take on Area Office Suppliers."
19. Kim Gorman, interview by Jeffrey L. Rodengen, audio recording, 23 March 2006, Write Stuff Enterprises.
20. Larry Brock, interview by Jeffrey L. Rodengen, audio recording, 11 January 2006, Write Stuff Enterprises.
21. David Fuente, interview.
22. Kissel Goldman, interview by Jeffrey L. Rodengen, audio recording, 27 March 2006, Write Stuff Enterprises.
23. Robert McCabe, "Giving At the Office: Office Depot Penciled in David Fuente as CEO, and He's Led It to Superstore Status," *Sun-Sentinel*, 30 January 1994, 1D.
24. *Highlighter*, Summer 1991, 1-3.
25. Mark Albright, "President Quits at Office Depot," *St. Petersburg Times*, 13 February 1990, 2E.
26. Michael Selz, "Tough Days at the Office," *Florida Trend*, November 1990, 28.
27. "Office Depot President Resigns," PR Newswire, 12 February 1990.
28. "Office Depot to Open Nine Stores," PR Newswire, 29 May 1990.
29. Jack Kopkin, interview by Jeffrey L. Rodengen, audio recording, 23 April 2006, Write Stuff Enterprises.
30. Office Depot 1991 annual report, 2.
31. Mark Begelman, interview by Jeffrey L. Rodengen, audio recording, 3 May 2006, Write Stuff Enterprises.
32. Ellie Lingner, "Boss by Day, Rocker by Night: Office Depot is Run by an Eraserhead," *Palm Beach Post*, 29 January 1995, 1E.
33. Brian Benge, interview.
34. Bill Snyder, interview by Jeffrey L. Rodengen, audio recording, 11 January 2006, Write Stuff Enterprises.
35. Mark Begelman, interview.
36. James A. McConville, "Pending Merger Could Give Office Depot California Clout," *HFD–The Weekly Home Furnishings Newspaper*, 7 January 1991, 168.
37. Scott Hedrick, interview by Jeffrey L. Rodengen, audio recording, 15 June 2006, Write Stuff Enterprises.
38. "Office Club Stores to Become Office Depots," PR Newswire, 20 April 1992.
39. "Pending Merger Could Give Office Depot California Clout."
40. Jean Dimeo, "Office Club to Become Unit of Office Depot," *Dallas Times Herald*, 21 December 1990.
41. Associated Press, "Office Supply Chain Agrees to be Acquired by Office Depot," Associated Press, 21 December 1990.
42. Beth Reinhard, "Office Depot Pays $16 million for Headquarters," *Palm Beach Post*, 23 February 1994, 5B.
43. Kieran Doherty, "Boca's Office Depot Remains an Enticing Stock," *South Florida Business Journal*, 18 November 1991, 21.
44. John Waggoner, "Office Depot: Investor Sees Boon in Hard Times," *USA Today*, 11 October 1993, 3B.

45. Office Depot 1989 annual report, 4.
46. *Office Depot Ink*, Spring 1992, 7.
47. "Office Depot Pays $16 million for Headquarters."

Chapter Three: Global Expansion

1. Office Depot 1995 annual report, 3.
2. James A. McConville, "Florida Retail Showdown Looms," *HFD–The Weekly Home Furnishings Newspaper*, 9 March 1992, 73.
3. Lynn Graebner, "Office Depot to Open Rancho Cordova Store," *The Business Journal*–Sacramento, 29 March 1993, 8.
4. Ibid.
5. "Office Supply Shakes Out, Leaving Big 3," *HFD–The Weekly Home Furnishings Newspaper*, 4 October 1993, 176.
6. Office Depot 1995 annual report, 20.
7. Angel Alverde, interview by Jeffrey L. Rodengen, audio recording, 25 May 2006, Write Stuff Enterprises.
8. Ibid.
9. Ibid.
10. Zach Fishbein, interview by Jeffrey L. Rodengen, audio recording, 30 May 2006, Write Stuff Enterprises.
11. Ibid.
12. Elisa Williams, "Empty Stores Open Door for Office Depot Chain," *Washington Times*, 28 July 1992, D3.
13. Ibid.
14. Mark Harrington, "Office Depot to Open Large Format in New York," *Computer Retail Week*, 24 April 1995, 3.
15. David Fuente, interview by Jeffrey L. Rodengen, audio recording, 9 March 2006, Write Stuff Enterprises.
16. David Altaner, "Office Depot Looking at Internet," *Sun-Sentinel*, 24 May 1996, 3D.
17. "Office Depot Cans Furniture Plans," *Press Journal*, 28 May 1998, D1.
18. *Office Depot Ink*, Spring 1995, 11.
19. *Office Depot Ink*, Fall 1992, 1.
20. Mark Begelman, interview by Jeffrey L. Rodengen, audio recording, 3 May 2006, Write Stuff Enterprises.
21. Office Depot 1994 annual report, 12.
22. "State's Largest Road Race Comes to Orlando," PR Newswire, 13 February 1995.
23. "Office Depot Leads Launch of Windows 95®," PR Newswire, 22 August 1995.
24. Mary Wong, interview by Jeffrey L. Rodengen, audio recording, 29 November 2005, Write Stuff Enterprises.
25. "Software Support Inc. and Uptime Services," Business Wire, 1 November 1995.
26. Office Depot 1993 annual report, 10.
27. *Office Depot Ink*, Spring 1992, 1.
28. Reuters, "Sales up at Office Depot," *Sun-Sentinel*, 20 March 1994, 12G.
29. *Office Depot Ink*, Spring 1992, 1.
30. Brian Benge, interview by Jeffrey L. Rodengen, audio recording, 11 January 2006, Write Stuff Enterprises.
31. *Office Depot Ink*, Spring 1996, 1, 15.
32. *Office Depot Ink*, Spring 1992, 1.
33. Venna Tredway, interview by Jeffrey L. Rodengen, audio recording, 23 March 2006, Write Stuff Enterprises.

34. David Altaner, "Office Depot Chief Honored," *Sun-Sentinel*, 20 March 1993, 14C.
35. Robert McCabe, "Giving At the Office: Office Depot Penciled in David Fuente as CEO, and He's Led It to Superstore Status," *Sun-Sentinel*, 30 January 1994, 1D.
36. *Office Depot Ink*, Spring 1993, 1.
37. Herald Staff, "Cordis, Office Depot Crack Magazine's 100," *Miami Herald*, 23 September 1995, 1C.
38. "Giving At the Office … ."
39. Office Depot 1993 annual report, 4.
40. "Giving At the Office … ."

Chapter Three, Sidebar: "Takin' Care of Business"— The Legend Behind the Song

1. E-mail correspondence from George Bryan to Brian Levine, Office Depot, 19 January 2006.

Chapter Four: Breaking New Ground— Business Services

1. Office Depot 1994 annual report.
2. Mark Holifield, e-mail correspondence, Office Depot, 2 February 2006.
3. Tracy Kolody, "Ambitious Office Depot Eyeing Large Corporations," *Sun-Sentinel*, 13 May 1993, 1D.
4. Cindy Campbell, interview by Jeffrey L. Rodengen and Melody Maysonet, audio recording, 11 January 2006, Write Stuff Enterprises.
5. Monica Luechtefeld, interview by Jeffrey L. Rodengen, audio recording, 29 November 2005, Write Stuff Enterprises.
6. Bill Bowen, "Paper-clip Pushers Try New Tactics: Office Depot Reorganizes," *Dallas Business Journal*, 7 January 1994.
7. Office Depot 1993 annual report, 5.
8. Ibid, 17.
9. Ibid, 13.
10. Tom Stieghorst, "Office Depot Eyeing Contract Supply Market," *Sun-Sentinel*, 19 July 1993, 21A.
11. Office Depot 1994 annual report, 15.
12. Don Finefrock, "Strong Office Depot Sales Boost Earnings for Fourth Quarter," *Miami Herald*, 9 February 1994.
13. *Office Depot Ink*, Spring 1994, 1, 2.
14. "Office Depot Acquires Yorkship Press," PR Newswire, 23 February 1994.
15. "Office Depot Acquires Two Contract Stationers," Associated Press, 25 May 1994.
16. Ibid.
17. Douglas Bolton, "Kindel Cost Office Depot $36 million," *Greater Cincinnati Business Record*, 28 November 1994.
18. Jim Talley, "Office Depot Acquires Pair of Stationers," *Sun-Sentinel*, 27 August 1994, 11B.
19. Ibid.
20. Cindy Campbell, interview.
21. Monica Luechtefeld, interview.
22. David Altaner, "Office Depot Picks Boss for $1 Billion in Business," *Sun-Sentinel*, 24 June 1994, 3D.
23. Office Depot 1995 annual report, 7.

24. Ibid, 14.
25. Ibid, 1, 3, 14.
26. Ibid, 3.
27. Robert McCabe, "Giving At the Office: Office Depot Penciled in David Fuente as CEO, and He's Led It to Superstore Status," *Sun-Sentinel*, 30 January 1994, 1D.
28. Keith Newman, "How Office Depot Can Outmaneuver the Pack," *Computer Retail Week*, 27 February 1995, 15.
29. Ibid.
30. Dale K. DuPont, "Office Depot President Quits," *Miami Herald*, 26 May 1995, 1C.
31. Alina Matas, "Former Office Depot Exec Acquires Ace Music Shares," *Miami Herald*, 9 December 1995, 1C.
32. "You Make It Happen," *The Link: The newsletter of Office Depot's Business Services Division*, Winter 1995, 1.

Chapter Four, Sidebar: The Office Depot Foundation

1. Mary Wong, interview by Jeffrey L. Rodengen, audio recording, 29 November 2005, Write Stuff Enterprises.
2. Robert McCabe, "Giving At the Office: Office Depot Penciled in David Fuente as CEO, and He's Led It to Superstore Status," *Sun-Sentinel*, 30 January 1994, 1D.
3. "Born Out of Disaster, Office Depot Foundation is Now a Great Tradition," *Office Depot Ink*, 22-23, Summer 1996.
4. "Giving At the Office ... ."
5. "Born Out of Disaster ... ."
6. Ibid.
7. "Office Depot Foundation Helps Associates and Local Communities," *Office Depot Ink*, Spring 1988, 18-19.
8. Ibid.
9. Mary Wong, interview.

Chapter Five: Growing Pains

1. "The Challenge of Being the Best," *Office Depot Sales Link*, July 1998, 1.
2. Lisa Gibbs, "Office Depot Executives Stock Up After Stock Price Dives," *Palm Beach Daily Business Review*, 14 August 1996, A9.
3. Office Depot 1996 annual report, 1.
4. David Sedore, "Bad Day at the Office," *Broward Daily Business Review*, 21 August 1996, A1.
5. Mark Holifield, e-mail correspondence, Office Depot, 2 February 2006.
6. Bill Seltzer, interview by Jeffrey L. Rodengen, audio recording, 6 March 2006, Write Stuff Enterprises.
7. "Office Depot Announces Restructure of Management Organization," PR Newswire, 26 January 1996.
8. "Office Depot Executives Stock Up After Stock Price Dives."
9. Steve Halpern, "Insider Buying Signals Faith in Office Depot," *Miami Herald*, 2 September 1996, 30BM.
10. *Office Depot Ink*, Summer 1996, 24.
11. Office Depot 1996 annual report, 1.
12. Ibid.
13. Dale K. DuPont, "Office Depot Execs Take Hit in Their Bonuses," *Miami Herald*, 24 April 1996, 7B.

14. Monica Luechtefeld, interview by Jeffrey L. Rodengen, audio recording, 29 November 2005, Write Stuff Enterprises.
15. Kathy Fajardo, interview by Jeffrey L. Rodengen, audio recording, 28 March 2006, Write Stuff Enterprises.
16. Annie Frye, interview by Jeffrey L. Rodengen, audio recording, 12 January 2006, Write Stuff Enterprises.
17. Cindy Campbell, interview by Jeffrey L. Rodengen, audio recording, 11 January 2006, Write Stuff Enterprises.
18. Ibid.
19. Ibid.
20. "Bad Day at the Office."
21. David Altaner, "Office Depot Looking at Internet," *Sun-Sentinel*, 24 May 1996, 3D.
22. Cindy Campbell, interview.
23. Ibid.
24. Ibid.
25. "Bad Day at the Office."
26. Dale K. DuPont, "Office Depot Stock Plummets," *Miami Herald*, 17 July 1996, 7B.
27. Office Depot 1996 annual report, 2.
28. Dale K. DuPont, "Office Depot Stock Plummets," *Miami Herald*, 17 July 1996, 7B.
29. "Rapid Growth Requires Third Telecenter," *Office Depot Ink*, Summer 1996, 1, 11.
30. Office Depot 1996 annual report, 1.
31. Bloomberg News, "Staples, Office Depot Merger Would Raise Prices," *Newsday*, 31 May 1997, A23.
32. "Office Depot Bought; $3.4 Billion Deal Puts Staples Back on Top," *St. Louis Post-Dispatch*, 5 September 1996, 1C.
33. "#2 Staples to Acquire #1 Office Depot: FTC Problems Likely," *Corporate Growth Weekly*, 9 September 1996.
34. Office Depot 1996 annual report, Securities and Exchange Commission, Form 10-K, 1.
35. Office Depot 1996 annual report, 1.
36. Julie Waresh, "Office Depot, Staples Merger May Be Dead," *Palm Beach Post*, 1 July 1997, 1A.
37. David Altaner, "Rival Pays $3 Billion for Office Depot," *Sun-Sentinel*, 5 September 1996, 1A.
38. Julie Waresh, "Penciling in the Future; 1,900 Office Depot Workers May Find Out What's in Store for Them This Week," *Palm Beach Post*, 13 October 1996, 1F.
39. Herald Staff and Bloomberg News Reports, "Office Depot Seeks OK for New Stock Option Plan," *Miami Herald*, 1 September 1997.
40. Darcie Lunsford, "Office Depot's Loss Becomes Job Fund's Gain," *South Florida Business Journal*, 10 April 1998, 4A.
41. Henry Sauls, interview by Jeffrey L. Rodengen, audio recording, 14 February 2006, Write Stuff Enterprises.
42. Paula Randolph, interview by Jeffrey L. Rodengen, audio recording, 17 March 2006, Write Stuff Enterprises.
43. "Penciling in the Future ... ."

44. Julie Waresh, "Office Depot to Keep 1,100 Delray Workers," *Palm Beach Post*, 16 October 1996, 6B.
45. "Penciling in the Future ... ."
46. David Fuente, interview by Jeffrey L. Rodengen, with Melody Maysonet and Stanimira Stefanova, audio recording, 9 March 2006, Write Stuff Enterprises.
47. Ibid.
48. Aixa M. Pascual, "Can Office Depot Get Back on Track?" *BusinessWeek*, 18 September 2000, 74.
49. "Staples, Office Depot Are Better Off Apart," *Computer Retail Week*, 7 July 1997.
50. Cindy Campbell, interview; Charlie Brown, interview by Jeffrey L. Rodengen, audio recording, 30 November 2005, Write Stuff Enterprises.
51. David Fuente, interview.
52. Julie Waresh, "Company in Top Financial Shape," *Palm Beach Post*, 2 October 1997, 4B.
53. "Office Depot, Staples Merger May Be Dead."
54. "Bad Day at the Office."
55. Cindy Campbell, interview.
56. Ibid.
57. Ibid.
58. Ibid.
59. Ibid.
60. "Office Depot—Developing a Coherent Data Architecture," *Chain Store Age*, October 1998, 28.
61. Cindy Campbell, interview.
62. Bill Seltzer, interview.
63. Ibid.
64. "Office Depot—Developing a Coherent Data Architecture."
65. Thomas Hoffman, "Short-Term Sacrifices: Office Depot Endures App Dev Delays to Ensure Tech Future," *Computerworld*, 16 March 1998.
66. "Office Depot—Developing a Coherent Data Architecture."
67. Office Depot 1996 annual report, Securities and Exchange Commission, Form 10-K, 7.
68. Monica Luechtefeld, interview.
69. Ibid.
70. "Quality Olympics Raises the Torch of Superior Customer Service," *Office Depot Ink*, Summer 1996, 10-11.
71. "Office Depot Appoints Dick Bennington President of Its Business Services Division," PR Newswire, 2 September 1997.
72. "The Challenge of Being the Best."
73. David Altaner, "Office Depot Looking at Internet," *Sun-Sentinel*, 24 May 1996, 3D.
74. David Rocks, "Why Office Depot Loves the Net," *BusinessWeek*, 27 September 1999.
75. Monica Luechtefeld, interview.
76. Monica Luechtefeld, "Office Depot Pioneers Electronic Commerce," *Office Depot Ink*, Fall 1998, 3.
77. Office Depot 1997 annual report, 12, 18.
78. Ibid, 18.
79. "Office Depot Pioneers Electronic Commerce."
80. Mike Troy, "Web Presence Key Strategy for Office Depot," 26 October 1998.

81. Jeffrey D. Zbar, "Office Depot Taking Care of Advertising," *Sun-Sentinel*, 29 March 1996, 3D.
82. Jeffrey D. Zbar, "Office Depot's New Slogan Means Business," *Sun-Sentinel*, 29 July 1996, 11.
83. Jeffrey D. Zbar, "Office Depot Opts for the Family Way," *Advertising Age*, 29 July 1996, 24.
84. Bob Garfield, "Office Depot's Nice Try Tries Just a Bit Too Hard," *Advertising Age*, 19 August 1996, 33.
85. Office Depot 1997 annual report, 20.
86. Troy Flint, "Wyse Wins Office Depot Account," *Plain Dealer*, 22 October 1997, 1C.
87. "Dilbert to Star in New $30 Million Ad Campaign for Office Depot," Business Wire, 21 November 1997.
88. Office Depot 1997 annual report, 21.
89. Ibid, 20.
90. Ibid, 21.
91. "Bay Hill Invitational Golf Tournament is a Spectacular Hole-in-One for Office Depot," *Office Depot Ink*, Summer 1996, 1, 8.
92. Office Depot 1997 annual report, 22.
93. Ibid, 23.
94. Office Depot 1996 annual report, 2.
95. Dale K. DuPont, "Office Depot Will Expand in Far East," *Miami Herald*, 14 February 1996, 9B.
96. "Office Depot Inc. to Set Up Discount Chain in Japan," *Asian Pulse*, 16 July 1996.
97. Office Depot 1997 annual report, 23.
98. Julie Waresh, "Company in Top Financial Shape," *Palm Beach Post*, 2 October 1997, 4B.
99. Office Depot 1997 annual report, 2-3.
100. Ibid, 2.

Chapter Six: Jockeying for Position

1. Office Depot 1999 annual report, 3.
2. Office Depot 1998 annual report, 6.
3. Ibid, 2, 3, 23.
4. "Office Depot to Buy Mail Order Supply Firm," *Arlington Morning News*, 19 May 1998, 2C.
5. Lee Ault III, interview by Jeffrey L. Rodengen, audio recording, 16 June 2006, Write Stuff Enterprises.
6. Constance L. Hays, "Office Depot in Deal for Direct Marketer," *New York Times*, 19 May 1998, D2.
7. Bruce Nelson, interview by Jeffrey L. Rodengen, audio recording, 27 April 2006, Write Stuff Enterprises.
8. Ibid.
9. Elaine Walker, "Office Depot Stock Drops in Wake of Merger Plans," *Miami Herald*, 27 May 1998.
10. Elaine Walker, "Office Depot to Acquire Viking; $3B Deal Could Boost Global Expansion," *Miami Herald*, 19 May 1998, 7B.
11. Neil Weinberg, "Bull in a Stationary Shop," *Fortune*, 24 August 1998, 90.
12. "Office Depot to Acquire Viking … ."
13. Elaine Walker, "Office Depot's Purchase of Viking Gets Final Approval," *Miami Herald*, 27 August 1998, 1C.
14. "Office Depot to Acquire Viking … ."
15. "Office Depot in Deal for Direct Marketer."

16. Karen Robinson-Jacobs, "Office Depot to Buy Viking for $2.6 Billion," *Los Angeles Times*, 19 May 1998, D3.
17. David Fannin, interview by Jeffrey L. Rodengen, audio recording, 29 November 1005, Write Stuff Enterprises.
18. Monica Luechtefeld, interview by Jeffrey L. Rodengen, audio recording, 29 November 2005, Write Stuff Enterprises.
19. Ibid.
20. Tim Toews, interview by Jeffrey L. Rodengen, audio recording, 29 October 2005, Write Stuff Enterprises.
21. Office Depot 1998 annual report, 4.
22. Clinton Wilder, "Profile Office Depot Inc.—E-commerce Pays Off for Office Depot," *Information Week*, 11 September 2000.
23. Office Depot 1999 annual report, 2.
24. Office Depot 1998 annual report, 20.
25. Office Depot 1999 annual report, 2.
26. "Office Depot Online Opens for Business," *Office Depot Ink*, Spring 1998, 8.
27. "Office Depot Opens in Cyberspace," *Newsbytes*, 15 January 1998.
28. "Office Depot Online Opens for Business."
29. Mike Troy, "Web Presence Key Strategy for Office Depot," *Discount Store News*, 26 October 1998.
30. Office Depot 1999 annual report, 14.
31. Office Depot 1998 annual report, 20.
32. "Office Depot Recognized for Online Excellence," Business Wire, 1 July 1998.
33. David Rocks, "Why Office Depot Loves the Net," *BusinessWeek*, 27 September 1999.
34. Monica Luechtefeld, interview.
35. Office Depot 1998 annual report, 4.
36. Ibid, 13.
37. Office Depot 1999 annual report, 4.
38. Ibid, 13.
39. Ibid, 16.
40. "Interview with Bruce Nelson," *Office Depot Ink*, Summer 1999, 12.
41. Office Depot 1999 annual report, 13.
42. Maria Joyce, "Customer Service Task Force Gets off to a Quick Start," *Office Depot Sales Link*, August 1998, 1.
43. Office Depot 1999 annual report, 13.
44. Monica Luechtefeld, interview.
45. Carol Sliwa, "Office Depot Learns from Experience; Upgrades Web site for Corporate Customers," *Computerworld*, 5 October 1998, 45.
46. Tim Toews, interview.
47. Office Depot 1998 annual report, 20.
48. Office Depot 1999 annual report, 13.
49. Ibid, 10.
50. Ibid, 18, 25.
51. Ibid, 18.
52. Ibid, 19.
53. Ibid, 18.
54. "Interview with Bruce Nelson."
55. John Deaton, interview by Jeffrey L. Rodengen, audio recording, 30 November 2005, Write Stuff Enterprises.
56. Elaine Walker, "Song Brings Back Memories—and Sales—for Office Depot," *Miami Herald*, 13 December 1999, 15BM.
57. Paul Owers, "Office Depot Dumps Dilbert," *Palm Beach Post*, 8 December 1998, 6B.

58. Office Depot 1998 annual report, 26.
59. Kirby Salgado, interview by Jeffrey L. Rodengen, audio recording, 12 January 2006, Write Stuff Enterprises.
60. Office Depot 1998 Annual Report, Management's Discussion and Analysis of Financial Condition and Results of Operations, 35.
61. Office Depot 1999 annual report, 9.
62. John Deaton, interview.
63. Office Depot 1998 annual report, 29.
64. Ibid, 3.
65. Ibid, 33.
66. Julie Waresh, "Office Depot Makes S&P 500 Listing," *Palm Beach Post*, 3 June 1999, 1D.
67. David Sedore, "Office Depot, FPL March Up List of Fortune 500," *Palm Beach Post*, 6 April 1999, 5B.
68. Office Depot 1998 annual report, 12.
69. Aixa M. Pascual, "Can Office Depot Get Back on Track?" *BusinessWeek*, 18 September 2000, 74; Office Depot 1999 annual report, 6; Julie Waresh, "Office Depot Earnings Off Mark," *Palm Beach Post*, 31 August 1999, 5B.
70. Gregg Fields, "President of Office Depot Quits," *Miami Herald*, 15 October 1999, 1C.
71. "President of Office Depot Quits."

Chapter Six, Sidebar: Supporting the National PTA

1. "Office Depot Partners with National PTA on 'Supporting School Values' Campaign," *Office Depot Ink*, Summer 1998, 1, 15.
2. Ibid, 1.

Chapter Seven: The Challenge

1. Jeff Malester, "Office Depot Shuts Stores, Takes Charge," *TWICE*, 22 January 2001, 8.
2. "Office Depot Shares Fall," Associated Press, 26 May 2000.
3. Aixa M. Pascual, "Can Office Depot Get Back on Track?" *BusinessWeek*, 18 September 2000, 74.
4. John Deaton, interview by Jeffrey L. Rodengen, audio recording, 30 November 2005, Write Stuff Enterprises.
5. Office Depot 1999 annual report, 6.
6. Charlie Brown, interview by Jeffrey L. Rodengen, audio recording, 30 November 2005, Write Stuff Enterprises.
7. David Fannin, interview by Jeffrey L. Rodengen, audio recording, 29 November 2005, Write Stuff Enterprises.
8. Ibid.
9. Rick Lepley, interview by Jeffrey L. Rodengen, audio recording, 14 February 2006, Write Stuff Enterprises.
10. "Can Office Depot Get Back on Track?"
11. David Fuente, interview by Jeffrey L. Rodengen, audio recording, 9 March 2006, Write Stuff Enterprises.
12. Elaine Walker, "New Era at Office Depot," *Miami Herald*, 19 July 2000, 1C.
13. Ibid.
14. Paul Owers, "Office Depot CEO Says Progress Slow," *Palm Beach Post*, 13 October 2000, 1D.

15. Office Depot 2001 annual report, 2.
16. "New Era at Office Depot."
17. Ibid.
18. Office Depot 2000 annual report, 2.
19. Karen-Janine Cohen, "Bruce Nelson: Office Depot Inc.," Sun-Sentinel, 25 January 2004, 12E.
20. Office Depot 2000 annual report, 3.
21. Ibid.
22. "A Message from Irwin Helford," Office Depot Ink, Fall 2000, 2.
23. Office Depot 2000 annual report, 8.
24. Tami Luhby, "Office Depot to Close All 6 LI Stores," Newsday, 4 January 2001, A46.
25. Office Depot 2000 annual report, 8.
26. "Office Superstores Scale Back Openings," DSN Retailing Today, 23 October 2000, 6.
27. Office Depot 2001 annual report, Management's Discussion and Analysis, 18.
28. Jeff Ostrowski, "Office Depot to Shut Money-Losers," Palm Beach Post, 28 December 2000, 1D.
29. "New Era at Office Depot."
30. Ibid.
31. Office Depot 2001 annual report, 15.
32. Chuck Rubin, interview by Jeffrey L. Rodengen, audio recording, 29 November 2005, Write Stuff Enterprises.
33. "Office Depot to Close 70 Stores," HFN–The Weekly Newspaper for the Home Furnishing Network, 8 January 2001, 85.
34. Clinton Wilder, "E-commerce Pays off for Office Depot," InformationWeek, 11 September 2000.
35. Susan Salisbury, "Out of the Box," Broward Daily Business Review, 6 September 2000, A1.
36. Neil Cavuto, "Office Depot CEO-Interview," Fox News Network, 15 February 2001.
37. Amy Martinez, "Office Depot Not Hit Hard by Profit Drop," Palm Beach Post, 20 April 2001, 1D.
38. Elaine Walker, "Office Depot's Long Journey," Miami Herald, 12 May 2001, 1C.
39. Barbara Powell, "Office Depot Plots Course Through Turbulent Economy," Sun-Sentinel, 2 December 2001, 1G.
40. Ibid.

Chapter Eight: The Beginning of a Journey

1. Office Depot 2002 annual report, 2.
2. Office Depot 2001 annual report, 2; Paul Owers, "Office Depot Investors Happy with Turnaround," Palm Beach Post, 26 April 2002, 1D.
3. Office Depot 2002 annual report, 12.
4. Office Depot 2001 annual report, 2; "Office Depot Investors Happy with Turnaround."
5. Office Depot 2001 annual report, 2-3.
6. Office Depot 2000 annual report, 4.
7. "Jerry's Letter," Wyn2k, March/April 2002, 8.
8. James Heskett, interview by Jeffrey L. Rodengen, audio recording, 15 June 2006, Write Stuff Enterprises.
9. Office Depot 2001 annual report, 16; 2002 annual report, 10.
10. Randy Pianin, "Special Month Contributes to City of Hope," Wyn2k, Summer 2002, 21.
11. Office Depot 2001 annual report, 16; Office Depot 2002 annual report, 10.
12. Office Depot 2001 annual report, 16.
13. Paul Owers, Cox News Service, 23 August 2001.
14. Office Depot 2001 annual report, 4.
15. Robert McCormes-Ballou, " 'Why Vendor Diversity?' It's Essential for Growth," Wyn2k, Summer 2002, 16.
16. Office Depot 2001 annual report, 6.
17. "Office Depot Creates Council to Target Women," South Florida Business Journal, 2 March 2001.
18. Ibid.
19. Lynn Connelly, interview by Jeffrey L. Rodengen, audio recording, 12 January 2006, Write Stuff Enterprises.
20. "Office Depot's Second Annual Women's Conference More Than Doubled in Attendance," Business Wire, 11 February 2002.
21. Lynn Connelly, interview.
22. "Office Depot Targets Women," Palm Beach Post, 20 January 2001, 10B.
23. "Office Depot Creates Council to Target Women," South Florida Business Journal, 2 March 2001.
24. "Office Depot is Awarded the 2001 President's Award by Florida Regional Minority Business Council," Business Wire, 14 March 2001.
25. Office Depot 2001 annual report, 4.
26. "Office Depot Completes Remerchandising in All of Its U.S. Retail Stores," Business Wire, 25 June 2001.
27. Bruce Nelson, interview by Jeffrey L. Rodengen, audio recording, 27 April 2006, Write Stuff Enterprises.
28. Office Depot 2001 annual report, 8, 10.
29. Elaine Walker, "Office Depot's Long Journey," Miami Herald, 12 May 2001, 1C.
30. Office Depot 2001 annual report, 8.
31. "Office Depot's Long Journey."
32. "Office Depot's Long Journey"; Elaine Walker, "Office Depot Tries New Format," Miami Herald, 9 August 2001, 1C; Karen-Janine Cohen, "Office Depot Hints At Its Redesign," Sun-Sentinel, 22 April 2003, 1D; "Office Depot's Main Man," Palm Beach Post, 26 November 2001, 1D; "Office Depot Rolls Out New Look," DSN Retailing Today, 20 August 2001, 1.
33. "Office Depot Tries New Format."
34. John Deaton, interview by Jeffrey L. Rodengen, audio recording, 30 November 2005, Write Stuff Enterprises.
35. Office Depot Ink, A Special Branding Issue, 1.
36. Office Depot 2002 annual report, 4.
37. "Office Depot Launches European Business Services Division to Better Serve Medium to Large U.K. Business Customers," Business Wire, 13 September 2000.
38. Ibid.
39. Office Depot 2002 annual report, 8.
40. Rolf van Kaldekerken, interview by Jeffrey L. Rodengen, audio recording, 14 April 2006, Write Stuff Enterprises.
41. Office Depot 2002 annual report, 8.
42. Ibid, 8.
43. Ibid, 2.
44. Ibid, Management's Discussion and Analysis, 14.
45. "Office Depot Closing 67 Stores in 18 States," Tulsa World, 4 January 2001.
46. "Office Depot Announces Plans to Upgrade Its Customer Service Organization," Business Wire, 6 November 2000.
47. Jim Emerson, "Virtual is its Own Reward; Office Depot Puts Phone Centers Online to Save Money," Direct, June 2001.
48. Jim Emerson, "Virtual is its Own Reward; Office Depot Puts Phone Centers Online to Save Money," Direct, June 2001.
49. Mathew Schwartz, "Getting IT Out of the Loop," Information Gatekeepers, Inc., 1 July 2002, 13.
50. Office Depot 2002 annual report, 6.
51. Stephen Pounds and Paul Owers, "Office Depot Acquiring Web Sites," Palm Beach Post, 23 June 2001, 10B.
52. Ibid.
53. Office Depot 2001 annual report, Management's Discussion and Analysis, 19; Bloomberg News, "Office Depot Grows on the Web," 10 July 2001, E1.
54. Monica Luechtefeld, interview by Jeffrey L. Rodengen, audio recording, 29 November 2005, Write Stuff Enterprises.
55. Lynn Craska, "Tech Depot Offers 100,000 Reasons," Wyn2k, Summer 2003, 44.
56. Monica Luechtefeld, interview.
57. Ibid.
58. "Office Depot Launches Newly Redesigned Web Site," Business Wire, 31 October 2000.
59. Kathleen Stockham, "Pardon Our Dot-Com Dust!" Wyn2k, Summer 2002, 19.
60. Office Depot 2002 annual report, 6.
61. "Berkshire Hathaway Buys 5 Million Shares of Office Depot," Associated Press, 14 August 2001.
62. "Office Depot Names New Executives, Shares Hit New 52-Week High," Broward Daily Business Review, 17 October 2001, A3.
63. Office Depot 2002 annual report, 2.
64. Office Depot 2001 annual report, 3; 2002 annual report, 2.
65. Office Depot 2001 annual report, 12.

Chapter Eight, Sidebar: Sponsoring the Olympics

1. Lynn Connelly, interview by Jeffrey L. Rodengen, audio recording, 12 January 2006, Write Stuff Enterprises.
2. "Office Depot: Proud Sponsor of the 2002 Games," Office Depot Sales Link, January/February 2001, 5.
3. Lynn Connelly, interview.
4. "Office Depot Announces U.S. Olympic Sponsorship," Business Wire, 1 December 2000.

Chapter Eight, Sidebar: The Office Depot Center

1. Sarah Talalay, "Sunrise Arena Renamed Office Depot Center," *Sun-Sentinel*, 14 September 2002, 1B.
2. Ibid.
3. Lynn Connelly, interview by Jeffrey L. Rodengen, audio recording, 12 January 2006, Write Stuff Enterprises.
4. "Sunrise Arena Renamed Office Depot Center."
5. Ibid.

Chapter Nine: Facing Challenging Times

1. Office Depot 2004 annual report, 3.
2. Greg Gatlin, "Office Depot Buy Pushes Staples Down," *Boston Herald*, 9 April 2003.
3. Mike Troy, "Office Depot Puts $900 Million Faith in European B2B Market," *DSN Retailing Today*, 5 May 2003.
4. Paul Owers, "Office Depot CEO Nelson Paid $12.6 Million in 2002," *Palm Beach Post*, 25 March 2003, 8B.
5. Karen-Janine Cohen, "Office Depot Aspires to No. 1 Position," *Sun-Sentinel*, 2 April 2003, 1D.
6. Karen-Janine Cohen, "Office Depot Plots Strategy for Rebound," *Sun-Sentinel*, 18 April 2003, 1D.
7. "Message from the Chairman & CEO," *Wyn2k*, Winter 2003, 4.
8. "Office Depot Aspires to No. 1 Position."
9. Karen-Janine Cohen, "Office Depot Hints At Its Redesign," *Sun-Sentinel*, 22 April 2003, 1D.
10. Mike Troy, "Office Depot Churns Out New Ideas," *DSN Retailing Today*, 6 January 2003.
11. Myra Hart, interview by Jeffrey L. Rodengen, audio recording, 6 March 2006, Write Stuff Enterprises.
12. Office Depot 2003 annual report, 2.
13. Ibid, 1.
14. Elaine Walker, "Office Depot Deals to Regain No. 1 Spot," *Miami Herald*, 9 April 2003, 1C; Charles E. Brown, "The Long Road Home," *Wyn2k*, Summer 2003, 4; "Defining Moments As We Turn 18," *Wyn2k*, Fall 2004, 4.
15. Samer Iskandar and Donna Block, "Office Depot Targets PPR Unit," *Daily Deal*, 9 April 2003.
16. Greg Gatlin, "Office Depot Buy Pushes Staples Down," *Boston Herald*, 9 April 2003.
17. "Office Depot Deals to Regain No. 1 Spot."
18. David Fannin, interview by Jeffrey L. Rodengen, audio recording, 29 November 2005, Write Stuff Enterprises.
19. Ibid.
20. Ibid.
21. Rolf van Kaldekerken, interview by Jeffrey L. Rodengen, audio recording, 14 April 2006, Write Stuff Enterprises.
22. Karen-Janine Cohen, "Voila! Office Depot Gets a French Connection," *Sun-Sentinel*, 9 April 2003, 1D.
23. Ibid.
24. "Office Depot Puts $900 Million Faith in European B2B Market."
25. Office Depot 2003 annual report, 1.
26. Office Depot 2004 annual report, 11.

27. "An Unbeatable Team," *Wyn2k*, Summer 2004, 18.
28. Stephen Pounds, "Office Depot Launches Site in Spanish," *Palm Beach Post*, 17 January 2003, 11B.
29. Ibid.
30. Ibid.
31. Office Depot 2003 annual report, 9.
32. "Message from the Chairman & CEO," *Wyn2k*, Spring 2004, 3.
33. Office Depot 2004 annual report, 3.
34. Ibid, inside cover.
35. Jay Eisenberg, "Magellan Sets Sail for Success," *Wyn2k*, Fall 2003, 14.
36. Office Depot 2004 annual report, 10; "Rick Coro, VP Merchandising Systems," *Wyn2k*, Summer 2003, 8; Jay Eisenberg, "Voyage of Discovery," *Wyn2k*, Summer 2003, 6.
37. "Foundation Release Builds Strong Base for Further Wins," *Wyn2k*, Fall 2004, 12.
38. Jay Eisenberg, "Voyage of Discovery," *Wyn2k*, Summer 2003, 6.
39. Ibid.
40. Ibid.
41. Office Depot 2003 annual report, 8.
42. "Office Depot Puts $900 Million Faith in European B2B Market."
43. Ali Velshi and Pat Kiernan, "Office Depot Brings the Supplies," CEO Wire, 4 July 2003.
44. "Office Depot Puts $900 Million Faith in European B2B Market."
45. "Office Depot Rolls Out Ink Depot," *Wyn2k*, Summer 2003, 16.
46. Office Depot 2003 annual report, 8.
47. "Office Depot Hints at Its Redesign."
48. Chad Mikula, Joe Jeffries, Jay Eisenberg, "Behind the Scenes: M2 Development: Stealthy, Intense, Revolutionary," *Wyn2k*, Fall 2004, 6-7.
49. Ibid.
50. Ibid.
51. "M2: The Future is Now," *Wyn2k*, Fall 2003, 5.
52. Rick Lepley, interview by Jeffrey L. Rodengen, audio recording, 14 February 2006, Write Stuff Enterprises.
53. "Behind the Scenes: M2 Development ...," *Wyn2k*, Fall 2004, 6-7.
54. Ibid; Stephen Frater, "Office Depot Debuts New Concept in Venice," *Sarasota Herald-Tribune*, 1 July 2004, D1.
55. Rick Lepley, interview.
56. Office Depot 2004 annual report, 10.
57. Brian Levine, "M2 Positioning," Office Depot internal document, 15 June 2004.
58. Karen-Janine Cohen, "Office Depot Unveils New Look Interior for Northeast Expansion," *Sun-Sentinel*, 1 July 2004; Steve Smith, "New Format, NE Expansion Set for Office Depot," *TWICE*, 12 July 2004, 5; Office Depot 2004 annual report, 6; Mike Troy, "Office Depot Shifts Store Expansion to M2 Format," *DSN Retailing Today*, 19 July 2004, 43.
59. "New Format, NE Expansion Set for Office Depot"; Office Depot 2004 annual report, 6.
60. Office Depot 2004 annual report, 6; Stephen Frater, "Office Depot Debuts New Concept in Venice," *Sarasota Herald-Tribune*, 1 July 2004, D1.

61. "New Format, NE Expansion Set for Office Depot."
62. Henry Sauls, interview by Jeffrey L. Rodengen, audio recording, 14 February 2006, Write Stuff Enterprises.
63. Karl Kunkel, "Office Depot Officially Unveils Christopher Lowell Office Line," *HFN–The Weekly Newspaper for the Home Furnishing Network*, 9 February 2004, 19.
64. Ibid.
65. "Office Depot Partners with Christopher Lowell," *Wyn2k*, Winter 2004, 10; "Christopher Lowell Collection PR Plan," Office Depot internal document.
66. "Designer Christopher Lowell Teams Up with Office Depot to Market Furniture," *Palm Beach Post*, 17 November 2003, 3D.
67. "Office Depot Debuts Line of Christopher Lowell Accessories," *Retail-Merchandiser.com*, 21 May 2004.
68. "Office Depot Expands Christopher Lowell Collection," *Retail-Merchandiser.com*, 19 November 2004.
69. Kirby Salgado, interview by Jeffrey L. Rodengen, audio recording, 12 January 2006, Write Stuff Enterprises.
70. "What You Need to Know About Chuck Rubin," *Wyn2k*, Summer 2004, 20.
71. Ibid.
72. "Private Branded Products Feature a Fresh New Look," *Wyn2k*, Summer 2004, 28.
73. "Defining Moments As We Turn 18," *Wyn2k*, Fall 2004, 4.
74. "Office Depot Begins Northeast Expansion with New Stores," *Retail-Merchandiser.com*, 21 October 2004.
75. Mike Troy, "Office Depot Churning up Change," *DSN Retailing Today*, 22 March 2004, 1.
76. Elaine Walker, "Office Depot to Buy 124 Stores," *Miami Herald*, 4 March 2004, 1C.
77. "New Format, NE Expansion Set for Office Depot."
78. Office Depot 2004 annual report, 10.
79. Karen-Janine Cohen, "Office Depot Plans Offensive," *Sun-Sentinel*, 15 May 2004; "M2 Format: The Future is Now," *Wyn2k*, Fall 2004, 5.
80. Mike Troy, "Office Depot Shifts Store Expansion to M2 Format," *DSN Retailing Today*, 19 July 2004, 4.
81. "1,000 Pages of Bigger ... Brighter ... BETTER!" *Wyn2k*, Fall 2003, 10.
82. "Big Wins for Big Book!" *Wyn2k*, Summer 2004, 27.
83. Linda Rawls, "Office Depot Rewards Loyalty," *Palm Beach Post*, 23 February 2004, 1F.
84. "Office Depot is Launching its 2004 Back-to-School Integrated Marketing Campaign Featuring New TV and Radio Spots," *Retail-Merchandiser.com*, 26 July 2004.
85. Karen-Janine Cohen, "Office Depot Makes Promotional Deal with Donald Trump," *Sun-Sentinel*, 8 June 2004.
86. "It's the Real Deal!" *Wyn2k*, Fall 2004, 24.
87. Seth Dreyfuss, "Office Depot Celebrates 18-Year Anniversary!" *Wyn2k*, Fall 2004, 21.

88. "Office Depot Expands 'Office for the Environment'; Tyler J. Elm Named Director of Environmental Affairs," Business Wire, 17 September 2003.
89. Tyler Elm, interview by Jeffrey L. Rodengen, audio recording, 12 January 2006, Write Stuff Enterprises.
90. Office Depot 2004 annual report, 13.
91. "New Paper Policy Helps Protect the Future of Our Planet," Wyn2k, Summer 2003, 14.
92. Ibid.
93. Tyler Elm, interview.
94. "Toner Cartridge Reuse at Office Depot," Wyn2k, Summer 2003, 15.
95. "Office Depot and HP Offer Nationwide In-Store Electronics Recycling Program," Wyn2k, Fall 2004, 45.
96. "Office Depot Announces Green Book Catalog," Business Wire, 22 December 2003.
97. Joe Truini, "Office Depot Opens Books," Waste News, 6 December 2004, 1.
98. Chuck Rubin, interview by Jeffrey L. Rodengen, audio recording, 29 November 2005, Write Stuff Enterprises.
99. Karen-Janine Cohen, "Sales of Computers Fuel Office Depot Earnings," Sun-Sentinel, 23 July 2004, 1D.
100. "Office Depot Lowers Earnings Expectations," Associated Press Online, 14 September 2004.
101. Charlie Brown, interview by Jeffrey L. Rodengen, audio recording, 30 November 2005, Write Stuff Enterprises.
102. Kor de Jonge, interview by Jeffrey L. Rodengen, recording, 20 April 2006, Write Stuff Enterprises.
103. Charlie Brown, interview.
104. Bruce Ackland, "Pressure: Office Depot Had a Q3 to Forget with Business Taking a Massive Dent from Slow Sales and Tropical Storms," Office Products International, 1 October 2004, 38.
105. Linda Rawls, "Storms, Sales Slam Office Depot," Palm Beach Post, 15 September 2004, 1D.
106. Neil Austrian, interview by Jeffrey L. Rodengen, audio recording, 23 June 2006, Write Stuff Enterprises.
107. Linda Rawls, "Office Depot Jettisons CEO," Palm Beach Post, 5 October 2004, 1D.
108. Ibid.
109. Mike Troy, "Office Depot Seeks New Direction, New CEO," DSN Retailing Today, 25 October, 2004, 8.
110. "Office Depot to Eliminate 800 More Jobs," Associated Press Online, 13 November 2004.
111. "Office Depot Seeks New Direction, New CEO."

Chapter Nine, Sidebar: Weathering the Storms

1. "Office Depot Responds Quickly As Hurricanes Slam Southeast U.S.," Wyn2k, Fall 2004, 34.
2. "Office Depot Offers Service," Pensacola News Journal, 16 October 2004, 10C.

Chapter Nine, Sidebar: Corporate Giving

1. "Office Depot Named to the 2004 'Companies That Care' Honor Roll," Business Wire, 8 April 2004.
2. Office Depot 2004 annual report, 4.
3. Suzanna Mahler, "Office Depot Sends Kids to School Packing," Palm Beach Post, 11 August 2004, 5.
4. "Office Depot Reaches Out to More Than 650,000 Teachers with Its Star Teacher Program," Business Wire, 8 July 2003.
5. Eugene Sutherland, "Teacher Appreciation Held at Office Depot," Daily Town Talk, 10 August 2003, 8A.
6. "Office Depot Pledges $1M to the Scripps Research Institute," Retail-Merchandiser.com, 3 May 2004.

Chapter Ten: A New Era

1. Steve Odland, analyst conference call, 15 February 2006.
2. Carol Krol, "Office Depot Puts Focus on 'Business' in New Year," B to B, 17 January 2005, 3.
3. Brian Levine, interview by Jeffrey L. Rodengen, audio recording, 26 May 2006, Write Stuff Enterprises.
4. Tony Ueber, interview by Jeffrey L. Rodengen, audio recording, 12 January 2006, Write Stuff Enterprises.
5. Ibid.
6. Jeffrey D. Zbar, "Office Depot Motto Returns to Taking Care of Business," Sun-Sentinel, 3 January 2005.
7. Tony Ueber, interview.
8. "Office Depot Motto Returns to Taking Care of Business."
9. Neil Austrian, interview by Jeffrey L. Rodengen, audio recording, 23 June 2006, Write Stuff Enterprises.
10. "Steve Odland Brings Significant Retail Expertise and Strong Track Record to Office Depot," Office Depot newsletter (unnamed), April 2005, 1.
11. Michael Myers, interview by Jeffrey L. Rodengen, audio recording, 6 March 2006, Write Stuff Enterprises.
12. "Wall Street Approves of Office Depot's CEO Move," Broward Daily Business Review, 15 March 2005, 3.
13. Elaine Walker, "Office Depot Names Chief Exec," Miami Herald, 15 March 2005, 1C.
14. "Wall Street Approves of Office Depot's CEO Move."
15. Paul Owers, "Office Depot's New Chief Shuffles Team, Sets Goals," Palm Beach Post, 13 April 2005, 1D.
16. "Steve Odland ... at a Glance," Office Depot newsletter (unnamed), April 2005, 2.
17. "Office Depot Welcomes New CEO Steve Odland," Retail-Merchandiser.com, 24 March 2005.
18. Stephen Pounds, "Corporate America Working to Fix Image, Office Depot Chief Says," Palm Beach Post, 9 December 2005, 1D.
19. "Office Depot Welcomes New CEO Steve Odland."
20. "Office Depot Names Dirk Collin Executive Vice President & Managing Director, Europe," Business Wire, 15 February 2006.

21. Cindy Campbell, interview by Jeffrey L. Rodengen, audio recording, 11 January 2006, Write Stuff Enterprises.
22. Brian Levine, interview.
23. Lee Ault III, interview by Jeffrey L. Rodengen, audio recording, 16 June 2006, Write Stuff Enterprises.
24. George Hill, interview by Jeffrey L. Rodengen, recording, 14 February 2006, Write Stuff Enterprises.
25. Monica Luechtefeld, interview by Jeffrey L. Rodengen, audio recording, 29 November 2005, Write Stuff Enterprises.
26. Daisy Vanderlinde, Breakthrough Performance Visions & Values Update, recording, 11 January 2006.
27. Chuck Rubin, Breakthrough Performance Visions & Values Update, recording, 11 January 2006.
28. Steve Odland, interview by Jeffrey L. Rodengen, with Melody Maysonet, audio recording, 11 January 2006, Write Stuff Enterprises.
29. Ibid.
30. Ibid.
31. Office Depot 2004 annual report, 4.
32. Paul Owers, "Angelou, Walters, Ireland Headline Office Depot's Women's Conference," Palm Beach Post, 24 January 2005.
33. "Office Depot Announces Recipients of Prestigious 2005 'Businesswomen of the Year' Award," Business Wire, 28 February 2005.
34. "Office Depot and Xerox Present $25,000 Grant to National Ovarian Cancer Coalition," Business Wire, 1 March 2005.
35. Robert McCormes-Ballou, interview by Jeffrey L. Rodengen, audio recording, 14 February 2006, Write Stuff Enterprises.
36. Ibid.
37. AnneMarie Richards, "Office Depot Named to Top 50 Corporations for Multicultural Business Opportunities List," Office Depot newsletter (unnamed), April 2005, 14.
38. Marcia Heroux Pounds, "Office Depot Ranked Among Corporate Elite," Sun-Sentinel, 23 March 2005, 1D.
39. "Office Depot Championing Environmentally Friendly Products," Retail-Merchandiser.com, 13 January 2005.
40. "Office Depot Wins Environmental Award," Retail-Merchandiser.com, 2 March 2005.
41. "Steve S. Odland Speaking Points for S.E.E. Change Press Event," internal document, 21 September 2005.
42. "Yalmaz Siddiqui New Office Depot Environmental Strategy Advisor," Financial Wire, 18 April 2006.
43. "Office Depot Names Yalmaz Siddiqui Environmental Strategy Advisor; Position Designed to Further Enhance the Company's Global Environmental Performance," Business Wire, 17 April 2006.
44. "Office Depot Receives 'Outstanding Retailer' Award, Retail-Merchandiser.com, 22 April 2005.
45. Paul Owers, "Office Depot Stock Soars," Palm Beach Post, 22 July 2005, 1D.

46. Joe Buckley, interview by Jeffrey L. Rodengen, with Melody Maysonet, audio recording, 11 January 2006, Write Stuff Enterprises.
47. Ibid.
48. "Q4 2005 Office Depot Inc. Earnings Conference Call," FD (Fair Disclosure) Wire, 15 February 2006.
49. Steve Odland, interview.
50. Joe Buckley, interview.
51. Paul Owers, "Office Depot Stock Soars," *Palm Beach Post*, 22 July 2005, 1D.
52. Neil Austrian, interview.
53. Susan Salisbury, "New Office Depot CEO Meets Shareholders, Execs," *Palm Beach Post*, 14 May 2005.
54. Ibid.
55. Mike Seemuth, "Two at Office Depot Exercise Options on Profit News," *Broward Daily Business Review*, 1 March 2006, 3.
56. Karen-Janine Cohen, "CEO is Bullish on Office Depot," *Sun-Sentinel*, 13 April 2005, 1D.
57. "New Office Depot CEO Meets Shareholders, Execs."
58. "CEO is Bullish on Office Depot."
59. Dan Mearns, "Office Depot Closing 27 Stores," *Sun Herald*, 14 September 2005.
60. "Office Depot Opens 1,000th North American Store," *Retail-Merchandiser.com*, 1 June 2005.
61. Ibid.
62. Mike Troy, "Office Depot Rolls Out Store No. 1,000 amidst Fanfare to Steal Staples' Thunder," *DSN Retailing Today*, 13 June 2005, 5.
63. "Office Depot Closing 27 Stores."
64. "Office Depot Leads the Pack in 'e-tailing'," *Miami Herald*, 11 July 2005, G27.
65. Brian Quinton, "Office Depot's Multichannel Challenge," *Direct*, 1 May 2005, 10.
66. David Trudnowski, interview by Jeffrey L. Rodengen, audio recording, 12 April 2006, Write Stuff Enterprises.
67. Cindy Campbell, interview.
68. "Q4 2005 Office Depot Inc. Earnings Conference Call," FD (Fair Disclosure) Wire, 15 February 2006.
69. "Office Depot Announces First Quarter Results," press release, 25 April 2006.
70. Cindy Campbell, interview.
71. Jeff Ostrowski, "Office Depot Reports Loss," *Palm Beach Post*, 20 October 2005, 1D.
72. Brian Skoloff, "Office Depot Posts Higher Fourth-quarter Profit as Costs Decline," Associated Press State and Local Wire, 15 February 2006.
73. "Office Depot Cuts Losses in Spain," *Expansion*, 20 October, 2005.
74. Charlie Brown, interview by Jeffrey L. Rodengen, audio recording, 30

November 2005, Write Stuff Enterprises.
75. Pat Beall, "Depot Hops Despite Missed Mark," *Palm Beach Post*, 27 April 2006, 3D.
76. "Office Depot Takes on Europe," *Daily Deal/The Deal*, 20 May 2005.
77. "Q4 2005 Office Depot Inc. Earnings Conference Call."
78. "Office Depot Posts Higher Fourth-quarter Profit as Costs Decline."
79. "Q4 2005 Office Depot Inc. Earnings Conference Call."
80. "Office Depot Becomes Majority Holder Of Israeli Subsidiary," Financial Wire, 5 April 2006
81. "Office Depot Announces First Quarter Results," press release, 25 April 2006.
82. "Magellan Supports Taking Care of Business," Office Depot newsletter (unnamed), April 2005, 15.
83. Mark Holifield, interview by Jeffrey L. Rodengen, audio recording, 14 February 2006, Write Stuff Enterprises.
84. Bruce Fong, interview by Jeffrey L. Rodengen, audio recording, 23 March 2006, Write Stuff Enterprises.
85. Gerry Lebel, interview by Jeffrey L. Rodengen, audio recording, 3 April 2006, Write Stuff Enterprises.
86. Bruce Fong, interview.
87. Niala Boodhoo, "When Charity Begins at Work," *Sun-Sentinel*, 10 March 2005, 3D.
88. "Office Depot Contributes $4.5 Million to Florida Universities, NonProfits," Financial Wire, 3 February 2006.
89. Bill Griffeth, "Office Depot—Chairman & CEO Interview," CNBC, Global News Wire, 21 July 2005.
90. Angela Moore, "Office Depot Profit More Than Doubles; Revenue up 7%," MarketWatch, 15 February 2006.
91. "Office Depot Announces Fourth Quarter and Full Year Results," press release, 15 February 2006.
92. "The Hottest Stocks of 2005," *CNNMoney.com*, 28 December 2005.
93. Mike Seemuth, "Two at Office Depot Exercise Options on Profit News," *Broward Daily Business Review*, 1 March 2006, 3.
94. "Staples, Office Depot Hit Highs," Associated Press, 23 March 2006.
95. Pat Beall, "Depot Hops Despite Missed Mark," *Palm Beach Post*, 27 April 2006, 3D.
96. Scott Hedrick, interview by Jeffrey L. Rodengen, audio recording, 15 June 2006, Write Stuff Enterprises.
97. George Hill, interview.
98. Henry Sauls, interview.
99. Robert D. Johnston, "Office Depot Looks to Move Headquarters from

Delray to Boca," *Broward Daily Business Review*," 15 March 2006, 1.
100. "Q4 2005 Office Depot Inc. Earnings Conference Call," FD (Fair Disclosure) Wire, 15 February 2006.
101. Steve Odland, interview.

Chapter Ten, Sidebar: NASCAR Sponsorship

1. Lynn Connelly, interview by Jeffrey L. Rodengen, audio recording, 12 January 2006, Write Stuff Enterprises.
2. Jeffrey D. Zbar, "Office Depot Motto Returns to Taking Care of Business," *Sun-Sentinel*, 3 January 2005.
3. Ibid.
4. Elaine Walker, "Let's Give the Little Guys a Chance, Says Office Depot," *Miami Herald*, 10 February 2005, 4C.
5. "Office Depot Partner with NASCAR," *Retail-Merchandiser.com*, 3 January 2005.
6. Alan Tays, "Office Depot to Become Full-Time Sponsor of Edwards," *Palm Beach Post*, 8 July 2005, 8C.
7. "Office Depot-Sponsored NASCAR Driver Named Ambassador For Youth," Financial Wire, 12 April 2006.
8. "Office Depot to Become Full-Time Sponsor of Edwards."
9. "Office Depot Partner with NASCAR."
10. Paul Owers, "Office Depot to Sponsor NASCAR," *Palm Beach Post*, 28 January 2005.
11. Anne Green, "Edwards' Debut Turns NASCAR Upside Down," *The Greenville News*, 26 January 2006, 1C.
12. Michael Bush, "Partnerships Drive Office Depot Business," *PR Week*, 13 February 2006, 7.

Chapter Ten, Sidebar: Helping Hurricane Victims

1. Steve Odland, interview by Jeffrey L. Rodengen, audio recording, 11 January 2006, Write Stuff Enterprises.
2. "Office Depot Pledges $1 Million for Relief in the Wake of Hurricane Katrina," PR Newswire, 28 August 2005.
3. Ibid.
4. "Office Depot Announces Newest Contributions to Hurricane Katrina Relief," PR Newswire, 7 September 2005.
5. Michelle Caruso-Cabrera, "Office Depot, Inc. Chairman & CEO Interview," CEO Wire, 1 September 2005.
6. "Office Depot Announces Newest Contributions to Hurricane Katrina Relief," PR Newswire, 7 September 2005.
7. Paul Larkin, interview by Jeffrey L. Rodengen, recording, 12 January 2006, Write Stuff Enterprises.

INDEX

Page numbers in italics indicate photographs.